Heritage

God Family Country

Jerry E. Humphrey

Heritage & Hope

———·———

Table of Contents

4

Photo of the book Author as a baby on top of our family bath tub in 1944.
Right photo taken during my elementary school years (circa1951).
Eight brothers shared two bedrooms when we were all still living at home.
We had two bunk beds in each room for eight of us in two bedrooms.
I was 13 in 1956 when we first moved into a house with an indoor bathroom.

I graduated from Plant City Senior High School in June 1960.
At age 16 in September 1960, I was enrolled in the first class entering USF.
After a journey of eight years, I graduated from Auburn University in 1968.
On June 9, 1967, I married Karen Davis and have lived happily thereafter.

Heritage & Hope

———·———

Prelude

For many years, I kept asking myself if I should write this book. Will anyone read it? If they do so, will they gain anything from it? Wouldn't it be better if we just left well enough alone and not bring up any memories of the past? Will people find what I write about interesting to read? Will it be within the Lord's will? I now believe that the book can be of value to whoever reads it. I also believe it will be in God's will as I trust He is inspiring me on what to write.

I want to include some of my personal experiences and memories mixed in with some history and culture of our county, state and country as far back as the American Revolution. We want to see our present and future generations being grounded in our heritage and culture. I believe God works through it all for the purpose and destiny He has for each of us.

"Jesus said to him, *I am the way, the truth, and the life. No one comes to the Father except through Me.*" (John 14:6). There is no other way for our salvation. Being in Christ, we are to proclaim the gospel of Jesus and make disciples of all the nations. I will also be including Judeo-Christian values, American exceptionalism, and the American dream.

This book will focus on the family history for Allan Rufus Humphrey, Sr. and Francis Caroline Blazer. In addition to our county, state and country, I have a deep regard for the history of mankind through the past 6,000 years or so. It speaks volumes for us to consider on the past, present and future.

I believe the history of Israel is recorded in God's Word for us to seriously consider. In His timing, Israel will be completely restored, all to His glory and honor. I believe it is recorded for Christians to grow in the grace and knowledge of Jesus Christ, and for all mankind to realize our need for redemption in Jesus, and no one else.

My desire for writing this book is first for my family to read it. I would be very pleased if all of my immediate and extended family members (along with future generations) do so also. Without any doubt, my father and mother would have been the first ones to read it. Additionally, I hope and trust many outside of our family will read the book, or portions thereof, and benefit from it for themselves in their ongoing journey here on earth. Please feel free to skip over the "begets" listed thorough out the book. Portions of this book will be entertaining only to true history buffs.

As I finished writing Heritage & Hope, I think all we did as a nation throughout our history included consistent fighting for peace, freedom and justice, not only for our country but for others around the world also. Men and women serving in each branch of our armed forces have shed their blood, many in death and many more with wounds to the body, soul and spirit. These wounds also include many with Post-traumatic Stress Disorder (PTSD).

We help our Wounded Warriors to recover their health. We believe with them for their healing and recovery. So many men and women have given their all so we, on the home front, may continue to enjoy living peacefully in freedom and prosperity.

On February 23, 1945, three of the five Marines and one Navy Corpsman raising the USA flag on Iwo Jima Mount Suribachi would soon afterwards give their ultimate sacrifice for us on that island. During the thirty five day battle, almost 7,000 men died on Iwo Jima in one of the most intense battles in the history of the Marine Corp.

I believe our heritage is peaceful living through a strong economy with military strength that provides freedom, liberty, and justice with a pursuit of prosperity for our families. I chose raising the American flag on Iwo Jima as a symbol of our heritage. The flag represents this exceptional Republic we call America. We respect our flag, always!

I believe the cross is a symbol of our Hope in Christ. His blood was shed for the redemption of mankind, to those receiving the gift of salvation by faith in Him. We thank God for our freedom in Christ.

It is my hope you will enjoy all I have been led to write about these past two hundred plus years with some of us being included at one time or another. We will also consider the time we may experience as we move onward in God's eternity, beyond America's crucial crossroads on the election dates of November 8, 2016 and November 6, 2018 (MidTerm Elections).

I truly believe our 2016, 2018 and 2020 Elections will be three of the most important elections in the history of our country. The die will be cast on whether we as a country will choose Socialism or Capitalism for America's future. Regardless of the outcome from these elections, will this conflict continue into future generations? I believe Socialism is slavery resulting in poverty while Capitalism is freedom providing strength in military power and abundant economic prosperity. As every vote is valuable, please vote, always!

I believe the present eroding freedom in our capitalism heritage is in serious jeopardy. The direction we choose through our voting will be decided through these two elections (2018 and 2020) along with the upcoming five elections from 2022 thru 2030. Our future generations will be depending on what we will do with this beautiful Republic that God has so generously blessed us with. I believe the die will be cast between now and the election in 2030.

Do I start at the beginning, the end, or some-where in between? I chose a life journey approach. I hope to be accurate with factual information along with being respectful of others. Please feel free to contact me at JHJhumphrey@aol.com on any questions, corrections or comments you may have as you read Heritage & Hope.

Jerry E. Humphrey
October 30, 2018

Book Cover Photograph.
Photograph was taken at the Parris Island Marine Corp Boot Camp Base Flag Raising Monument. Our family of wife Karen, daughter Kim, son Greg and I attended his Marine Corp boot camp graduation on March 9, 2001. Brick barracks replaced wooden barracks that I had at boot camp in 1962. Greg, a Staff Sergeant, accepted an early retirement option after serving fourteen years in the Marines, including four tours in Iraq and Afghanistan.

Heritage & Hope

Eastern Hillsborough County Communities

Crystal Springs

Kathleen

Antioch

Knights

Midway

Cork

Shilow   Mount Enon

Snows Corner

Dover   Plant City   Youmans   Winston

Seffner   Coronet

Turkey Creek   Trapnell   Springhead

Sydney   Beatty's Corner   Bealsville

Valrico   Hopewell

Durant   Pleasant Grove

Bloomingdale

Lithia Springs   Alderman's Ford   Keysville

Pinecrest   Welcome

Approximate Layout of the Area Communities

Area covers 12 miles West to East and 25 miles North to South. Highway 92 goes West/East and Highway 39 goes North/South. Both highways crisscross in the area's only town, Plant City.

Heritage & Hope

———————•———————

Introduction

As my journey on earth continued onward at full speed, it was slowly dawning on me that my generation is now the elderly generation. No longer could I refer to the older generation as being someone else, such as my parents, uncles or aunts. They are no longer with us. As a matter of fact, my youngest brother Donald and I are the only two of eleven siblings still living our journey here on earth. If our family history is to be recorded for our past and present generations, it would best be accomplished by my generation. A book on our family history does not exist. With that in mind, I have another reason to write this book about our family, all centered on our history, heritage, memories and hope.

During the journey for my generation, we had the Greatest Generation (enduring the Great Depression and World War II) going before us and the Baby Boomers Generation (and let's not forget the Flower Children) following right behind us. I personally arrived on the world stage September 16, 1943, a couple of years before the Baby Boomers and some twenty years after the Greatest Generation. I guess I am a Pre-Baby Boomer and our parents were the Pre-Greatest Generation. I have always identified with the Greatest Generation more so than the Baby Boomers. Quite often I wonder what exactly the Baby Boomers will be leaving as a legacy.

Whether we thought about it much or not during the past fifty years or so, our parents and my siblings grew into adulthood during the harsh "Old South" gradually changing into President Lyndon B. Johnson's Great Society with his 1964 War on Poverty (the "New South?"). We lived through the changes even though it was a slow and challenging process. God's grace was with us through it all. In Heritage & Hope, I will focus on the lineage for our father Allan Rufus Humphrey, Sr. and mother, Frances Caroline Blazer. I desire to lay a foundation for this book to be meaningful to the reader.

In retrospect, I now realize my life was forged on the education and culture we experienced in "strawberry schools". A small area of land in and around Plant City was formed through the ages with a rich top soil excellent for growing a variety of crops, especially strawberries. Mild winter weather with low temperatures in the mid 30 degrees made for perfect conditions to grow sweet strawberries in the winter.

This strip of land goes west to east from Dover and Turkey Creek to Youmans and Springhead, north to south from Knights Station and Cork to Trapnell and Hopewell. Portions of Bealsville, Pinecrest, Ruskin and Kathleen are also included.

The area's only town originally inherited the Indian village name, Ichepuckesassa. However, our non-native residents have enough trouble pronouncing "Kissimmee" correctly. For the sake of simplicity, the name was changed to Cork. Finally in 1886 as the city was incorporated, the name was changed again to Plant City in honor of Henry B. Plant as he ran his railroad track through the area on his route from Jacksonville to Tampa. Without doubt, his railroad was extremely instrumental in expanding the commerce and population of this eastern Hillsborough County agricultural area.

In the 1880's, phosphate was discovered in the area east of Dover Road, following along Highway 60 to Mulberry, Ft. Meade, Bartow, and adjacent small communities. The production of strawberries, vegetables and oranges, along with livestock were on the increase in the area. New cigar factories were rapidly being built in Ybor City and West Tampa at about the same time.

Prior to the Indian Wars in the 1830s, native Indians roamed the territory of Florida freely, as they had for thousands of years. People had been moving into the area from other parts of the South after the Indian Wars were finally over in the 1850s, (and a few before the wars). After the War Between the States ended in 1865, the movement of settlers increased substantially with families homesteading plots of land for their families. The land was referred to as "Islands". The homesteading movement grew quite rapidly, especially during the period between the 1880's through 1917, at which time the United States joined with the Allies in World War I.

Mother's parents moved to the Kissimmee area in 1910 from Point Pleasant, West Virginia when her mother's doctor told her she had to move to Phoenix or Florida to help relieve her breathing difficulty. A year later they moved further south as she was still having discomfort. They took the train to the most southern point of the southwest coast, Fort Myers. They settled in Punta Gorda where they operated a boarding house on main street (Highway US 41). It was twenty five miles north of the existing Thomas Edison winter home and laboratory. I believe it was at that boarding house Father met Mother in the mid 1920s. Her parents were planning for her to attend Florida Southern College in Lakeland.

In 1928, Marjorie Rawlings left her position as a reporter for the Rochester Journal and moved to the remote village of Cross Creek, Florida. She had a cracker house with an orange grove she purchased in the back woods of Cross Creek. It is here that she wrote the award winning books The Yearling and Cross Creek, among other books. Movies were made of both books in later years. She wrote about the struggles that families in her community would endure as they lived in the harsh Great Depression years.

About 10 years later in 1945, another writer, Lois Lenski, wrote a fictional book she entitled Strawberry Girl. It was written about a family that settled, I believe, in the Kathleen area (small community northwest of Lakeland) around 1905. The family owned and operated a small family farm with their children helping with the house and farm chores along with attending "strawberry schools" and a neighboring church.

The year this school system was established is questionable. The school year would run from March till mid December. This school schedule would allow the children time off during the strawberry season to pick the strawberries during the harvesting time of January through March. Instead of getting the summer months off like the regular schools did, those children would get the winter months off so they could help their family harvest the strawberries.

In the fictional novel The Yearling, Jody's father settled in the scrub land wilderness northeast of Ocala after he was discharged from the Southern Army and a few years after the war. We read about other families settling in the Kathleen area in the early 1900s in the fictional novel Strawberry Girl. The farms were family owned and operated. Whatever work that needed to be accomplished had to be performed by the parents, children and grandparents.

We had elementary and high schools with those schedules along with elementary and high schools providing their regular winter schedules. As I was growing up, I know the following elementary schools were "strawberry schools" – Springhead, Trapnell, Pinecrest, Dover, and

Cork. Turkey Creek and Pinecrest had junior high (7th thru 9th grades) and senior high schools (10th thru 12th grades). The system worked fine as the families, including the children, worked the strawberry crops every year.

In the 1950s, times began to change and our culture began to change rapidly. As the local economy grew and expanded, the family farms fell by the wayside quickly. Families had so many more opportunities to earn income than working the family farms. Social pressures and economical feasibilities forced the shutdown of the "strawberry schools" in 1956.

There was a lot of resistance from the local citizens, mostly from adults that had grown up in the schools and wanted them to continue, just for the sake of tradition. The county school board won the argument and the decision was plain and simple, no more "strawberry schools". The schools were closed when the students started the winter schools schedules in September. The students could stay in their present school year class or choose to move up to the next year class. They would be skipping their present school year months of September thru mid-December.

Our family could have been one of the families identified and written about in Cross Creek or even Strawberry Girl. We identified more with the families in the latter since the setting was close to Lakeland and they had family farms with strawberries, our primary cash crop.

At age 23 in 1925, our father moved from the tobacco farms of eastern North Carolina to the farm land of West Central Florida. Two of his granduncles served in the Confederate Army. During wartime serving, his granduncles died of pneumonia. Our mother was raised in a well-established family moving down from Point Pleasant, West Virginia. Her grandfather was from Ohio and had served in the Northern Army during the War. I thought Jody's mother in The Yearling was very similar to our mother in nature and outlook on life. Our mother was definitely identifiable with the women in the Strawberry Girl.

They had to be courageous and enduring in their share of the work load along with the men. Whether it was by hunting and farming or by working for wages, the men were responsible for providing the food and other necessities for living. We experienced a transition from the Farmer/Hunter to the Farmer/Employee work lifestyle in the early 1900s. Father was a Farmer/Employee with his children being the farm hands doing the work on the farm and mother doing all of the house work and cooking. That lifestyle for our family lasted from the late 1930s till we dis-continued farming forever in 1960.

Mother was never employed throughout her adult life. Karen and I both became employed full time as we each graduated from college. She was an elementary teacher and I entered into an industrial and commercial construction career. Family farms were quickly fading out during the late 50s and the 60s. We entered a whole new world during those few short years. Even young Amish adults were leaving the farm life in northern states.

With all of the moving around our family did throughout central Florida over the years, we never once moved north of the eastern Hillsborough County area. What if our father had moved to Cross Creek to see if the grass would be greener north of the Hillsborough County line? What if Marjorie Rawlings had settled into a Plant City countryside farm rather than Cross Creek? I find those questions intriguing due to how close we came to being possible neighbors. It was only about a hundred mile difference. Instead of going north, we went one hundred miles south to Moore Haven for a brief time. I firmly believe if our mother did not insist on returning to Florida after Allan Jr.'s death, the family, along with our next generations would have most likely stayed in North Carolina. And we would all be *Tar Heels*. We would be cheering, "*Go North Carolina State*"

Our nation's most famous inventor, Thomas Edison discovered Florida during his young adult years as he purchased a section of land on the Caloosahatchee River in Ft Myers. In the mid 1880's he designed and pre-fabricated his house in New Jersey and shipped it to Florida and erected it on his Florida property. He also built an in ground concrete pool (most likely one of the first ones to be built) and his lavatory along with his experimental trees to be used to make new potential tires, fuels, etc. He worked at his New Jersey laboratory in the summers. His friend, Henry Ford joined him as he built his winter home next to Edison's compound.

The two compounds are like diamonds in the rough. I am amazed at how few people have ever heard of them, let along taken the few hours of time they would need to tour them. I am writing about the people living in Florida now plus tourist planning to visit the west coast of Florida. Since WW II, many of our northern friends have adopted a lifestyle of maintaining two homes, with one up north during the summer months and one in Florida during the winter months. This lifestyle was popular during the 50s and 60s.

In 1932, country singer and song writer Mel Tillis was born in the local area and raised in Pahokee, Florida (a small community on the southeast edge of Lake Okeechobee). After serving in the Air Force and before going to Nashville to start his musical career, he worked for the Atlantic Coast Line Railroad in Tampa. About the time his future country singer daughter, Pam, was born in Plant City on July 24, 1957, Mel was beginning to be established in Nashville country music. Some of his relatives lived in the Dover area where we owned a thirty acre farm during World War II. In 1957, we were living in Youmans. A father and daughter going from rural Florida to their tremendous success in country music is truly a story in itself. Actually his stuttering handicap enhanced his success tremendously.

I believe our family was also similar to the Walton family with John "John-Boy" Walton, Jr. (Richard Thomas) growing up in rural Virginia during the depression and WW II days. He was the eldest of seven children. It was a very popular television series during the 1970s. They used the fictional name "Waltons" based on stories of the Earl Hamner, Sr. family as written by Earl Jr. They even had family photographs.

At home, we called our parents *"Mama"* and *"Daddy"*. I decided to use Mother and Father in this book. Our Father gave each sibling a nickname that we would use when we were at home. However in public, we always used our given names.

In the book, I only used our given name as listed here from the oldest to the youngest: Mary, Allan Jr., Charles, Robert, Lloyd, Philip, Harry, Jerry, Michael and Donald. Our third oldest child was an unnamed boy living for a few minutes after birth. Between 1929 and 1947, Mother birthed eleven children. The first one was a girl. Afterwards, she birthed ten boys.

Oh yes, we had that well known southern accent. However, I think accents like the ones in Brooklyn, Long Island, Boston, Maine, etc. are a lot more entertaining than we had in rural Florida. We also have unique accents in states like Georgia, North Carolina, Tennessee, Alabama, and Texas. Some of my dialect was so strong that I carried it into adult life. It took decades for me to stop saying simple statements like *"I'm fixin to do it rite now." "Y'all look over yonder." "I reckon so."* Sadly, dialects and accents are quickly vanishing as our culture evolves rapidly for the better or worse.

"...to give you a future and a hope. Then you will call upon Me and go and pray to Me, and I will listen to you. And you will seek Me and find Me, when you search for Me with all your heart." (Jeremiah 29: 11b -13)

Four Generations of Mother's Family (circa 1917).

Great Grandfather Philip Blazer (1832-1921).
Grandfather Harry Benton Blazer, Sr. (1858-1938).
Uncle Sanford Deems Blazer, Sr. (1893-1958).
First Cousin Sanford Deems Blazer, Jr. (1917-1972).
Photograph was taken in 1917 at their family homestead in Punta Gorda.
Our mother Frances Caroline Blazer (1907-1969) had two brothers, Uncle Sanford Deems Blazer, Sr. and Uncle Harry Benton Blazer, Jr. (1903-1968).
Great Grandfather Philip Blazer fought in the Civil War as a First Lieutenant in the 7th Regiment Ohio Volunteer Cavalry Company M.

Our Mother's family two story house in Punta Gorda (circa 1930).
Large front porch convenient for spontaneous visitations from neighbors.

Our Mother's Mother, Mary Aurelia Hannan Blazer
and Mother's Aunt Elizabeth Engle Hannan (circa 1927).

Heritage & Hope

———·———

Dedication/Acknowledgments

Dedication

I dedicate Heritage & Hope to my Father and Mother, Allan Rufus Humphrey, Sr. and Frances Caroline Blazer. It is without doubt to do so, as they kept our large family together from their wedding day in 1928 till their death during the space age of the 60s. They kept the family together in unity throughout the hardships and challenges we endured. They were both born during a history timeline when the automobile was ushered in and the horse and buggy lifestyle was ushered out. I also dedicate Heritage & Hope to my wife Karen for faithfully being the unifier and encourager for our family.

Acknowledgments

I acknowledge Karen for allowing me the tons of lonesome time that was required to write this book along with her encouragement and meticulous proofreading work. I am thankful for Karen's sister, Dorothy Davis, in her editing work and encouragement. Other editing team members include daughter Kim, son Greg, brother Donald, and the "Bloomingdale YMCA Writing Memories Group".

I thank sister-in-law Mildred (Lloyd) for allowing me to include her poem *"Church at the Crossroads"* and Karen's sister, Dorothy Davis, for allowing me to include two of her poems, *"Legacy" and "Fencing"*. I am thankful for one of Karen's aunts, Pauline Davis Colson, for giving me a copy of her 1914 speech dedicating a new two story brick building with administration offices and classrooms for Springhead Elementary School. She was 15 when she gave the speech and 74 when she gave me a copy forty four years ago. It was a miracle her speech survived without becoming lost in that long storage time.

I thank the Life Story Writer's Class Instructors Spence Autry and Val Perry for their instruction and encouragement to write my life story. The course was held at the Bloomingdale Regional Library. Also, I

18

thank my life story writer's class small group Facilitator Allan Osburn for exhorting me to keep on writing.

I appreciated my monthly writing group "Writing Memories" Moderator/Facilitator Mary Novus along with group writers Maryann Hunt, Dotty Hon, Kelly Kelly, Olga Finch, and Gretchen Spoko for their encouragement and helps in writing my life story. I appreciate Alien Handley for his computer formatting guidance. I give a very special thank you to "Joy" Diane Lakner for her work and guidance in my self-publishing <u>Heritage & Hope</u>.

Most of all, I acknowledge and thank my brother, Dr. Donald Humphrey (an Optometrist), for the information he gathered on our family. He has been collecting this data throughout some forty five plus years of research through interviews, online genealogy websites, and research at courthouses in Florida, North Carolina, West Virginia and Ohio. Most likely I would never had written <u>Heritage & Hope</u> if I didn't have access to the information and photographs he has discovered throughout his decades of research during personal time off from his business, Eyecare of Plant City.

I used Don's family tree information with associated dates on births, marriage and death for members of our father and mother's direct ancestor and descendants. He wants to write a family tree historical account with a broader family tree outreach. My book is only focused on the Allan Rufus Humphrey, Sr. and Frances Caroline Blazer lineage. Our two accounts will be complimentary.

Resources for historical information included The World Book Encyclopedia, Wikipedia, and articles in the Tampa Bay Times and Tampa Tribune through the past forty five years. Biblical verses were taken from the New King James Version (NKJV). Historical photographs were provided at the courtesy of Plant City Photo Archives & History Center.

I thank God for His inspiration and grace in this endeavor.
"In everything give thanks; for this is the will of God in Christ Jesus for you."
(1Thessalonians 5:18)

Heritage & Hope

————•————

Chapter 1

The "Tar Heel" State Connection

What in the world is a "Tar Heel"? Here is one possible answer. Before the outbreak of the War Between the States, North Carolina worked at preserving the Union. However, after the state did withdraw, it did it's best to fight for the Southern cause. Over ten battles were fought within the state. According to legend, during one fierce battle, some soldiers retreated, leaving the North Carolina forces to fight alone. The North Carolinians threatened to put tar on the heels of the other soldiers so they would "stick better in the next fight." Henceforth, it became "The Tar Heel State".

This chapter includes considerable history that I think is pertinent to the purpose of Heritage & Hope. Feel free to skim through the history paragraphs. However, if you do carefully read the historical accounts, it will enrich the importance and admiration of our family's heritage all the way back in history to the 1700s America.

Also, please feel free to skim through the "begets" throughout the book. I do hope that our immediate family members will take the time to carefully ponder the listings as it reflects our immediate family tree through our father, Allan Rufus Humphrey Sr. Our brother, Dr. Donald Humphrey, has worked throughout his adult life spending years and years of vacation time researching records in county courthouses in Ohio, West Virginia, North Carolina and Florida.

He collected data and information that I have listed in this book. An invaluable amount of information would be missing from Heritage & Hope if he had not spent all of those never ending years of research. Our immediate family members will want to spend some extra time reading and re-reading the last five generations that are recorded from Lewis Humphrey to Allan Rufus Humphrey, Sr.

In 1585, English settlers built colonies on Roanoke Island off the coast of North Carolina. Then they disappeared within five years.

Incidentally, traces of the lost colony were discovered in August of 2015. The island is now part of a national wildlife refuge. The Wright Brothers National Memorial is a few miles north of the island. Cape Hatteras is to the southeast. In 1629, King Charles I of England granted what is now North Carolina and South Carolina to his attorney general, Sir Robert Heath. He did not settle this granted land. The first permanent white settlers moved from Virginia to the Albemarle Sound region around 1650.

In 1663, King Charles II granted the Carolina colony to eight lord proprietors. The Colonists fought and defeated the Tuscarora Indians from 1711 – 1713. During this time, pirates terrorized the state coastline. Most of the piracy along the Atlantic coast line ended with the death of the famous pirate Blackbeard in a battle near Ocracoke Island in 1718. North Carolina came under direct royal rule in 1729.

In 1734, the American explorer and frontiersman, Daniel Boone, was born in a log cabin near Reading, Pennsylvania. He led an expedition and discovered a trail to the far west through the Cumberland Gap in 1769. The trail would be used by people to reach the new frontier area of Kentucky and all points westward. Scottish Highlanders settled around Fayetteville, North Carolina in 1746, after Bonnie Prince Charlie was defeated in Scotland.

At age 15 in 1749, Daniel Boone moved with his parents to Rowan County, North Carolina, on the Yadkin River, where he started his own hunting business. Rowan County is between the cities of Charlotte and Winston Salem. He married Rebecca Bryan and they raised ten children, during a twenty four year period of domestic family life, in the Yadkin Valley.

North Carolina entered the Revolutionary War against England in 1771 at the Battle of Alamance. Most of the Revolutionary War was fought outside of the state. They did fight the British in neighboring states of Virginia, Georgia and South Carolina. In 1781, British forces withdrew from North Carolina and surrendered in Virginia.

The state's population grew from 36,000 people in 1729 to 350,000 in 1775. Most likely when Daniel Boone heard about that 1775 population statistic, he couldn't leave the state fast enough for more "elbow room" in the new frontier area of Kentucky. In the meanwhile,

North Carolina would ratify the Constitution and become the 12th state on November 21, 1789.

In 1775, Daniel Boone led a group of colonists to an area in Kentucky he named Boonesborough. He established a fort and claimed the area from the Indians. He brought his family to live in the settlement and he became the community leader. One year later, Shawnee and Cherokee Indians kidnapped his daughter Jemima. He rescued her without any harm to her. Two years later, he had to rescue himself when he was also captured by the Shawnee tribe. He would eventually move on to Femme Osage Creek, west of St Louis.

As Daniel Boone was moving from Rowan County, North Carolina to Boonesborough, Kentucky in 1775, along with having to fight Indians in his new place of residence in Kentucky; our great, great, great grandfather, Lewis Humphrey (1772-1839), was a three year old toddler, most likely growing up on a Craven County, North Carolina family farm. (Rowan County is approximately 100 miles west of Craven County).

By 1788, Daniel Boone moved his family to Point Pleasant, West Virginia for a brief time. As an interesting family tree side note; our grandparents, on Mother's side, moved from Ohio to Point Pleasant after the War Between the States. Mother was born there in 1907.

A few years later, her family moved to Punta Gorda, Florida to help improve Grandmother's breathing. Boone would move one more time in his life to an area just west of St. Louis, Missouri, where he continued to hunt until his death in 1820. He is remembered as one of the greatest woodsmen in American history.

The state economy was so depressed from about 1800 to 1835 it was called the "Rip Van Winkle State" because it seemed to be asleep. The state was lacking in commerce, industry, seaports, and transportation facilities. Most of the people worked on farms using inferior tools and farming methods. Many people left the state for better opportunities elsewhere.

In his research, Don found the following information on our great, great, great grandfather. His name was Lewis Humphrey (1772-1839). He lived in Craven County, in Wintergreen and Perfection areas. He lived to age 67. As a time in history reference, Lewis was 48 years old in 1820, when Daniel Boone died in Missouri at age 86. To date, he has not been able to find any more information on the Humphrey family tree prior to Lewis Humphrey.

Based on the information we have, I believe Lewis Humphrey (1772-1839) had to deal with the extremely depressed state economy that was ongoing throughout his adult life. I can only imagine he lived a life of hunting and farming in the community he was born, always struggling to make ends meet, similar to Daniel Boone and mostly everyone else in that time. He most likely sold furs to make extra income also. We think he may have owned at least two or three slaves at one time or another during his adult life.

Considering the information we do know about Lewis and the depressed state economy, I suspect he lived his entire life in the log cabin and farmed the land he inherited from his father. Like all other small family farmers, he had to compete with the large plantation owners having large numbers of slaves in the production of their marketable farm crops. I think he would have lived a very harsh life.

According to our father's side of the family tree, most of his ancestors pretty well lived their lives close to their birth places. Deductive thinking leads me to believe our unknown great, great, great, great grandfather (the father of Lewis) grew up in the area, but was born in Wales. Based on the information we do have on the Humphrey family tree since 1772, I believe our ancestors were more likely to be very cautious and conservative people, always trying to live safely with as much comfort as possible.

Unless someone can prove otherwise, this leads me to believe that our Humphrey ancestry did not attempt to leave Wales for the colonies until after the area they wanted to settle in was totally safe of the early Indian wars and the piracy fighting along the Atlantic coast line. All of these conflicts were over by 1729. I believe also that is why the area's population surged by 314,000 from 1729 to 1775.

That thinking would be true for a large population of people, along with our Humphrey ancestor, deciding it was now safe to settle in the colony. I deduce that Lewis Humphrey's father arrived in the North Carolina colony from Wales sometime around 1750. That would also allow for another twenty years of waiting on a very safe time to immigrate. I believe the birthdate record for the father of Lewis is unknown in North Carolina because his birth occurred in Wales.

I believe the father of Lewis would be born in Wales where Father had told us many times the family immigrated from. I think he may have been born in Wales around 1745 and traveled to North Carolina as a toddler with his parents and older siblings. He could have married by age 26 in 1771. One year later, their son, Lewis (1772-1839) would be born in 1772.

The following factual information on our direct lineage was listed from Don's research notes. Lewis Humphrey (1772-1839) was 29 when he had his first son, Hiram Humphrey (1801-1869). The first wife of Lewis is unknown. Then, they had three more sons; Daniel Humphrey (1804-1847), Lott William B. Humphrey (1813-1862), and unknown son (1814-?).

Lewis would marry his second wife, Nancy Burke (1780-1850). They had Druscilla Ann Humphrey (1818-?), Ozaida Humphrey (1820-?) and Joseph H. Humphrey (1825-?). Lewis had a total of five sons and two daughters. Many of these sons and daughters would live to experience the War Between the States. Some of their sons likely fought in the war.

Our great, great grandfather, Hiram Humphrey (1801-1869) married his first wife, Nancy Jones (?-?) at an unknown date. They had six children as follows: Jesse Humphrey (1833-1861), William Humphrey (1834-1862), Holland Humphrey (1839-?), (Micajah Humphrey (1840-?), Jemima Humphrey (1843-?), and Mary Humphrey (1844-?). Hiram married his second wife,

Eliza Harrison (1809-?). They had three children as follows: Hannah Humphrey (1849-?), and Rufus A. Humphrey (1853-1917), Carrie Anne Humphrey (1854-?). Hiram had a total of nine children over a twenty three year period. He was 32 at the birth of his first child in 1833. There is an observation that I ponder. Jemima was born in 1843. One hundred years later, I was born in 1943.

It appears that Hiram Humphrey (1801-1869) lived a life with plenty of heartache. His father was 29 when Hiram was born. He would be 38 when his father, Lewis, died. He would also live the first half of his life working toward his American dream within a state deep in a depressed economy. By age 48, he will have lost his first wife, re-married, and was having his seventh child, Hannah. He would be 52 years old and Eliza would be 44 when the eighth child, Rufus was born. He worked as a carpenter as well as farming. Another interesting observation we may ponder. Eliza was born in 1809. Almost one hundred years later, Mother was born in 1907.

An age of progress began in 1836 for the state and continued until 1861. Then the War Between the States brought death, despair and destruction to the state. The abolition of slavery caused a loss of inexpensive farm labor. We believe Hiram did not have any slaves on his farm.

The war period was particularly hard on Hiram as he lost two sons from illnesses in the war. His son, Jesse, died in 1861 at age 28 and William in 1862 at age 28. Those two brothers were our great grand uncles. We don't have any information on the deaths of their siblings or mothers. Their father, Hiram would die a few years after the war in 1869, at age 68. Hiram lived to see the war's end and the beginning of a horrible reconstruction program forced on the Southern states. He would die four years later during that tumultuous period. Another thought to ponder is the fact that Hiram was born in 1801, and Father was born one hundred years later. Father died in 1967 at the age of 64, one hundred years after our great, great grandfather Hiram died at age 68 in 1869.

Books of history were written on those one hundred years of the 19th century. The Allan Humphrey family would live through it all within the same close knit area with deep roots in North Carolina's cotton and tobacco country. The same holds true for the 20th century and it looks like more of the same for the 21st century. And let's don't forget the last half of the 18th century also.

On July 4, 2016, we celebrated our country's 240th birthday since the birth of our country in 1776. Our family has lived in this country throughout those same years, and some. People come and go while the land remains the same for all times.

More or less, Hiram lived the same time period as President Abraham Lincoln. Lincoln was born in 1809 in a one room log cabin in Hardin County, Kentucky. His family moved to southern Indiana in 1816, and then on to southern Illinois in 1830. He had to work hard to support his family. As President, he preserved the union and brought freedom to the slaves through winning the War Between the States. Without question, the war was obviously hard on him and his family. His young son, Willie, died of typhoid fever in 1862. And as the war ended, he was assassinated April 14, 1865, at age 56.

The following statistics reflect the magnitude of that national tragedy. In 1865, the United States population was 35.2 million. Soldiers killed included at least 110,000 Union combat deaths and 250,000 other deaths. The Southern combat deaths and other deaths included at least 95,000 and 165,000 respectively. Combined combat deaths for both sides were at least 205,000 and 415,000 which equals total deaths of at least 620,000.

The exact number of soldiers killed or wounded on both sides is not known. These statistics are minimal and they could be as much as 20% higher. The total war deaths equaled 17.6% of the country's 1865 population of 35.2 million people. Keep in mind; these statistics do not include the number of soldiers that were wounded.

We, along with future generations, dare not forget this horrific time in our history. Our country was harshly tested during those four years of war. God's grace and mercy was in the midst of it all. Like so many in the summer of 1865, our family had to pick up the pieces and move on with their lives. The Reconstruction program was implemented by the Federal government.

Some four million slaves were now free to pursue their own dreams. Large plantations were divided into small farms. The number of farms grew from some 75,000 in 1860 to 150,000 in 1880. By the late 1800's, farm production equaled what it had been before the war. Tobacco and cotton crops led the growth. Furniture manufacturing also became large scale industries.

Hiram's son, Rufus A. Humphrey (1853-1917), our great grandfather, married Manalcy Phillips (1852-1923). They had a son, John Council Humphrey (1878-1947), daughter Mary Humphrey (1881 - ?), daughter Lillie Humphrey (1884 - ?), son Edward James Humphrey (1885 – 1950), and daughter Mimie Idora Humphrey (1893-1918). They had two sons and three daughters over a period of fifteen years from 1878 -1893.

Our Great Grandfather Rufus A. Humphrey lived to age 64. He was 8 years old as the war began. Two of his uncles, Jesse and William, died in the war. He was only 16 years old when his father died. His mother, Eliza, probably died about the same time. Most likely at that age, he dropped out of school to help operate the farm. His remaining six brothers and sisters between ages 30 and 15, were also likely living on the family farm in 1869.

The family probably had a few slaves to help them on the farm until they were freed after the war. I believe they were able to obtain some more land at a cheap price during the reconstruction era when federal agents were helping to restart local economies. After the reconstruction time, they probably had enough land in order to operate separate farms. I believe the family prospered fairly well from 1865 till Rufus died in 1917. As the plantation owners lost their slave labor, small family farms became more competitive in the production of farm crops. The number of small farms would double within the next fifteen years. During that time, the state economy was prospering fairly well.

Father was 15 years old when his grandfather Rufus died. He would be 21 when his grandmother Manalcy died in 1923 at age 71. I would hope our father would have had many fond memories of his grandfather and grandmother. With one exception, I don't remember anything about Rufus our Father may have shared with us during our meal time conversations. He would tell us that our grandfather, John Council (1878-1947), named him Allan Rufus Humphrey (1902-1967) after his father, Rufus A. Humphrey (1853-1917).

Father was always mindful to tell us that Rufus was a Biblical name, as we find in Romans 16:13, *"Greet Rufus, chosen in the Lord, and his mother and mine."* There was a great spiritual revival in the north as well as the south during the 1840s. It has been considered that God was preparing America for the troubled times waiting at her doorstep. Actually, during that time in history, Rufus was a popular name.

I wonder if Hiram and Eliza named their first born son, Rufus, for a spiritual significance in their lives. I tend to think they may have had a strong spiritual revival and awaking. Why else would a person name their son Rufus? Father thought the name was so special, that he named his first born son Allan Rufus Humphrey, Jr. (1930-1932) and Father's name became Allan Rufus Humphrey, Sr. So we had three generations of first born sons with the name Rufus. In 1932, when Allan Rufus, Jr. died from pneumonia in North Carolina at the age of 2, Mother insisted that the family move back to Florida.

John Council Humphrey (1878-1947) was the first son of Rufus A. Humphrey (1853-1917) and Manalcy Phillips (1852-1923) Rufus was 23 and Manalcy was 26 when John Council was born. John Council married Mary Elizabeth Stocks (1879-1911). They had a daughter, Annie Olivia Humphrey ((1899-1972) and two sons, Allan Rufus Humphrey Sr., (1902-1967) and Johnnie W. Humphrey (1907-1984).

Mary Elizabeth Stocks (1879-1911) died at age 32, and within a couple of years, John Council married Apsley Ethel Fulford (1891-1938) in 1913. They had a stillborn daughter, Irene Humphrey (1914-1914), son, Woodrow Wilson Humphrey (1916-1990), son, Richard Lee Humphrey (1918-1985) and daughter, Julia Janie Humphrey (1921-2003). Apsley Ethel would die in 1938 when Julia Janie was age 17.

John Council was 32 when his father, Rufus, died at age 64 in 1917. Father was 15 years old when his grandfather died in 1917, 9 when his mother died in 1911, 12 when his stepsister was stillborn in 1914, 36 when his stepmother died in 1938, and 45 when his father died in 1947. Father was 30 when his son, Allan Rufus Humphrey, Jr. died in 1932 and 31 when his next son was stillborn in 1933.

He moved his family from North Carolina to Seffner, Florida in November or December of 1932. In summary, our family's direct Father lineage includes Allan Rufus Humphrey, Sr. (1902-1967) as our Father, John Council Humphrey (1878-1947) as our Grandfather, Rufus A. Humphrey (1853-1917) as our Great Grandfather, Hiram Humphrey (1801-1869) as our Great Great Grandfather, and Lewis Humphrey (1772-1839) as our Great Great Great Grandfather. Our Great Great Great Great Grandfather is unknown at this time.

Large families were intertwined in our family tree over time. Lewis Humphrey (1772-1839) had seven children within twenty four years from 1801-1825, Hiram Humphrey (1801-1869) had nine children within twenty one years from 1833-1854, John Council Humphrey (1878-1947) had seven children within twenty two years from 1899-1921, and Allan Rufus Humphrey, Sr. had eleven children within eighteen years from 1929-1947. The family of Allan Rufus Humphrey, Sr. has a multitude of relatives in the eastern coast area of North Carolina and the central west area of Florida.

Also in summary, our Humphrey family's direct mother lineage includes Frances Caroline Blazer (1907-1969) as our mother, Mary Elizabeth Stocks (1879-1911) as our Grandmother, Manalcy Phillips (1852-1923) as our Great Grandmother, Eliza Harrison (1809-?) as our Great Great Grandmother. Plus, we have an unknown Great Great

Great Grandmother. Our Great Great Great Great Gandmother is also unknown.

By the late 1920's the state led the nation in the production of cotton textiles, tobacco products and wooden furniture. The Great Depression brought drops in prices and wages. Businesses and banks closed. Workers lost their jobs and farmers lost their farms. The economy improved during World War II and the decades following the war. Father and Grandfather were both born and raised in North Carolina tobacco country. As the country entered the Industrial Revolution, more non-farm related work opportunities opened up for people at the turn of the 20th century.

Father dropped out of school after the eighth grade. He was too young to sign up for the military during World War I. For the next seven years, I would think that he worked in tobacco farming along with earning some income working part time for local businesses.

The 1911 marriage between John Council and Apsley Ethel Fulford ended in a divorce in 1922. John Council received some money from a former lumber business in Ayden, North Carolina. Florida was entering a booming expansion in the '20s enticing people to move there. In circa 1924, he traveled alone to an area near Punta Gorda, where he started a citrus business. In 1925, our father, Allan Rufus, and Uncle Johnnie William joined him in the business.

In the middle of the Great Depression, the business shut down in 1935. Grandfather John Council and his son, Johnnie, went back to North Carolina. I would think that John Council resumed working in the tobacco industry along with being employed periodically as a carpenter as long as he could work.

Uncle Johnnie would soon afterwards leave the area to serve his country with a career in the U. S. Army. I believe he served with General Patton. Father stayed in Florida as he had married Frances Caroline Blazer of Punta Gorda and was gainfully employed with Phoenix Utility Company as a lineman. During Grandfather's business years in Florida, our father, with his young family, was on the move; living for brief periods in Tampa, Punta Gorda, Seffner, and in the North Carolina towns of Winterville and Farmville.

Father would tell us about the time his father took him to see the Buffalo Bill Wild West Show when it came to their area. He also talked about going to Billy Sunday Tent Revival meetings. At one time during the depression days, John Council lived with our parents in Florida at different times. They shared about how he was at times set in his ways and hard to please.

We have seventy five years of history from 2018 to 1943. Going back another sixty nine years will take us to 1874. Grandfather John Council Humphrey was born in 1878 and died in 1947 at age 69. He could have made the same reflection of memories over the past sixty nine years that he had lived.

Growing up in the 1880s, Grandfather John Council (1878-1947) would hear vivid stories about the War Between the States days and the Reconstruction era. He personally lived through the horse and buggy days, the Industrial Revolution, Spanish American War, the Teddy Roosevelt "*Speak Softly and Carry a Big Stick*" Presidency, the invention of cars, trucks, planes and radio, World I, the Roaring 20's, the Great Depression, World II, and the beginning of the Cold War and television.

Grandfather John Council had two uncles that died while serving in the Confederate Army during the War Between the States. He was 39 when his father died in 1917. John Council Humphrey lost his first wife when she was a young age of 32. He lost a 2 year old Grandson, Allan Rufus Humphrey, Jr. in 1932 and he lost another Grandson one year later. His second wife's first child was stillborn in 1914. She died at age 47 in 1938. Her husband, John Council died nine years later in 1947 at age 69.

Having never seen my grandfather in person, I was four years old when he died in North Carolina. He was living with relatives when he died. He had been a widower from his second wife for nine years. I always wondered how Grandfather adapted to the rapidly changing society and culture he experienced.

Our Father lived sixty five years from 1902 till 1967. Throughout his life, Father also had to deal with that rapidly changing society. He was 45 when our grandfather died. I always wonder if they both would resist the changes they were constantly challenged to make throughout their lives. I know I have not escaped the challenges of change that still occurs in my lifetime. That would make it the last three generations. We have our generation, the generations before us, and the generations that follow us. Every generation is eternal in time.

The Allan Rufus Humphrey Sr. family had 150 years of a North Carolina southern heritage before he married a *"Yankee"* in 1928 with Florida sand (and sandspurs) in her shoes. During the war, Mother's Grandfather served in the Union Army. Two of Father's Grand Uncles served in the Southern Army. He, along with his offspring, would end up with sand in our shoes. I have included only the direct lineage in our family tree to our father, Allan Rufus Humphrey, Sr. Donald has more Humphrey family data that I have not included.

Mother's mother was told by her doctor around 1910 that she had to move from Point Pleasant, West Virginia to an area of the country that would be best for her breathing. He said it could be either Phoenix, Arizona or Florida. She chose Florida. Ironically, if Mother had not insisted on the family moving back to Florida after her first born two year old son, Allan Rufus Jr., died of pneumonia in 1932, the family most likely may have stayed in North Carolina. Instead of being Florida *"Crackers"*, we would be North Carolina *"Tar Heels"*. In a society and culture where the man of the house had the final say in major considerations, this was one decision that was strongly persuaded by our mother. I believe it is God's destiny that we are in Florida for His purpose.

"Bless the Lord, O my soul; And all that is within me, bless His holy name! Bless the Lord, O my soul, and forget not all His benefits: Who forgives all your iniquities, Who heals all your diseases, Who redeems your life from destruction.
Who crowns you with lovingkindness and tender mercies," (Psalm 103:1-4).

Our Father's Father, Grandfather John Council Humphrey (circa 1945).

Heritage & Hope

———•———

Chapter 2

"Buckeyes" & "Mountaineers" Connection

Since writing the chapter on our father's ancestry, I realized how much our family had always considered father's ancestry more than our mother's blood line. In startling reality, our heritage is 50% "Tar Heel" (North Carolina) and 50% "Yankee" (Ohio and West Virginia). In our pure blood line, we are as much "Yankee" as we are Southern. In Heritage & Hope I use the terms "Tar Heels", "Buckeyes" (Ohio), "Mountaineers" (West Virginia) and "Yankees" with a high level of honor and respect, just as I do also with Florida "Crackers".

Our brother Donald recorded extensive notes on quite a bit of ancestor history that he discovered in his research. With his permission, I have included his findings in this chapter along with mixing in bits of history for Ohio and West Virginia.

Based on Don's research, I will list Mother's lineage through her father's first and then her mother's lineage. Our mother, Frances Caroline Blazer (1907-1969) is a descendant of Thomas Hannan (1757-1835). Thomas Hannan (1757-1835) married Elizabeth Henry (1767-1832) and they had eight children (five sons and three daughters). Their youngest child, Jesse Hannan (1800-1888) married Frances Waugh (1795-1860). They had a son, Erastus Demetrius Hannan (1836-1893). Erastus Hannan married Frances Prince (1845-1872) and they had a daughter, Mary Aurelia Hannan (1870-1935). Mary Hannan married Harry Benton Blazer, Sr. (1858-1938). They had two sons, Sandford Deems Blazer, Sr. (1893-1958) and Harry Benton Blazer, Jr. (1903-1968). They also had one daughter, Frances Caroline Blazer (1907-1969).

That daughter would become our mother. Her oldest brother, Sandford (1893-1958) married Claudia Reynolds (?-1950) and they had one son, Sandford. Deems Blazer, Jr. (1917-1972). Sandford, Jr. married Rosa Catherine Wilson, 1921, and they had two sons and two daughters; Rosa Catherine Blazer, 1939, Sandford Deems Blazer III,

1943, Thomas Allen Blazer, 1948, and Cynthia Mary Hannan Blazer, 1953, Sandford Deems Blazer III and I were both born in 1943. Imagine, another book could be written on their family.

The following family tree information shows our mother's lineage through her mother's ancestry. Our mother, Francis Caroline Blazer (1907-1969) is a descendant of Jacob Blazer (1760- ?). Jacob Blazer (1760-?) had one known son, Peter Blazer (1790-1854). Jacob's wife is unknown. Peter married Frances Atkinson (1791-1875) and they had Philip Blazer (1832-1921) along with nine other children. Philip married Caroline Safford (1836-1896) and they had Harry Benton Blazer, Sr. (1858-1938) along with four other children. Harry Blazer, Sr. married Mary Aurelia Hannan (1870-1935). They had two sons and one daughter: Sandford Deems Blazer, Sr. (1893-1958), Harry Benton Blazer, Jr. (1903-1968), and our mother, Frances Caroline Blazer (1907-1969).

Sandford Blazer, Sr. (1893-1958) married Claudia Reynolds (?-1950) and they had one son, Sanford Deems Bazer, Jr. (1917-1972). He married Rosa Catherine Wilson (1921-   ). They had two daughters and two sons, all born between 1939 and 1953. One son, Sandford Deems Blazer III (1943-   ) was born the same year I was born, 1943. Due to a prohibitive travel distance, we had almost zero contact with their family. Mother's other brother, Harry Benton Blazer, Jr., disappeared as a young adult and was never heard from again. He was one of two uncles on our mother's lineage. Our parents could only wonder what ever happened to him.

To the best of our knowledge, Harry Benton Blazer, Jr. (1903-1968) never married. Don found his death certificate, which provided us valuable information. He was born on January 14, 1903, in West Virginia. He was a veteran of World War II as he served in the war during his early 40s.

He was admitted to the Chicago, Illinois Veterans Administration Research Hospital on August 29, 1968, where he would die on September 4. His cause of death was listed as an Intra-Cerebral Hemorrhage. Our mother died one year later in 1969, without ever knowing about his death. He was living at 22 West Ontario in Cook County Chicago and working as a restaurant counter man. He is buried at Mt. Carmel Cemetery in Hillside, Illinois. Mother's oldest brother, Sandford Blazer, Sr. had died ten years previously in 1958. Both uncles died at age 65, and mother died at age 62.

Mother's father, Harry Benton Blazer, Sr. and mother, Mary Hannan Blazer, died in 1938 and 1935, at ages 80 and 68 respectively. Grandmother, Mary Hannan Blazer, Sr., died on April 5, 1935. Three years later on June 14, our Grandfather Harry Benton Blazer, Sr. died. Her parents lived in Punta Gorda at the same time that Mother gave birth to a daughter and five boys between 1929 and 1938.

One son died two months shy of his second birthday and one son died a few minutes after birth. She gave birth to five more sons after her father's death in the spring of 1938. During certain periods of time in 1930 and 1937, our family lived at our grandparent's boarding house in Punta Gorda. They had a great opportunity to spoil their three living grand children during these brief times, in spite of the ongoing economic depression. By the year 1937, Mary was 8, Charles was 3, Robert was a baby, not yet 1.

Grandfather was 79, Grandmother 67, Father 35 and Mother 30. Our Grandmother died in 1935 and Grandfather died three years later in 1938 when we were living in Moore Haven. Lloyd was born there on March, 13, 1938. I can only imagine how Mother dealt with a new born baby, the recent loss of her mother (and now her father) along with the isolation she felt after they had moved to the small farming town of Moore Haven.

Her only surviving brother, Sanford, Sr. had married and had one son who had also married and was beginning to start his family of four children. Sanford Sr. and wife Claudia visited us one afternoon in 1948 when we were living on Clay Turner Road in Springhead. We still have two photographs they took of us during that visit. As we never had a camera, the photograph was one of the few taken of me as a child, except for some school photos we saved. The pose included me standing barefoot, wearing dirty coveralls, in a strawberry field with four of my brothers. All five of us were squinting into the fading sun light. It is one of my favorite snapshots. I remember the visit as being startlingly and awkward.

In 1938, our family would drive the seventy miles back to Mother's childhood home for Grandfather's funeral. The four children making the trips would include three of them being under the age of three, and were not yet potty trained. Incredible, Lloyd was a three week old baby at the time of our Grandfather's death. This funeral would also bring back sad memories of the loss of Allan Jr. in October, 1932 and her unnamed new born son in January, 1933. The spring and summer of 1938 had to be a very harsh time for our mother.

The year 1938 was also the year they should have been celebrating their tenth wedding anniversary. That year would also be remembered throughout the nation as the tenth year since the destructive hurricane that pushed the Lake Okeechobee water into flooding the south shore areas of the lake, killing thousands of people. That deadly 1928 hurricane hit Lake Okeechobee during the same week our parents were being married in Punta Gorda. Less we forget, the nation and state were still struggling through a very depressed economy.

In 1939, we moved to Wauchula, 50 miles north of Punta Gorda, on US Highway 17, where Philip and Harry were born. I have vivid memories of Mother telling us in the 50s how happy she was to move out of the Lake Okeechobee area for good. Regardless of their difficult and painful life, our parents stayed together and did not abandon the family. Because of their commitment to marriage, our family unit stayed intact through all of our trials and tribulations.

After we moved to Wauchula in 1939, we basically lost contact with her remaining brother, Sanford Blazer Sr. Between the four grandchildren of his own to enjoy along with the travel distance, we pretty much lost any contact with his family for the next twenty years until his death, at age 65, in 1958. Mother did visit with a couple of cousins in West Virginia.

Other than Mother, Donald, Lloyd and Mildred; our family never had contact with her relatives in West Virginia. Looking at the past is like Monday morning coaching. We could have done better if we had done such and such. The biggest reason was the distance from Hillsborough County was closer to father's relatives in North Carolina than mother's relatives in West Virginia. We thought of West Virginia as being a faraway land. And it was before the Interstate highway system was completed. And you had to drive through all of those mountains. Airline and train travel was too expensive.

Ohio, the Buckeye State, has a very rich heritage. Eight of our country's presidents hailed from Ohio at the time of their elections, ranging from Ulysses Grant to Warren Harding. In 1847, our Florida snow bird friend, Thomas Edison, was born in Milan, Ohio. His family moved to Port Huron, Michigan when he was 7 years old.

In 1787, the Ohio Northwest Territory was established to provide land to the Revolutionary War veterans and other settlers. One year later, the first area settlement was established at Marietta. The Battle of Fallen Timbers in 1794 ended the Indian Wars in the area. The Ohio Territory established in 1799 gained statehood as the state of Ohio in 1803. Land was ceded by the territory Indian tribes during the time period of 1805 through 1818.

Chillicothe (in southern Ohio) served as the capital of Ohio from statehood in 1803 until 1810. The capital was moved 70 miles northeast to Zanesville for two years. In 1812 it was moved back to Chillicothe. In 1816 the capital was moved again, 40 miles north to Columbus. At that time Columbus was considered the geographic center of the state, accessible to most state residents.

Early in the 19th century, the wilderness of Ohio isolated the state from the eastern markets. The 110 mile Ohio & Erie Canal constructed in the 1820s and 1830s from Lake Erie in Cleveland to New Philadelphia provided a valuable link to areas like New York and New Orleans. It helped to transform a wild frontier into a booming and populous state, taking it from almost bankruptcy to one of the most prosperous states in the country within 20 years. Ohio became a major manufacturing state in addition to producing abundant agricultural products. The state had a strong economy as the country approached the War Between the States. Ohio would provide 320,000 men to serve in the Union forces during the War.

Jacob Blazer (1760-?), of German descent, was living in Pennsylvania at age 40. His known son, Peter Blazer (1790-1854) was born in Washington County, Pennsylvania in 1790. In 1800, at age 10, he traveled to Gallia County, Ohio with his father at age 40. The family settled on a farm. Two years later, Peter's son Philip Blazer (1832-1921) was born in Gallia County Ohio, likely on the family farm. Peter Blazer remained with his father, Jacob Blazer for twenty four years.

At age 24 in 1814, Peter married Frances Atkinson (1791-1875). They had 10 children, including Philip Blazer (1832-1921). They all remained in Gallia County Ohio, except for Permelia Blazer moving to Omaha Nebraska. Peter Blazer was a solider in the War of 1812, and he was a farmer. His wife Frances Atkinson was a native of Shenandoah Valley, Virginia. Most likely, she had a deep concern for the families living in the valley during the war. She died in 1875 at age 84. Her husband, Peter, died in 1854 at age 64, leaving her a widow for twenty one years.

Philip Blazer (1832-1921) married Caroline Safford (1836-1896) in 1856. He was 24 and she was 20. Philip lived with his father Peter Blazer until his father's death in 1854, when Philp was 22. As an adventurous young man, he operated a boat on the Ohio River for two years after which he traveled to California in 1859 during the gold rush fever days. Two years later, he gave up digging for gold in 1861 and went back to his Gallia County home.

In September 1862, at age 30, Philip Blazer enlisted in the 7th Regiment Ohio Volunteer Cavalry Company M as it was being organized for battle at that time. As an interesting note, I enlisted in the Marine Corp Reserves one hundred years later in 1962, at age 18. He was quickly promoted from Private to Sergeant, then Second Lieutenant and once more to First Lieutenant. He remained in the army throughout the war. The regiment saw action in campaigns and raids as part of the Army of the Ohio primarily in Kentucky, Tennessee, and western North Carolina. They also served as part of the Union forces hastily sent northward in the summer of 1863 in pursuit of Morgan's Raiders, seeing action at the Battle of Buffington Island where much of Morgan's command was captured. Participating in the Knoxville Campaign in the autumn of 1863, the 7th suffered a significant setback in a small skirmish with numerous prisoners being seized from the 7th Ohio Cavalry.

In July 1864, the regiment moved into Georgia and joined the forces of General William T. Sherman during the Atlanta Campaign. It participated in skirmishes and engagements with the Confederate cavalry until the fall of Atlanta in July, They again engaged in skirmishes in Tennessee. As the war was ending, the regiment pursued retreating Confederates in Alabama and Georgia as far south as the Anderson Prison in southern Georgia. .News was received that Robert E. Lee had surrendered in Virginia.

The regiment was mustered out on July 4, 1865, and returned home to Ohio. Great Grandfather Philip Blazer would, most likely, see his 7 year old son Harry for the first time since he enlisted in the Army. He was now 33 years old himself. During the war, they lost 2 officers and 26 enlisted men killed and mortally wounded. Similar to Southern forces, they suffered 4 officers and 197 enlisted men dying by disease.

Following the war, veterans would frequently meet to remember the war and their fallen comrades. As I reflect on this chapter, I can only wonder how close my Great Grandfather, Philip Blazer, came to fighting one of our Southern relatives, or acquaintances, in battle. He lived with our grandparents in Punto Garda till his death in 1921.

Even worse, is the reality that his mother (and our great, great grandmother), Frances Atkinson (1791-1875), not only had to worry about his safety, but also for the Southern folk she knew in Shenandoah Valley. She also had nine other sons and daughters along with an unknown number of grandchildren that were most likely exposed to the war in some way or another.

She was 70 when the war started and she would live another 10 years after the war ended. As her husband Peter Blazer died seven years before the war, she would also have to endure the war years as a widow. She was our mother's Great Grandmother.

The war had a very direct effect on their family and friends from both sides of the Mason Dixie Line, as the Southern states fought the Northern states. Philip Blazer (1832-1921) was married to Caroline Safford (1836-1896), a Granddaughter of Colonel Robert Safford (1765-1863). Caroline Safford was our mother's Grandmother.

At age 25 in 1790, Colonel Robert Safford served as a guide for hundreds of French investors wanting to settle in the Ohio River wilderness. French aristocrats, known as the "French 500" escaping punishment in post-Bastille Day, pre-revolutionary France, saw the promise of a new life in the boundless American frontier as tempting.

The French settlers named the community Gallipolis, meaning "City of the Gauls". They quickly established a thriving river trade. The small town is located on the west side of the Ohio River, about forty miles north of Huntington, West Virginia and the Kentucky state line. Colonel Safford was said to have cut the first tree in clearing the land where the city of Gallipolis was established with log cabins.

In 1803, their county was named "Gallia" in honor of the county's first settlers, the "French 500" as they are known. Gallipolis still bears the mark of the French as a reminder of the county's heritage.

Point Pleasant, West Virginia is located on the east side of the Ohio River and Gallipolis, Ohio is located on the west side of the river. It is the county seat for Mason County, West Virginia, at the meeting point of the Ohio River and Kanawha River. The Kanawha River starts at the Ohio River in Point Pleasant and runs southeastward through Charleston and north of Beckley, West Virginia. Today, Point Pleasant and Gallipolis have less than 5,000 people in each town.

Colonel Safford was considered a key frontiersman in the settlement of Gallipolis and Point Pleasant. He would also serve his country as a Colonel in the War of 1812. Later, he represented Gallia County, Ohio in the State Legislative Assembly. He was a well-known Indian Scout in his younger years. He roamed the wilderness hunting and fighting with Daniel Boone. Legend has it that a wolf trap used by Colonel Stafford and Daniel Boone is on display in Columbus, Ohio.

The descendants of Colonel Safford have a cane that he made on the day that his son, Robert Safford, was born on July 4, 1800. Colonel Safford was 35 at that time. He would live almost 100 years till his death in 1863, at the age of 98. He lived from a time of establishing settlements in the Ohio River wilderness to dying before he knew for sure if America would continue as one united country.

Generations would be blessed regardless of their challenges. However his son, Robert Safford, a farmer by occupation, did get to see the war's end as he died in 1865. His wife lived till 1877. In 1874, Mr. and Mrs. Philip Blazer settled in Mason County, West Virginia. One of their sons, Harry Benton Blazer, Sr., (1858-1938) was the father of our mother, Frances Caroline Blazer (1907-1969). He worked as a telegraph operator in Mason County. One son farmed in Cherokee County, Missouri and another son had a lumber business.

A neat historic fact discovered by Don was that The Hannan Trace was blazed from St Albans, West Virginia to Chillicothe, Ohio, by our mother's Great Great Grandfather, Thomas Hannan (1757-1835). The trace became a trail and eventually a road. Our mother's mother would die 100 years later in 1935. She had moved from Point Pleasant, West Virginia to Punta Gorda, Florida with her husband, Harry Benton Blazer, Sr., circa 1910.

The trace went west from St Albans (in the western section of the state near Charleston) 35 miles to Point Pleasant West Virginia and then crossing the Ohio River into Gallipolis, Ohio. The trace then went northwest 60 miles to Chillicothe. Ohio. The trail provided a direct entrance into southern Ohio from the West Virginia area. The trail is called "Hannan Trace Road" today. He married Elizabeth Henry (1767-1832) and they had eight children.

The famous pioneer and trailblazer, Daniel Boone (1734-1820), blazed the Wilderness Road from Cumberland Gap Virginia to Boonesborough Kentucky in 1775. Boonesborough is only 120 miles southwest of Chillicothe. Thomas Hannan and Boone were acquaintances in their hunting and trailblazing adventures. During his times of moving deeper and deeper into the wilderness, Daniel Boone personally wanted to move to Florida. He had visited the area and he liked the government's offer of giving free land to settlers. However, his wife, Rebecca, insisted that they stay near her family and friends.

In 1749, the French explorer, Pierre Joseph Celoron de Blainville claimed the area for France and named the meeting point of the Ohio and Kanawha Rivers "Point Pleasant". However, legend has it that when George Washington surveyed this area in the 1740's, he referred to it as the Pleasant Point. Celeron's expedition failed since the local tribes remained pro-English, and English population in the region refused to give up their possessions. The British remained in control of the area following the defeat of France in the French and Indian War (1754-1763).

The Battle of Point Pleasant was fought on October 10, 1774, at the connection of the Kanawha and Ohio Rivers. The battle was fought on the future site of the town between some 1,000 Virginia militiamen led by Colonel Andrew Lewis (1720-1781) against an equal number of Indian warriors led by Shawnee Chief Cornstalk. He named the location "Camp Point Pleasant". At that time, Virginia included all of West Virginia. This was a large territory of land.

Considered a landmark in frontier history, some believed the battle to be the first of the American Revolution also. Their defeat broke the power of the Indians in the Ohio Valley and calmed a general Indian war on the frontier. It also prevented an alliance between the British and Indians, one which could very possibly have caused the Revolution to have a different outcome, altering the entire history of the U.S. In addition, the ensuing peace with the Indians enabled western Virginians to return in a more bearable atmosphere.

The event is celebrated locally as the "First Battle of the American Revolutionary War". In 1908 the U.S. Senate authorized erection of a local monument to commemorate it as such. Our Great Great Great Grandfather, Thomas Hannan's (1757-1835) name is listed on that monument. He was 17 when he fought in that one day battle. Most historians regard it not as a battle of the Revolution (1775–1783), but as a part of a war between Virginia and local Indians.

"Camp Point Pleasant" was established by Col. Lewis at the time of the Battle and the settlement that followed also took that name. Although not certain, Point Pleasant may have been permanently settled by whites as early as 1774. Prior to that, hostilities between whites and Indians all along the Ohio River Valley prevented any possible settlements being established. Forts were built to help protect settlers. The settlement at Point Pleasant did not receive an official charter until 1794. Point Pleasant was incorporated in 1833.

If it may not have been the beginning of the War Between the States, John Brown's Raid on the federal arsenal at Harper's Ferry in 1859, certainly added fuel to the ongoing heated debates on slavery. Harper's Ferry, West Virginia is located at the intersection of Maryland, Virginia and West Virginia. The federal arsenal and armory, built in 1796, manufactured muskets and rifles used in the War of 1812 and the War Between the States.

On the night of October 16, 1859, Brown, with eighteen men, captured the armory and arsenal. His intent was to incite slaves to insurrection and arm them to fight for their freedom. After a bloody battle, U.S. Marines, under the command of Colonel Robert E. Lee, captured the raiders. Brown and six of his followers were tried for treason, convicted and hanged.

In 1861, a small federal garrison destroyed the arsenal before abandoning the town as a force of Virginians approached them. It was never re-built. One year later, General "Stonewall" Jackson captured the garrison, taking 12,500 Union soldiers as prisoners, before joining Lee at Antietam.

West Virginia was the only state in the Union to separate from a Confederate state (Virginia) during the War Between the States in 1861. Two years later, the territory achieved statehood in 1863.

Circa 1910, the family doctor told our grandparents, Harry Blazer Sr. and Mary Aurelia Hannan Blazer they had to move Mrs. Blazer to either Phoenix or Florida to provide relief for her breathing difficulty. They chose Florida. As the family had ancestors living in Point Pleasant area over 100 years, I can only imagine how sad it was for the family to sell their Point Pleasant property and move to Florida for the rest of their lives, leaving behind family and friends.

Especially sad was our Great Grandfather, Philip Blazer (1832-1921) leaving behind his Northern Army Seventh Ohio Calvary comrades he had served with as an officer during the War Between the States. He was also leaving four other children and their families behind as he went with our mother's parents, our mother and her two brothers.

The family traveled by train to the beautiful Kissimmee, Florida area where they thought would be an acceptable location for Grandmother's health. As she continued to have difficulty through their first year in Florida, they decided to take the train as far south as the Henry B. Plant Railroad would take them to the southwest coast of Florida. They got off the train at the last stop in Fort Myers.

They built a house in a sleepy village called Punta Gorda, located 20 miles north of Fort Myers. Grandfather owned and operated a wood pallet business in Arcadia, about 25 miles north on US Highway 17. I would deduct that he had a successful business in Point Pleasant, as he appeared to be a confident entrepreneur. With the help of his family, he would also operate a boarding house in their home.

The family was active in community events, and especially their local Methodist Church. They could walk the short distance to the church centrally located in their town. At the time of their move to Florida, Mother was 3 years old and her grandfather Philip Blazer, father, mother, and two brothers; were 78, 52, 40, 17, and 7 respectively. Like so many families, they were a typical three generation family.

Great Grandfather Philip Blazer lived 11 years after their move to Florida, as he was well cared for by his son and daughter in law. He lived as a widow for 25 years after his wife, Caroline died in 1896. Grandfather lived 28 years and Grandmother lived 25 years in Florida. So, evidently, the warm humid climate was just what the doctor ordered for her to live out a full 68 years here on earth. Ironically, our Uncle Johnnie Humphrey lived his final years in Phoenix, Arizona. He was a retired Army Captain serving in World War II. He suffered war wounds of which he received a purple heart.

In 1935, Harry Blazer Sr. purchased 8 burial lots at Indian Springs Cemetery on South Taylor Road, about 3 miles south of Punto Gorda. Most likely, he thought their 3 children and possible spouses would want to be buried there also. For whatever reasons, they are the only 2 relatives buried in that family burial space. Their graves are about 50 feet from their beloved Governor Albert Gilchrist, our 20th Governor of Florida; serving from 1909 to 1913. The Governor was like family to the community. He died in 1926.

Great Grandfather Philip Blazer died in 1921, at age 89. At that time in our family history; Grandfather was 63, Grandmother 51, as they had been local residents for ten years. I believe they all would have many fond family memories that no doubt could have been recorded as a best seller. Grandmother died later in 1935 at age 65 and Grandfather died in 1938 at age 80. Mother was 31, Sandford 45, and Harry Jr. 35, respectively. Father was 36. His father, John Council Humphrey, died 9 years later while living with North Carolina relatives in 1947 at age 69. After Grandfather Blazer died, his property was sold and the children and spouses left the area to live elsewhere. The 6 family burial lots remain empty. Since then, no family member has lived in the immediate Punta Gorda area.

As I wrote this chapter on our family history, I became very fascinated with the adventurous life of our Great Grandfather, Philip Blazer. We only have one photograph of him taken in his final years on earth, and very limited folklore of him shared by our mother. However, with what little we may know, to me he was a mix of movie actor Errol Flynn and Lieutenant Colonel George Custer.

I can see him as Mark Twain operating a river boat up and down the Ohio River, and as a "forty-niner" panning for gold in California. I can see him leading his cavalry horse men, waving his officer's sword as they charged into battle against Morgan's Raiders. I think it was his adventurous spirit that persuaded him to go to Florida with his son Harry and family in lieu of staying in Point Pleasant with his other four children and families, plus his army comrades. Was he always looking for one more *"Hurrah"*?

His adventures took him from Ohio to California, to various southern states, and on to Florida. His ultimate test of reality with courage was on the battle field. We read in Stephen Crane's novel, <u>The Red Badge of Courage</u>, about a Union soldier who struggles to find the courage to fight in the heat of battle. I think our Great Grandfather would tell us that he had a lot more than one chance to test this struggle that is within us.

His life story began well into the horse and buggy days (with trains and ships galore). He got to see the birth of automobiles and airplanes. He had to remiss the fact that he would witness bio-fold airplanes with machine guns replacing men riding horses in full charge as they waved their swords and pistols into battle.

Robert (Bob) Humphrey, Jr. discovered extensive research on my Great Great Great Grandfather Jacob Blazer (1760-?) He has shared it with me for <u>Heritage & Hope</u> . Jacob Blazer (4th great grandfather to Bob) came to Ohio from Germany. He and his wife were both born in Germany. They had 21 children in 30 years. His mother (Bob's 5th great grandmother) was 13 when she had her first child. She was 61 at Jacob's birth. According to records, both his father and mother died the year he was born.

The Blazer family originated east of Bern Switzerland in a town called Langnau, 20 miles east of Bern. It is interesting to note that the family name started as Blaser in Switzerland. They were living in Langnau in 1475 and the family remained there. Somehow he was born in Germany in 1750 and then found himself in the US around 1770. He fought in the American Revolution and membership can be gained in the SAR Sons of the American Revolution organization for his descendants. He is listed in the Official roster of the soldiers of the American Revolution buried in the state of Ohio Repository. He is buried in Gallipolis, Gallia County, Ohio.

This information adds to and compliments the research discovered by Don. Our mother did share with us that she was from German descent. I would believe Jacob Blazer and his Grandson, Phillip, could have written a Best Seller book on their life experiences. It is sad to know we only have a slight glimpse in appreciating what all our founding fathers (and families) accomplished in establishing America in total freedom and hope.

On December 15, 1967, the Silver Bridge that spanned the Ohio River from Gallipolis, Ohio to Point Pleasant, West Virginia collapsed while it was full of rush-hour traffic, causing the deaths of 46 people. The collapsed bridge was replaced by the Silver Memorial Bridge two years later in 1969. The original bridge was built in 1928, the same year our parents were married. Mother recognized one name of the bridge collapse victims. They were family acquaintances when the family lived in Point Pleasant before moving to Florida. The disaster would occur 57 years after their move south.

In regards to some similar Florida history, we think that disasters like the Point Pleasant bridge collapse happens to someone else. However at 7:33 a.m. on Friday, May 9, 1980, it happened in our backyard. During a severe storm, the freighter Summit Venture was blown off course and rammed into one of the Sunshine Skyway Bridge piers.

The pier was destroyed and a section of the bridge roadway crashed into the Tampa Bay water. In a blinding rain, drivers in the southbound lanes were not able to see the missing roadway ahead. Six cars, one truck and a Greyhound Bus plunged into the waters below. Only one man survived the fall as 35 people were killed.

Actually, another four men survived the accident. Richard Hornbuckle was driving his car with three co-workers riding with him. As he was driving very slowly, he saw the missing roadway and slammed on his brakes just in time to stop, only 14 inches from the remaining bridge deck edge. That bridge section was on a slight incline also. They got out of the car and scrambled to safety.

In spite of the plea of a coworker, Richard went back to the car for his golf clubs. Miracles never cease from happening. The old 1954 Skyway Bridge was finally replaced by a new bridge in 1987. The new beautifully designed Skyway Bridge is sturdier, in a better location for ships, and surrounded by bumpers called "dolphins" that can protect the pilings from the impact of a ship like the Summit Venture.

Karen and I were newlyweds living in Auburn, Alabama as I was finishing my last year of college when the Silver Bridge collapsed in 1967. When the Skyway Bridge was hit and collapsed, I was driving to work in West Tampa from our home in Valrico and heard the news on my car radio. The weather was stormy with little visibility.

It was a moment like *"What were you doing when President Kennedy was shot?"* And I remember that day, November 22, 1963, like it was yesterday also. At age 20, I was setting between my plumbing crew supervisor driving a company truck and his plumber riding "shotgun" from work on that day. I was their "gopher and ditch digger". He was shot earlier in the afternoon but I didn't hear about it until we were going home. We were installing plumbing for a new strip mall shopping Center near Cypress Gardens in Winter Haven.

As I finished writing this chapter, I can only look back on the heritage of so many that were truly blessed abundantly by God. In spite of the wars, strife and hard times, I believe our ancestors lived with a desire to be in God's will for their purpose and destiny through their years as they would prepare the way for future generations.

The Great Commission for the Ecclesia of God is the same for our past, present, and future generations; proclaiming the gospel of Jesus Christ to the nations and making disciples in love. The Ecclesia of God in our generation and the generations before us was faithful in reaching the nations with apostles, prophets, evangelists, teachers, and missionaries, preaching and teaching the Word of God to people.

Billions of written copies of God's Word were provided to men, women, boys and girls (in their language) around the world. Also throughout our country's history, so many Americans with gifts of talents provided their skills and time to meet physical needs of people around the world. In Christ, we are freely given, we freely give. It is my hope that this will be true for our future generations as they may personally experience being in the Lord and the truth recorded in Colossians 1:28 *"...Christ in you, the hope of glory."*

I believe God has blessed America tremendously throughout our history as the Body of Christ reached out to the nations through the Great Commission of proclaiming the gospel of Jesus. They did this along with good works in love for people in so many nations. May we continue to do so in hope and faith.
"Then God said, 'Let Us make man in Our image, according to Our likeness...'" (Genesis 1:26a)

Our Father's Oldest Sister, Aunt Annie Oliva Humphrey Dennis (circa1960).
Oldest Child of Grandfather Humphrey and 1st Wife Mary Elizabeth Stocks.

Jerry and Karen visiting Aunt Margaret at her home in NC. (circa 1992)
Aunt Margaret (Bailey) Humphrey (Uncle Richard Lee)
They had four children: Stewart, Richard, Mary Ethel, and Sandra.

Heritage & Hope

———•———

Chapter 3

Humphrey Uncles, Aunts & Cousins

As a starting point, Grandfather John Council Humphrey (1878-1947) married Mary Elizabeth Stocks (1879-1911). Their first child was a daughter, Annie Olivia Humphrey (1899-1972). Annie married Fern Dail (?-?) and then later she married her second husband Charlie Roscoe Dennis (?-?).They had five children: Mary Alyce (?-?), Evelyn (?-?), Doris (?-?), Roscoe Wooten (1922-1985), and Boy Dennis (1931-?). Total of three daughters and two sons.

Their second child was a son, Allan Rufus Humphrey, Sr. (1902-1967). Allan married Frances Caroline Blazer (1907-1969). They had eleven children: Mary Elizabeth (1929-2013), Allan Rufus, Jr. (1930-1932), unnamed son (1933-1933), Charles Benton (1934-1975), Robert Lee, Sr. (1937-2013), Lloyd Allan, Sr. (1938-2017), Philip Eugene, Sr. (1939-2017), Harry Blazer (1940-1996), Jerry Ernest (1943-   ), Michael James (1946-2009), and Donald Patrick (1947-   ). Total of one daughter and ten sons.

Their third child was a son, Johnnie William Humphrey (1907-1984). He married Reba Louise Huston (1901-?), Ann, Sally and May. No children.

Mary Elizabeth Stocks died in 1911, when her three children ranged from 11 to 4 years old. John Council Humphrey then married Apsley Ethel Fulford (1891-1938). Their first child was a daughter, Irene Humphrey living five days (1914-1914). Their second child was a son, Woodrow Wilson Humphrey, Sr. (1916-1990). Woodrow married Gladys Lucille Baker (1920- ?) They had two children: Janet Marie (1939-1995) and a son, Woodrow Wilson, Jr. (?-1995). Total of one daughter and son.

Their third child was a son, Richard Lee Humphrey (1918-1985). Richard married Sallie Margaret Bailey (1923-1998). They had four children: James Stewart (1942-   ), Richard Carroll (1944-2017), Mary

Ethel (1948-   ) and Sandra Kaye (1955-   ). Total of two sons and two daughters.

Their fourth child was a daughter, Julia Janie Humphrey (1921-2003). She married Carson Henry David Baker (1917-1983). They had five children: Barbara Baker (1939-2016), Thomas Baker (1944-   ), Johnathan David Baker (1946-2017), Bonnie Ethelyne Baker (1951-1967), and Constance Ann Baker (1953-   ). Total of three daughters and two sons.

John Council Humphrey, had three children with his first wife Mary Elizabeth Stocks and four children with his second wife, Apsley Ethel Fulford, for a total of seven children.

Our Father, Allan Rufus Humphrey, Sr. and mother, Frances Caroline Blazer had eleven children. This is my immediate family. Our birth dates ranged over an eighteen year period, from 1929 through 1947. The three youngest children barely knew the four oldest living children. Our family had four groups of siblings as we grew up. They were Mary, and Allan Jr.; Charles and Robert; Lloyd, Philip and Harry; and me, Michael and Donald. Our sibling living five minutes was in the first group.

In the Humphrey family tree, we had three Uncles: Johnnie William, Woodward Wilson, and Richard Lee. We had two Aunts, Annie Olivia and Julia Janie. We had twenty one first cousins within the families of our three uncles and two aunts. Including our immediate family of eleven children, we have twenty seven first cousins within our immediate generation.

The work to publish our complete Humphrey family tree is being reserved for future generations to accomplish. Also, Donald is working on a book to include a complete tree to date with related information.

I did not realize that our family was totally isolated from the families of our uncles and aunts. As I grew up during the 1940s and 1950s, I never thought much about having an extended family on our father's family nor on our mother's family. We never had cousins living nearby to grow up with. They were like the old saying, *"Out of sight, Out of mind."*

We were living on Clay Turner Road in Springhead 1948, the first time we had extended family visit us. One day, Mother's brother and wife made a brief afternoon visit. They took photographs, which was extremely exciting to us as we never had a camera to take family photos. In one snapshot, I was standing in a strawberry field in coveralls and barefoot with four brothers. That was our only visit.

The next visits were from Uncle Johnnie and Reba around 1955 when we lived on Trapnell Road and again around 1957 when we lived in Youmans on Highway 92. Reba was confined to a wheel chair from an earlier health condition. As a retired Army Captain, Uncle Johnnie and Reba were free to travel in their silver Airstream Travel Trailer that he pulled behind his car.

He fought in World War II with, I believe, General Patton in North Africa and Europe. He received a Purple Heart medal for being wounded by exploding shrapnel. We were in awe as we viewed the medals he was awarded during his service. He enjoyed helping us with the farm chores.

As newlyweds in 1957, Charles and Barbara lived with us for a brief time as they found housing to move into after he served four years in the Marine Corp. Father was working up north at that time. They were like movie stars stuck with staying in an old frame house with three bedrooms and one bathroom full of six boys ranging from age 10 to 19, not knowing how to act around a girl living in our midst. With me being 14, I thought they looked like Rock Hudson and Elizabeth Taylor in the movie, "Giant". To say the least, that was a very awkward time for all of us. Overall, I believe Barbara found the ordeal quite amusing. It did have the makings for a good comedy.

Aunt Janie, Carson and children, Tom, Johnnie, Bonnie and Connie, visited Barbara and Charles about a year later. They visited us for a brief time also. Our farm was next to a large beautiful orange grove loaded with oranges. Tom and Johnnie enjoyed seeing the trees up close and climbing them. We jokingly debated on which state had the worst hurricanes.

Our parents, Donald, Michael and I drove to Long Island, New York in June of 1960, to work on a farm in Commack. I was 16. We stopped by to see Uncle Richard Lee and Aunt Janie's families for the afternoon with an overnight stay. We visited Uncle Richard Lee and Margaret's family along with Aunt Janie's family at his house in the afternoon. This visit was the first time we had met Uncle Richard Lee and Margaret, and their children, Stewart, Carroll, Mary Ethel and Sandra.

That was the infamous day that Uncle Richard Lee allowed Stewart to take us boys on a Sunday afternoon cruise. We had three families of seven teenaged boys: Stewart, Carroll, Tom, Johnnie, Michael, Donald and me: all piled into the family's 1956 four door Chevrolet. Stewart took us on a cruising tour of nearby small towns and then on some country clay roads.

He asked me if I wanted to drive on a clay road and I said ok. That was a big mistake as I did not realize how slick wet clay can be. Within minutes of driving, I felt the car back end slide to the left too much. In an attempt to correct the slide, I over compensated the sliding motion to the right till the car made a fast 180 degree turn and stopped on the side of the road embankment which had a steep slope down to the road ditch bottom.

Then the car started to roll over in slow motion downhill on the road shoulder until we were upside down. As we didn't use seat belts then, all seven of us were in a pile of bodies on the car roof interior. Guardian angels protected us from being injured. Needless to say, we did not have a pleasant time facing our parents and their displeasure at hearing what happened to us on what should have been a relaxing Sunday afternoon drive in the country. Even though it has been fifty five years, I can still see the accident in slow motion. I deeply regretted it happened. We stayed at Aunt Janie's house and left for New York early the next morning. During that next day, we visited Uncle Woodrow and Aunt Lucille in Norfolk, Virginia. He had moved to the area and was employed at the Naval Shipyard. The visit was very brief as we had to continue our trip to New York.

One Saturday in the summer of 60 while working on a farm in Commack, Long Island, Father drove us to Princeton, New Jersey to visit Aunt Annie. She was 61 and Father was 58. She was the oldest of her siblings with Father being the second oldest child. I remember her living alone in a house located in the college town of Princeton. She served us an early dinner on a table in her back yard.

I still remember her swatting flies with a fly flap as we all used our left hand shooing flies away from our food as we ate with our right hand. She was so nonchalant about the ordeal that it was downright comical. Without missing a beat, she carried on a conversation as if everything was fine. That visit was the only time I saw her in my life. She would live another twelve years. Father would live another seven years. I never did meet any of her five children.

My next visit with Uncle Woodrow occurred during the summer of '62. I had just finished boot camp at Paris Island and was assigned two months of assault amphibian vehicle training at Camp Lejeune in North Carolina I decided to take a bus trip to Norfolk, Virginia on a long weekend liberty leave to visit Uncle Woodrow and Lucille.

I arrived at the Norfolk bus station in the late afternoon. Uncle Woodrow was only 46 and was employed at the shipyard. He picked me up at the bus station and drove me back to the station after we had a brief visit with him and Aunt Lucille at their home. The drive from the station to their home took about forty five minutes or so. That visit was the last time I would see Uncle Woodrow and Aunt Lucille. Father left home for Florida by the time Woodrow started school. Woodrow had few memories of our father.

My first meeting with Cousin Woodrow (Woody) Wilson Humphrey, Jr. was providential. We met by coincidence at the Marine Corp Camp Lejeune base during that same summer of 62. One day I was on a "pick up" team of Marines playing each other in a game of volleyball. During the game, I kept hearing the opposing team players hollering out *"Humphrey this and Humphrey that"*. After the game was over, I approached him and told him I was a Humphrey also. We talked a little more and soon discovered that we were first cousins. We talked about getting together again soon. Time slipped by, then my six months of active duty was over, and I was shipped home. That visit on a Marine Corp base volleyball field was the first and last time I saw Cousin "Woody".

Looking back at my meeting with Uncle Woodrow and my coincidental meeting with Cousin Woodrow in the summer of 62, I think of both meetings as being providential. I don't think any other of my family siblings had the opportunity to meet Uncle Woodrow, Aunt Lucille, nor Cousin "Woody".

On another weekend liberty during my two months at Camp Lejeune, I hitched rides for the sixty so miles to the Farmville area of North Carolina to visit Uncle Richard Lee and family. It was dark as I arrived in the area and I was not sure how to find his house. And I didn't have a cell phone like today. I walked into a country store that was still opened. There were two men talking at the cash register and I asked them if they knew the Richard Lee Humphrey family and one of the men spoke up and said *"Yes, I know them. They live right down the road. I can drive you to their house."*

So off we went. In a few minutes I had arrived safely and sort of on time for my weekend visit. That was only two years after my infamous visit in the summer of 60. Once again I was treated to a tour of the area the next day as I also got to visit with them. I didn't get an offer to drive anymore.

Many years later in the 90s, Karen, Kimberly, Greg and I visited Aunt Janie, Cousin Stewart and his wife, Linda, in Ashville, North Carolina. Our visit was cut short a day as we had car trouble on the drive up from home. We all were disappointed in having to cancel a planned trip to the Biltmore Estate in Ashville with Aunt Janie. Stewart did take us on a tour of the North Carolina United Methodist Children's Home, where he was Director. Also during the 90s, Karen, Kimberly and Greg and I had an overnight visit with Aunt Margaret and Sandy on another trip we took to New England.

Around 1981, Robert and Donna took a vacation trip to see the Grand Canyon National Park and other nearby tourist sites. On the way out, they stopped by to visit Uncle Johnnie in Phoenix, Arizona. Even though his health was deteriorating, he raised the American flag daily in his front yard. He died a few years later in 1984 at age 77.

We had an opportunity to visit with extended family members around the Greenville area along with meeting a few more cousins of cousins for the first time at Aunt Janie's funeral in 2003. Once again, it was a one day visit including a lunch. Eventually, Connie moved into the Tampa Bay area to stay. Some years later, Tom moved to the *"Sunshine State"* also and is now living in Daytona Beach Shores.

As a cousin of cousins through marriages, I guess we have a distant kinship to movie actress Ava Gardner. She was born in nearby Smithfield, North Carolina, and also lived in Newport News, Virginia and Rock Ridge, North Carolina. Her parents, Mary Elizabeth (Molly) and Jonas Gardner, were originally cotton and tobacco farmers. Ava's mother maiden name was Baker.

Ava was born in 1922 and died in 1990 at age 67. Aunt Janie married Carson Baker, a relative of Ava Gardner. Carson was born in 1917 and Janie was born in 1921. All three were close in age and lived sort of close to each other. I wonder if they ever met at a reunion or special event. When she was discovered by MGM in 1941, her North Carolina accent was so thick, she had to work with a speech coach to overcome her Southern drawl before making her first movie. As they say in in some iconic cartoons, *"That's all folks"*.

"I will say of the Lord, "He is my refuge and my fortress; My God, in Him I will trust."" (Psalm 91:2).

Our Parents, Allan Rufus Humphrey, Sr. and Frances Caroline Blazer September 21, 1928 Wedding Day in Punta Gorda, Florida.

Allan Rufus Humphrey, Jr. born December 16, 1930 in Punta Gorda died of pneumonia on October 21, 1932 in Farmville, North Carolina (circa1931).

Jerry as a preteen in the mid 50s at Turkey Creek Junior High School.

Father's younger brother Johnnie William Humphrey (circa 1942).
Uncle Johnnie served in the Army during WW II in Africa and Europe.
He signed up as an enlisted man and retired as a Captain. He would visit us
quite often from his North Carolina home base during his retirement years.

Heritage & Hope

———•———

Chapter 4

Our Baseball Team

Whenever someone would ask me how many kids we had in our family. I mean siblings, as this was eons before political correctness. And yes, I do know a kid is a young goat. I could jokingly answer, *"We have ten little Indians"* (another PC dig). Or I would say, *"We have a baseball team of nine boys with our older sister being the team coach"*. With forever increasing PC regulations, I am afraid to call us anything now.

Actually, it didn't matter what you called us; as long as we were called to the supper table on time. Our family included nine boys and one girl with birth years ranging from 1929 through 1947. The first name was probably a more realistic identification.

Over the years we would ask the question to our parents at the dinner table on why we had so many kids. Our father would always answer, *"Well, if we didn't, you wouldn't be here."* Although he was directing his answer to the one asking the question, we all knew he was referring to each of us at that time also. This answer has always sort of satisfied my appetite for a reason of why so many kids.

Another thought would be the fact that many families living on farms had a large number of children to help with the farm chores. We know that large families were traditional and common. Child labor was prominent in family farms and businesses throughout the country right up until the 1950s decade.

And I have another possibility for consideration. Our parents moved to our father's home town area of Winterville, North Carolina in 1932. Their first boy, Allan Jr. died from pneumonia at the age of 2 in North Carolina. In our mother's grieving, she insisted that they move back to Florida. Mary was the family's first born child and our only sister. Over the next twenty some years, they had ten boys with the second one dying a few minutes after his birth. Our parents did not officially name him. *"Before I formed you in the womb I knew you…"* (Jeremiah 1:5). I believe he has a name for eternity.

After the loss of their first two sons so early into their marriage, did they desire to have an abundance of children? Regardless, I do believe that God has a purpose and destiny for each of us in His eternal Kingdom on earth and in Heaven.

As it could have been; our baseball team would include our parents as Team Managers, our only sister Mary as Coach, Allan Jr - Pitcher, Charles - Catcher, Robert - First Baseman, Lloyd - Second Baseman, Philip - Third Baseman, Harry - Shortstop, Jerry - Left Fielder, Michael - Center Fielder, and Donald - Right Fielder.

My listing is in the order of each one's respective age with Mary always being the coach in our lives over the years, right up to her passing at age 84 in 2013. I would like to think of our third unnamed brother being our team "Honorary Coach". He is 85 years old now. This is the first time in my life that I have thought to list each family member in a respective team position. I listed the team from the oldest to the youngest. Could there be another consideration?

And we never played a single game as a full team of nine. However, we did play plenty of softball with teams made up of siblings and friends. I do remember we would make up teams with siblings and neighborhood friends to play backyard softball and football. Those backyard and pasture lot games were popular during the 50s especially as professional football was beginning to be shown more and more on television. Basketball was out of the question as it was not so popular in the day. Plus, it was impossible to play a basketball game on grass. Later in life, we played volley ball and horse shoes.

"Have I not commanded you? Be strong and of good courage; do not be afraid, nor be dismayed, for the Lord your God is with you wherever you go." (Joshua 1:9)

Heritage and Hope

———— · ————

Chapter 5

WW I/Roaring 20s/Great Depression

Father and Mother, born in 1902 and 1907 respectively, grew into adulthood in the midst of World War I, the Roaring Twenties, and the Great Depression. Our nation survived times of war and peace, deceptive wealth, excessive luxuries and great losses. Boom time in the Ft. Myers/Punta Gordo area went to an abrupt hard time. They went from their wedding year of 1928 into thirteen years of challenging times, and then they went right into World War II.

Men and women moved from rural areas to large cities looking for a way to start building their American Dream in the ever expanding industrial sector, while basically neglecting the nation's agriculture industry. World War I, also known as the Great War, began on July 28, 1914 and lasted until November 11, 1918. Our country remained neutral until 1917, when we joined the Allies, to turn the tide of the war to victory.

More than nine million combatants and seven million civilians died as a result of that war. It was one of the deadliest conflicts in the history of mankind. The Central Powers agreed to an armistice on November 11, 1918, ending the war in victory for the Allies. Father and Mother were respectively 15 and 10 years old, when America entered the war in 1917.

Although the war was "Over There" in Europe and they were both too young for military service, it still had to have a personal effect on their childhood development as they were growing into young adults. Our generation and all generations to come must never forget the sacrifices so many men and women made in this Great War as well as other wars that have been fought and will be fought to protect our freedom, and the freedom for all nations (as they may choose to be free). Let's always remember "*World War I was the war to end all wars.*"

After celebrating victory in a big way, people quickly turned their attention, as always, to their pursuit of prosperity with luxury following close behind as they entered into the Roaring Twenties. In 1920, the women's rights movement won passage of a constitutional amendment granting women's suffrage. Young women of the period expressing freedom from conventional conduct were called "Flappers". Overnight, Jazz music became very popular.

The radio, telephone and record player became popular for mass communications and entertainment. The public had extra money to spend on consumer goods such as record players, telephones, ready to wear clothes (rather than home-made) and house appliances like electric refrigerators, stoves and washing machines.

Evangelist Billy Sunday was the Billy Graham of that era. He held tent revivals and preached to the multitudes. Father told us that he attended a Billy Sunday crusade meeting one night with our grandfather. They attended other crusades also.

Prohibition was a law restricting the manufacturing, selling, exporting, importing, and transporting of any alcoholic beverage. As an ironic oversight, it did not include a statement that restricted the specific act of drinking any alcoholic beverages. The law was in effect from January 16, 1919 until December 5, 1933, at the time it was replaced by the 21st amendment. Speakeasies that resulted were definitely some of the most secretive and rebellious things to experience in the 1920s. They were basically secret alcoholic lounges with hidden doors for secret entry. Illegal transportation of liquor and gang activities skyrocketed during that time.

It did make for a lot of "cops and robbers" movies with stars like James Cagney and Edward G. Robinson. Cagney's fifth movie role made him an overnight star as he played a ruthless gangster in the 1931 movie, "Public Enemy". Robinson was forever identified with the snarling gangster role of "Little Caesar" in the 1930 movie. One of my favorite movies was "Key Largo" staring Edward G. Robinson as gangster Johnny Rocco. That 1948 movie was the last of five films he made with Humphrey Bogart. The good guy always won. The bad guy always lost. And we always left the theater knowing that crime does not pay!

Radio was the rage in that era also. Pittsburgh's KDKA was the first radio station established in 1920. Three years later, there were more than five hundred stations in the nation. Within ten years, over twelve million households had a radio. People also flocked to the movies. By 1930, seventy five per cent of the population was visiting a movie theater every week. We always had a few dimes and nickels to buy a theater ticket.

The most desired product to purchase was the automobile. In 1920, low prices made cars affordable luxuries. In 1924, a Model T Ford was priced at $260. By 1930, automobiles were practical a necessity. Twenty per cent of the population had a car at that time. The automobile industry cottage businesses such as service stations, restaurants, and motels were created to meet the traveling needs of the population.

The nations of the world were shaken for thirty one years; as (by the grace of God) we were victorious in two world wars, a deceptive time of prosperity, and a great depression.

And to think, our parents lived through every day of those terrible years from 1914 - 1945, one day at a time. I believe anyone living through those thirty one years should be given a medal of some kind and our upmost respect. Father and Mother were respectively 43 and 38 years old when WW II ended in 1945.

As I reflect on all those years of struggling, I thought about what Jesus said, as recorded in John 10:10: *"The thief does not come except to steal, and to kill, and to destroy, I have come that they may have life, and that they may have it more abundantly."* I believe our nation obtained victory in Jesus to God's glory and honor in each of those horrible events. We will want to trust in Him for our victory and freedom that already is in Christ for all things.

As we are being in Christ, we do His works in obedience to His Great Commission as recorded in Matthew 28:19-20: *"Go therefore and make disciples of all the nations, baptizing them in the name of the Father and of the Son and of the Holy Spirit, teaching them to observe all things that I have commanded you; and lo, I am with you always, even to the end of the age."*

In His Word, God promises blessings and prosperity to those individuals and nations observing His commandments. As individuals and as a nation, we will want His blessings and we will want to be confident that we are protected by Him.

This early 1900s church sanctuary, the Methodist Church, and Mother's family house were all located on the town's main street (Highway US 41).

John Council Humphrey 2nd Wife, Apsley Ethel Fulford Humphrey White. Woman on the left is un-identified. (circa 1928).

Heritage & Hope

———·———

Chapter 6

Some Ft. Myers/Punta Gorda History

After the world's most famous inventor, Thomas Edison, visited Ft. Myers during his young adult years, he fell in love with the area. At age 38 in 1885, he purchased a section of land on the Caloosahatchee River in Ft Myers. The tropical community had a grand total population of 349 people.

During the next two years, he designed and pre-fabricated a house in New Jersey. He shipped and erected it on his Florida property. He would also build an in ground concrete pool in his backyard. It was most likely one of the first ones to be built in our state. He built a laboratory building along with planting trees to be used to make various products such as tires.

He would use this compound for the winters and his New Jersey laboratory in the summers. He would live this lifestyle for some forty six years, till his death in 1931. The compound remains just as it did the very day he died. His friend, Henry Ford, would join him as he built a winter home next door to the Edison house.

These two properties (like diamonds in the rough) exist today as tourist attractions. I am flabbergasted at how few people have ever heard of these historic sites, let alone visited them. This includes the people residing in Florida as well as tourists visiting Florida. These men were instrumental in helping to make America great. Allow for at least a three hour tour.

This way of life would become very popular for many families. It would become common place after World War II, just like "snow birds" flying back and forth north/south every year. It still continues, even though our state population exceeds 20,600,000 people today. This number includes those moving to Florida to live as permanent residents. In comparison, our population was 750,000 and 2,770,000 in 1910 and 1950, respectively. And the growth still continues today.

In 1884, a severe freeze in the state resulted in much of the citrus industry moving farther south with some of it to the Ft. Myers/Punta Gorda area. The 20th century opened with 943 residents in Ft. Myers. The town was in a "building boom". The growth would increase in 1904 with the arrival of the Coast Line Railroad. Bradford Hotel was built that same year.

During the 1920s, the Seaboard Railroad expanded to Ft. Myers competing with Henry Plant's already established Coast Line to the city. Terminals from that period can still be seen today. In 1928, the same year our parents were married in Punta Gorda, the legendary Tamiami Trail (US Highway 41) was finally opened after extreme construction challenges in building the highway through wet lands infested with snakes and mosquitos.

That major civil engineering and construction feat provided a highway with no roadway interferences from SR 60 in Tampa, down the west coast to Naples, crossing the Everglades, and then going straight into Miami, ending at US 1. That highway gave the southwest gulf coast a wide opened door for development.

We now have I-75 as a speedy alternate route between Tampa and Miami. Regardless, everyone should take the time to drive leisurely down the Tamiami Trail; stopping to visit Everglades City, take an airboat ride, walk the Everglades national park walkway trails, and visit Indian exhibits.

In 1910, the family doctor told our mother's parents, Harry Blazer Sr. and Mary Aurelia Hannan Blazer they had to move Mrs. Blazer to Phoenix or Florida to relief her ongoing breathing difficulty. They chose Florida.

As the family had ancestors living in the Point Pleasant, West Virginia area since the early 1800s, I can only imagine how sad it was for the family to sell their house and move to Florida, leaving family and friends for the rest of their lives. One family member extremely sad had to be our Great Grandfather, Philip Blazer (1832-1921) as he was leaving behind his Northern Army comrades he had served with during the War Between the States, forty five years earlier.

The family traveled via train to the Kissimmee, Florida area where they thought would be an acceptable location for Grandmother's health. As she continued to have difficulty breathing through their first year in

Florida, they decided in 1911 to take the train as far south as the Henry B. Plant Railroad would take them to the southwest coast of Florida.

They got off the train at the last stop in Fort Myers. They would build a house and live in a small fishing village called Punto Gorda, a short distance north of Fort Myers. They took their two sons and daughter with them to that small village.

The daughter (our mother) was age 3. Her grandfather Philip Blazer, father, mother, and two brothers were 78, 52, 40, 17, and 7 respectively. Like many families in that time, they were a typical three generation family unit. They moved a long distance from Point Pleasant, West Virginia to a harsh life in a central Florida wilderness. Her grandfather was born in Ohio. He was 38 when he was discharged from the Northern Army after the war in 1865.

My mother's family home in Punto Gorda was about twenty five miles north of the Thomas Edison Fort Myers house. They owned and operated a boarding house on Highway US 41 in Punta Gorda.

I think it was at that boarding house our father and mother met in the mid 1920s. She considered attending Florida Southern College in Lakeland after graduating from school in 1927. They lived within walking distance of the Punta Gorda Methodist Church, where they were active members.

As a note of church history trivial, The United Methodist Church was formed from a union of the Methodist Church and Evangelical United Brethren Church in 1968.

In 1905, several downtown Punta Gorda buildings were destroyed by a fire. Like so many cities in our country, wood buildings almost touching each other in the late 1800s were powder kegs waiting to explode. After that disaster, the city council mandated that all new business structures be constructed of brick or concrete. The Methodist Church congregation built a beautiful modern brick sanctuary building in 1913. The church property had been purchased previously for $250 in 1887. As a price comparison for the time, a box of Kellogg's corn flakes cost nine cents in 1910.

With mother's family living so close to the Thomas Edison property for twenty one years (from 1910 till Edison's death in 1931) I often wondered if mother's family ever ran into Edison during any of their trips to Ft. Myers and didn't recognize him at that moment. The best of my memory, she told us that she never did have the opportunity of meeting Edison.

One resident of Ponta Gorda that our mother always proudly talked about was Albert Gilchrist. He was our 20th Governor of Florida, serving from 1909 to 1913.

She would tell us what a good man he was. His main platform issue was to improve the state's health. He was Governor during the first three years her family lived in Punto Gorda.

He was born in 1858 at Greenwood, South Carolina and died in 1926 at New York, New York. He attended the United States Military at West Point for three years, and served in the Florida state militia, reaching the rank of Brigadier General. He left the state militia to serve in the U. S. Army during the 1898 Spanish American War. He reached the rank of Captain in the regular army before being discharged in 1899.

He would work as a civil engineer and in real estate sales before settling down in Punta Gorda to become an orange grove grower. In 1893, he was elected to the Florida House of Representatives where he served until 1905.

The Florida Legislature passed a bill naming Gilchrist County (northwest of Gainesville) after him. The bridge for U. S. Highway 41 crossing over Peace River was named Gilchrist Bridge. A dormitory at Florida State University was named after the former Governor. Plant City named a street and a park Gilchrist in his honor also. Upon his death, the bachelor governor left a large portion of his estate to local orphans.

I would certainly think he had plenty of opportunities to see a future president in action during the 1898 Spanish American War. The flamboyant and very progressive Theodore Roosevelt would charge up San Juan Hill on his horse; while waving his sword (maybe?), leading his "Rough Riders" into battle against the Spanish Army. They had traveled on train to Tampa and then embarked on ships to Cuba. Sone Officers stayed in the Plant Hotel during their brief time in Tampa.

I pondered my mother's life as a 3 year old child growing up with her two older brothers, age 7 and 17, in that subtropical environment. I can only deduce that she lived her youth filled with tender loving care and happiness. I think she was completely protected in that small main street town. I believe she grew up as a shy, compliant, trusting girl in a small close knit community of people that cared for one another. It was all about family. I believe she knew and was known by most everyone living in Punta Gorda from the time the family moved into their house in 1911 till the day she left town with our father soon after their September 21, 1928 wedding.

Unfortunately, her paradise did not escape the Influenza Epidemic of 1918. That dreaded disease killed more people than the number of people dying in World War I. Our mother had a near death experience with influenza during that time. The epidemic created a panic rush for nurses. The Chicago School of Nursing was recruiting women as students, promoting potential earnings from $15 to $25 per week.

After their wedding day, our family moving would begin. Father and mother would make their first move to Tampa where our first sibling and only sister, Mary, was born on June 20, 1929. Of course they would take the newly completed Tamiami Trail with a record drive time to Tampa.

Just like the unexpected stock market crash only four months away on October 1929, the reality of hardships was soon to hit our nation, states, counties, cities; and definitely our newlywed family of three. It will be like a major hurricane striking with widespread devastation. For years, men would ask other men, *"Brother, can you spare a dime for a cup of coffee?"* That saying taken from a song written in 1930 by "Yip" Harburg and Jay Gorney was frequently heard during the depression.

"Trust in the Lord with all your heart, and lean not on your own understanding: in all your ways acknowledge Him, and He shall direct your paths."
(Proverbs 3:5-6)

Our House on Rice Road east of County Line Road.
I was in the 4th grade at Springhead Elementary when we lived here in 1952.
The house is still occupied as a residence (2018 Photo).

Photograph courtesy of Plant City Photo Archives & History Center.
Plant City State Farmers Market is located in the southwest area of the town.
Note the trucks and cars lined up to enter the open air market structure.
Our produce, including strawberries, would be auctioned to the highest bidder.
Memories of our market trips are very similar to this photo scene.

Heritage & Hope

————— • —————

Chapter 7

A Fantasy of Great Magnitude

Three of Thomas Edison quotes on how to achieve success are: "Opportunity is a chance missed by most people because it is dressed in overalls and looks like work." plus: "The three great essentials to achieve anything worthwhile are: Hard work, Stick-to-itiveness and Common sense." and my favorite of all: "There is no substitute for hard work".

I cannot help but think how the answer to one "what if" question would be very intriguing, especially based on Mother living only twenty five miles north of Thomas Edison on Highway US 41 for twenty one years. Although our mother never mentioned that she had met him personally, I can only envision a chance encounter with the famed inventor similar to the following story. It is a tale that could have been told by my mother. I look back in time as I consider the possibility of what could have happened almost a century ago.

"It was a warm winter Saturday morning in mid December 1922. The state economy at the time was in a sort of an expansion with a bright future. Florida was looking for a "Boom Time" along with Ft. Myers sharing in the good times.

As a fifteen year old ninth grader, I was riding with my parents on a day trip to Ft. Myers to see Christmas decorations and then window shop at the stores on Main Street. My two older brothers were preoccupied on that day. We planned to drive around the town to see the new commercial and residential buildings being construed throughout the town with the new Mediterranean Revival Design and Construction. We would also drive down McGregor Boulevard to see the recently planted majestic palms.

Best of all, we were going to see a movie at the local theater. I was excited for this part of the trip as Rudolph Valentino's latest role staring as a bullfighter in Son of the Sand was playing. In 1921, he had achieved the status of becoming the first male superstar actor for his role in Four Horsemen of the Apocalypse. Tragically, his charmed life had a sad ending. He would die in 1926 at the youthful age of 31 following surgery for peritonitis. I cried along with so many other girls on that day.

And I was looking forward to eating supper in Fort Myers. I wanted my favorite dishes of smoked mullet, grits, cold slaw, mustard greens, hush puppies, and sweet iced tea. The desert had to be a slice of Key Lime Pie.

After driving a very short distance south of the bridge, we passed an elderly man struggling to change a flat tire on his car. We pulled off the roadway and the man gladly accepted Father's offer to finish the task at hand. He looked to be about 75 years old with a shuffled look, wearing baggy trousers and a long sleeve shirt.

He quickly sat down on the running board. As he wiped the sweat and dirt off his face and hands with his handkerchief, he looked at my father and said, "I am very appreciative of your act of kindness." Once the tire was changed, we were ready to continue our journey. My father and I realized this stranger was none other than the famed Thomas Edison. He looked exactly like the photos we had seen of him through the years in newspaper articles.

Just like a curious teenager, I excitedly eked out "Are you Thomas Edison?" He answered in a monotone voice, "Yes, that's what I am told quite often." Then he laughed and said "I do appreciate your help in changing my flat tire. Will you allow me the opportunity to show you around my laboratory and property?" I was ecstatic when I heard my father quickly answer, "We would love to. Lead the way."

We were at his compound within a few minutes. He grabbed ice cold 6 oz. glass bottles of Coca Cola for each of us from a commercial Coca Cola ice chest in the laboratory.

The property was breath taking with the house and laboratory competing with the trees and plants that filled the landscape open spaces like a jungle. All of his experimental trees were growing like weeds reaching for the blue sky and sunshine. His below ground concrete swimming pool was full of clear water. He walked us down to the river bank to show us where he went fishing without a hook and bait. He said he only used his fishing time as a much needed nap time. So those napping stories were really true after all. The river bank with palms, cedars, oaks and pines were an untouched tropical paradise.

As he finished giving us a tour of his compound, a slight elderly man walked over briskly from the neighboring house to join us. As he approached us with piercing eyes, Thomas Edison announced, "I want you to meet Mr. Henry Ford, my good friend and neighbor." Mr. Ford noticed we were driving a three year old Model T Ford and he asked my father if he was completely satisfied with our car. Father said, "Yes, it has been a fine automobile to own and drive." Mr. Ford said, "Good, we want the next vehicle you purchase to be a Ford also. By the way, in a few years we will have a new model available for you to own, the Model A. "It's going to be 'The Car' for the roadways of America."

Just as abruptly as he had met us, Mr. Edison promptly excused himself from our short visit as he noted that he and Mr. Ford had a scheduled meeting with Harvey Firestone on how to improve on the lifetime of tires and engine belts.

After exchanging our good byes, we climbed into our Model T and continued the few blocks to downtown on main street (years later becoming the Tamiami Trail) with memories of a fantastic experience living history in such a personably way."

As I have stated, it is what could have happened! But the story does make for an insightful view into a precious time in our family and state history. However, my mother's sheltered youth in her paradise did not prepare her for the shocking hardships that she would experience very soon in her life.

Around 1975, as Karen and I visited mother's childhood house, an elderly couple living there gave us a tour. I was in awe as I walked around the very house my mother's family lived for so many years, some fifty years earlier.

 I visualized people coming and going in a hub of activity at their house through the years they lived there. This would be especially true for the years Punta Gorda resident, Albert Gilchrist, served as Governor of Florida, from 1909 to 1913, and the Tamiami Trail construction years until it's completion in 1928, along with traveling needs for so many during the boom time development era. The house also served as a place to stay for people during the depression years. When we add the mix of the family's active fellowship in the Methodist Church within walking distance, their boarding house was humming with activities for all sorts of people, including the many local friends of three teenagers in their youth group and school.

Grandfather's original concrete bench was still sitting in the front yard. Years later Mrs. Nellie Wells gave our brother Don a similar bench that now sets in his back yard. The bench reminds me of the wooden ones that were placed on the sidewalks of St. Petersburg during the 20th century.

By chance, I was able to obtain one of those original green wooden benches that looked like it would be from around 1930. It was in a St Petersburg scrap yard available to whoever wanted it. I took the bench and had it restored to its original condition. The bench now sits on our back porch with the beautiful deep green color and "St. Petersburg, FL" painted in white letters on the bench backrest (exactly like an original).

With a deep sadness, I regret to write that the house was demolished between the time of our first visit and our second visit around 2000. The concrete bench was gone also. Lloyd and Mildred had moved to the area and a convoy of us siblings with our wives and sister, Mary drove down to visit them one day. Then we toured the site where the house once stood. Next, we visited the Methodist church and then we finalized our trip at our grandparent's graves in Indian Springs Cemetery.

In 1935, our Grandparents purchased a family section with eight lots. They are the only family members buried at the cemetery. The other six lots remain unused to this day. Their beloved Governor Gilcrest is buried some 50 feet away. The cemetery is about three miles south of Punta Gorda. As we toured the graves, I felt an atmosphere of peace and grace.

It would be dismissive to include a history of the Florida southwest coast and not mention hurricanes. Punta Gorda and the surrounding coast area have always been in a very high risk area for hurricanes. Seventy five hurricanes have been recorded as hitting the area. Hurricanes between 1930 and 1949 were unnamed. The largest hurricane was an unnamed one in 1888. Did Mr. Edison wonder what he got himself into? On average, the area has been affected somewhat lightly or a little more, every two and half years or so by a hurricane. Average direct hit by hurricane winds is on an average of eight and half years.

A hurricane hit the area in October, 1910 with 110 mph traveling from the south. That was about the same time Mother's family was moving to Florida from West Virginia. Maybe we could call it their liquid sunshine welcome to Florida.

On September 10, 1960, Hurricane Donna, with 125 mph winds, traveled north from the southeast with a heavy storm surge. Water was pulled out into the Gulf then pulled back inland as the eye traveled northward causing heavy damage. Hurricane Donna would then travel north through the central section of the state. That hurricane is the same one that hit our house in Youmans a short time after we arrived home from our trip to Long Island, New York.

I think everyone living in Florida during the 2004 hurricane season remembers the big four in rapid hits from Charley 8/13, Frances 9/6, Ivan 9/24 and Jeanne 9/26. Charley hit Punta Gorda direct with 145mph winds causing heavy destruction in Charlotte & Desoto counties from wind and a storm surge. It was a small but powerful hurricane, killing thirty three people and causing fourteen billion dollars in damages.

"Are they not all ministering spirits sent forth to minister for those who will inherit salvation?" (Hebrews 1:14)

Front Row Lt to Rt, Jerry and Harry. Back Row, Philip, Lloyd and Robert. Our 1948 residence on Clay Turner Road in Springhead.
Photograph taken by mother's visiting brother, Sanford Blazer, Sr.
We squinted into a sunset with a strawberry field in the background.
The freedom of going barefoot in spite of cuts, rusty nails, sandspurs, etc.
We did not swim near bridges due to a potential broken beer bottle.

I attended grades 5 and 6 at Trapnell Elementary School in 1953 and 1954.
It was a typical early 1900's wood framed structure built in 1935.
We walked to school as it was a short distance west of our house.
Karen taught her first year as a 6th grade teacher at this school in 1966.

Lloyd and Robert on Clay Turner Road in Springhead, 1948.
Rolled up trousers prevent them from getting caught in their bicycle chain.

Heritage & Hope

————•————

Chapter 8

Cross Creek and a Hurting Family

In the flamboyant year of 1928, Marjorie Rawlings left her position as a Reporter for the Boston Globe and moved to the remote community of Cross Creek, Florida. She had her brother purchase a tract of land with a "cracker house" and orange grove in the back woods of Florida for her.

She, along with our family and everyone else, was in for a rude awakening of a great economic depression that would leave profound effects on everyone. During the years while she lived there, she wrote the award winning book, The Yearling and also Cross Creek, among other books.

Movies were made of both in later years. She wrote about families enduring hardships in that very harsh "Garden of Eden". Although she wrote other books, I want to focus on these two. They had time settings in the 1870s and 1930s respectively.

The homestead is now the Marjorie Kinnan Rawlings Historic State Park located in Cross Creek, between Gainesville and Ocala, on County Road 325, five miles east of US Highway 301. In Cross Creek, she summarized her feelings of the area, *"I do not know how anyone can live without some small place of enchantment to turn to."*

This park is a "must see" for all ages. I may also add, both of these books should be a "must read" for everyone calling Florida their home state. And please do enjoy the original movies for both books.

The house with her typewriter and library, the kitchen for gourmet cooking, bedrooms, the outhouse, vegetable and flower garden, tenant house, and the orange grove are all still existing the same as when she lived there. For fifteen or so years, she lived and wrote at that homestead till she finally moved from the area in the mid 40s.

Her fiction book, <u>The Yearling,</u> explored living conditions in the 1870's central Florida, about twenty miles north of Ocala. Characters in this book were based on those she had experiences with in her time at Cross Creek.

Her book, <u>Cross Creek</u> was nonfiction as she described life for several Cross Creek residents during the Great Depression. As we may ride through the country side in all four directions of her homestead today, amazingly we can notice that very little has changed over the some ninety years since the time she started writing about her Cross Creek enchantment.

Our father was born on August 2, 1902 in Hookerton, North Carolina, a few miles south of Greenville. He was raised and worked as a child in tobacco country. In 1922, at age 20, he traveled with his 44 year old father and 15 year old brother, Johnnie, to the Arcadia, Florida area looking for better employment opportunities.

Brothers Woodrow and Richard Lee, at ages 6 and 4, were placed temporarily in a Macon, Georgia children's home. Their mother kept 1 year old sister Janie at home in North Carolina.

Although Father dropped out of school after the eighth grade, he did learn the basic *"Three Rs of reading, riting and rithmetic"* for that 1916 time period. As he grew into an adult, he quickly added "street smarts" to his eight years of formal education.

He entered into a buying and selling produce business venture with his father and brother, I believe, in the fifty mile long area from Wauchula to Punta Gorda. They finally abandoned the business in 1925. His father and brother went back home, picking up Uncles Woodrow and Richard Lee from the Georgia children's home on their trip back to North Carolina. Our father stayed in Florida and eventually became employed with Phoenix Electrical Power Company, working on a crew installing overhead power lines. This work experience helped him to kick start his career in electrical construction work.

His later employment, working as an electrician in the World War II Tampa ship yard building Navy battle ships, also helped his overall electrical career training. He told us that he was too young to serve in WW I and too old to serve in WW II. Early in the economic depression; as he was not able to find adequate employment in Florida and being raised on a farm in the state's tobacco country, he thought he would have better work opportunities in his North Carolina home town.

After our young family of parents, sister Mary, and brother Allan, Jr. moved to North Carolina, our 2 year old brother, Allan Jr. suddenly died of pneumonia on October 21, 1932. Our mother was seven months pregnant with her third child. In her grief, she felt her only son's death was the result of harsh living conditions in North Carolina. Upon her adamant insistence, the family moved back to Florida; this time settling in Seffner. On January 23, 1933, their unnamed baby died a few minutes after birth. Quick as a flash of lighting, within a period of three months; Mother, at the young age of 26, experienced the death of two children.

For some unknown reason, the family went back to Winterville, North Carolina, where our brother Charles was born on August 25, 1934. Our father may have had a promising employment offer in North Carolina prior to leaving Seffner.

It was early spring of 1936; my parents were driving down US Highway 301, leaving Farmville, North Carolina area for the second time within a four year period. They were traveling back south in their Ford Model T headed for Punta Gorda with our sister, Mary, and brother Charles, aged 7 and 2 respectively. Mother probably did not know yet that she was into another pregnancy. On January 16, 1937, Robert would be born in Mother's hometown of Punta Gorda.

Since her marriage in 1928 at age twenty one, she had given birth to four children. In 1932, our brother Allan, Jr. died at age two and another unnamed child died one year later in 1933. The family lived in Farmville about three years before returning to Florida in 1936.

In a short span of eight years, life for Mother was drastically different than the pleasant social life she loved as a naive young lady growing up with loving parents and two older brothers in her beloved Punta Gorda paradise. Although her parents had to live within a very tight budget, their family life in that small community had more overall desirable living conditions than most other towns throughout the country. And her parents enrolled her to attend Florida Southern College in Lakeland. However, love and wedding bells won out.

But now they were headed to Florida again for good. Both Father and Mother had high hopes that things would be better once again in her home town. Their spirit soared as they sped by the sign, *"Welcome to Florida - The Sunshine State"* at a cruising speed of 45 mph, heading south on Highway 301. The sun was beaming with brilliant bright sun light. Their hope was renewed, just as brightly as the sun rays shining between the fluffy white clouds drifting slowly in the deep blue sky. Everything looked so bright and beautiful. They hoped their future would be like that bright sunshine.

"Train up a child in the way he should go,
and when he is old he will not depart from it." (Proverbs 22:6)

Boy Scouts

Turkey Creek Junior High School 7th grade in 1955.
I am the first student on the left side.
A total of 18 students with our Teacher/Scout Master.
I remember camping out one weekend at Lithia Springs.

Heritage and Hope

———·———

Chapter 9

A Cross Creek Fantasy

Large segments of unemployed poverty level income Americans were on the move as the country entered into the 20th century. Millions of African Americans migrated from the South to northern cities from around WW I through the 60s.

In Oklahoma, families losing their farms to the banks migrated from the Dust Bowl in the mid 30s to California, giving our country a new wave of western migration. Carl Steinbeck's best seller book, <u>Grapes of Wrath</u>, told the story of those families stacking their house hold goods and furnishings along with the family on their flatbed truck and making that move.

They would drive approximately one thousand miles on historic Route 66 to California with promises of employment and hope. They overcame the challenge of crossing the mountains and desert along with enduring the hostility of native residents.

During that depressed era, families also moved southward to Florida. Johnny Cash recorded the hit song "Orange Blossom Special" with the ballad of men illegally riding freight trains south, especially to Florida, looking for a new start in a destination considered the land of "milk and honey". These men, called "hobos," were constantly being chased off the trains by company security patrols using "Billy Sticks" (small baseball bats). Upon his election in 1932, President Franklin D. Roosevelt established the New Deal and the Social Security system in efforts to help improve the nation's economy.

As I wrote the 'Tar Heel State Connection' chapter, I began to realize the importance of tobacco farming in the agricultural history of North Carolina ever since the colonial days. Tobacco was not considered harmful to our health until recently. Regardless, I would be remiss to ignore its role in the heritage and hope of our ancestors.

Also, lest we forget, a cigar manufacturing industry was established in Ybor City and West Tampa during the 1880s. Over two hundred cigar factories were in full operation in the Tampa area at its manufacturing peak. Production dwindled from abundant production in the 50s until almost zero today. As of 2016, there is only one cigar factory struggling to stay in production in spite of extreme regulations. For some seventy years, a huge portion of the population in Tampa made their life hood in that industry

In her book, <u>Cross Creek</u>, Marjorie Rawlings wrote about families showing up at her doorsteps looking for employment. She wrote about families that were traveling through the area and also neighboring families that she would befriend and help.

I can envision our family's chance encounter with the famed writer similar to the following story that could have been a reality, but was not. It could have been a story similar to experiences the writer would eventually share about in her book, <u>Cross Creek</u>. Based on this train of thought, we begin our family story that could have happened eighty two years ago.

Midafternoon on a warm spring day in 1936, a young family turned off the road and drove up to my front porch where I was typing on my book, <u>The Yearling</u>. A man and woman got out of their Ford Model T, followed by a boy and girl. They came through my fence gate and up to the Porch. He boldly spoke up saying, "Good afternoon madam, I'm Allan Humphrey. This is my wife Frances, daughter Mary, and son, Charles. We are responding to your tobacco farming help wanted sign we saw on Highway 301."

The couple was in their thirtyish years, not much younger than me at age thirty nine. The children stood cautiously behind their mother with each one peeking around at me from their protected position. I answered back with a warm "Hello", told them my name, and confirmed my farm help need for the summer. I emphasized "I don't know how successful tobacco farming in Cross Creek can be, but I'm willing to give it a try for at least one crop." Mary and Charles had those big dark haunting eyes that had become so common place during the depression. He explained "We were traveling from Winterville, North Carolina to Punta Gorda. We saw the sign and thought it might be a good work opportunity. I was raised working on North Carolina tobacco farms and I am confident that I can produce a good cash crop of tobacco for you by August."

They were an adorable family. He was a tall, take charge type man with wavy red hair and piercing eyes. Frances was modestly attractive with wavy dark hair, although somewhat quiet and shy. Sadness was reflecting in her eyes as she listened compliantly. The never ending economic depression had made all four lean and gaunt. The attractive tomboy acting daughter and charming son stood shyly behind their mother.

I would learn the family ages later as 34, 29, 7 and 2, respectively. He said "Frances and Mary could handle the cooking and house work. I will work the tobacco farm, vegetable garden and tend the orange grove. All we will need is room and board plus a percentage of the crop profit. We will need enough cash to tie us over till I find work upon arriving in Punta Gorda after the tobacco is harvested in August. We will also need some cash for settling in expenses once we arrive there." All of a sudden, Mary blurted out in a feisty tone, "And I will take care of my baby brother." With a look of shock, Frances quickly rebuked her daughter, "Hush Mary. You know you shouldn't speak to an adult unless they speak to you first." Charles broke out with a big grin and giggled softly as he peeped up at me. He tried to stifle his laughter.

I had the tobacco seeds in my barn and was very anxious to start planting. Plus, there was no way I could refuse this intriguing family with a strong willed father, hurting mother and two adorable children. I quickly said "Ok, the deal sounds good to me. Let's do it. I'll help you settle into my tenant house." We spent the rest of the day getting them settled in the empty tenant house across the yard behind my house.

As a celebration, we prepared and ate a yellow rice and chicken with green beans dinner together as we got to know each other better. True to his word, he went to work bright and early the next morning as we enjoyed a colorful sun rise over the eastern horizon filled with large oaks and pine trees. Tobacco farming was like a promise of hope in a brand new venture for me. However, I would soon learn the three to four month tobacco farming process is labor intense and demands constant attention. Also, extreme summer storms could bring devastating consequences to the tobacco crop.

Allan would teach me as he worked the crop each day. He explained how dark soil is best for dark leaves. However light soil is ok, but it produces light colored leaves. Best weather conditions include 65 to 95 degree temperatures and 65-70% humidity. The Cross Creek area had these weather conditions more or less. And we had history on our side as tobacco had been successfully grown in north Florida. He disked the soil, prepared the nursery beds and sowed the seeds. With a little bit of watering and big help from the warming soil, seedlings shot up like weeds. Each seedling was transplanted as they grew to about 6" or so. Then once again after obtaining more growing time, he transplanted the developed seedlings to intervals of

2' apart. He watered each plant with a water bucket and a barrel of water hauled by mule from the creek. Irrigation systems were usually implemented on large farms.

He watered each plant as needed till they continued to grow in the summer rains. Then he did the required hoeing and weeding, taking extreme caution not to cut the surface roots directly below the soil. As the summer progressed, the chore of removing the tops (an undesired plant growth *at the top of the plants) began. Immediately following this work, suckers (undesirable plant growth on the stalks near the developing leaves) had to be removed one at a time. And as we approach harvesting time, flowers had to be removed from the plants. After all of the summer work, the leaves are ready for harvesting in August. He did five harvestings of the leaves at one to two week intervals. The bottom leaves were removed first, and then he worked his way up the stalk removing leaves during each of the five harvestings. Then he entered the curing process which gives the tobacco its aromatic smoothing flavor and smell. He hung the leaves in well ventilated hot and humid sheds that he built. The curing takes a few weeks.*

The arrangement worked out well for everyone. We were able to share the profits just as he projected. Francis was a big help with the house work and the flower garden. Mary was like a mother to Charles, tending to his needs and being his playmate. I was able to spend time with Frances during our breaks from her daily chores and my writing. I would empathize with her as she would confine in me on mourning the loss of her two year old son and stillborn son. She wanted to be back close to her hometown with her parents and friends. I believe her summer at Cross Creek helped her in finding closure for her grieving. I heard some ten years later that she gave birth to seven more sons as the family lived in various places like Punta Gorda, Moore Haven, Wauchula and Dover.

As I have noted, what could have happened never happened. However, it is good story on potential tobacco farming along with being a helpful hand in Cross Creek. For best results, tobacco farming requires a dry and warm climate in a frost free period of 3 to 4 months between transplanting and harvesting. Tobacco should be allowed to ripen without heavy rainfall. Excess water causes tobacco plants to become thin and flaky. Florida weather is usually more extreme than desired temperature and moisture levels.

The movie "Parrish" staring Troy Donahue focused on tobacco farming in Connecticut. Our nephews Keith and Kevin (Lloyd and Mildred's twins) worked on a tobacco farm in Windsor, Connecticut during the summers of 84 and 85. Our North Carolina cousins worked in tobacco fields throughout their school years.

At least once in a lifetime, visit an auction warehouse during the harvest time in a small town such as Farmville, North Carolina. Regardless of our stance on the potential ill effects of tobacco, we can definitely enjoy the unique aromatic smoothing smell of the cured tobacco leaves as they are auctioned off to the highest bidder. Whether we like it or not, tobacco farming was a vital livelihood throughout generations in our family history. During the 60s, our small tobacco family farms were discontinued as my generational cousins entered into careers other than growing tobacco.

"Before I formed you in the womb I knew you; Before you were born I sanctified you; And I ordained you a prophet to the nations." (Jeremiah 1:5).

Front: Father, Michael, Jerry, Donald, Mother. Back: Lloyd, Philip, Harry. Photo taken at our Youmans house front porch by Uncle Johnnie in 1957. At this residence, I attended the 9th grade at Springhead Junior High and grades 10 through 12 at Plant City Senior High. I graduated in June 1960.

Jerry with Ralph Moreland at Commack, New York, in 1973.
Karen and Jerry visited Mr. Moreland at his farm on Long Island.
Mother, Jerry, Michael and Donald worked on his farm in 1960.
Everyone except me worked for Mr. Moreland again in 61.

Aunt Julia Janie Humphrey (Carson Baker) (circia 2001).
She had five children: Barbara, Thomas, Johnathan, Bonnie and Connie.

Heritage & Hope

———•———

Chapter 10

1943 and Some

On my September 16, 1943 birthdate, the Allied countries had already been fighting Germany and Japan for several years as the United States had also entered into World War II after December 7, 1941. From that date in infamy, it would be three years and nine months before the war was over on August 15, 1945, about a month before my 2 year old birthday.

Some eighteen million women had to fill in for the men leaving manufacturing jobs to fight in the war. Manufacturers efficiently changed over from producing cars and other goods to making bombs, war planes, trucks, ships, tanks, etc. Our country established rationing due to shortages in common foods such as canned food, meat, cheese and butter. Movies and short clips were released to the public promoting rationing and the purchasing of war bonds. One of these documentary films was *"With the Marines of Tarawa".*

At the January 14-24, 1943 Casablanca conference with Winston Churchill, President Roosevelt announced the war can end only with "unconditional German surrender." Roosevelt met with Churchill and the Chinese leader, Chiang Kai-shek, at the Cairo Conference in November 1943, and then held the Tehran Conference to confer with Churchill and Stalin. They discussed plans for a postwar international organization, such as the United Nations. They were confident of a victory in that worldwide war.

During that same year, Churchill warned us of the potential domination by a Stalin dictatorship over Eastern Europe. During 1943, one of the world's largest office buildings, the Pentagon, was completed. The Germans were defeated in North Africa and the Japanese were defeated at Guadalcanal and Tarawa. U.S. General Dwight Eisenhower was named the Supreme Allied Commander. He would lead the Allies in the June 6, 1944 "D Day" Normandy invasion on the beaches of France. Seven years after the war, he would become President from

1952 – 1960. President Roosevelt led our country in prayer on D Day. His prayer closing included: *"...and a peace that will let all of men live in freedom, reaping the just rewards of their honest toil."*

Future President Lt. John F. Kennedy was commander of PT-109 sunk by a Japanese destroyer. He survived the attack, but his injuries plagued him the rest of his life. Another future president, almost killed in action, was George H, W. Bush. He was flying a bombing mission in a Pacific Ocean battle when his TBM Avenger plane was shot down. He had to parachute from the plane as it was going down into the ocean. He was rescued four hours later. He would parachute from an airplane on his milestone birthdays till his last jump at age 90.

The Glenn Miller Orchestra music was popular at that time. The average wage was about a dollar per hour. A new house cost $3,600, a new car $900, and house rent was $40 per month. Americans worked sacrificially to produce "guns and butter". We had only one option – that was to win! We did not have a Plan B.

On May 11, 2015, as I was leaving a doctor's office in Brandon, another patient leaving the building at the same time asked me if I were a Humphrey. He had heard my name called out in the waiting room and was curious if I was from the Humphrey family he had as a neighbor when he was a 10 year old child in Dover. I said "yes." As we continued our conversation, we confirmed that our two families were close neighbors and we knew each other very well during the WW II years.

He introduced himself as Roy Lott and that our families had farms close to each other on Dad Weldon Road for a period of time during the war. I was flabbergasted that we would meet again in this manner for the first time in seventy two years since those war time years. After a brief sidewalk visit, I obtained his telephone number and followed up with an informative telephone conversation on memories of times past.

The year 1943 was a very good year, as it was the year I entered this world on September 16, at 9:40 P.M. to be exact. Dr. Alsobrook was my mother's birthing doctor at our rural house. He died two years later in 1945. I was born in a cracker style farm house on Dad Weldon Road; about five miles north of the present residence where my family and I have lived on Beachmont Drive in Valrico for the past forty five years, since 1973. Our house is near the south dead end of Dover Road. Roy was 10 years old in the year I was born.

At that date, I arrived into a large rural family with one girl and five boys. Our one and only sister, Mary, was 14, brothers Charles was 9, Robert - 6, Lloyd - 5, Philip - 4, Harry - 3 and me as the sixth boy, in diapers as a new born. Two more brothers, Michael and Don would arrive a few years later in 1946 and 1947 respectively.

I was named Jerry Earnest Humphrey. Later in life, with much difficulty, I would spell my middle name as "Ernest". My Certificate of Birth document listed my place of birth as Florida, Hillsborough County, Rural, Rt.1, Dover. Father's occupation was listed as Farming/Shipyard Electrician and Mother's occupation as Housewife. As I wrote Heritage & Hope, I discovered that I may have been named after a neighbor, Earnest Williamson.

Dr. Alsobrook established his medical practice in Plant City as a young Vanderbilt University graduate in 1904. He added a private hospital to his second floor office in a brick building located in the southeast corner of Reynolds and Collins Streets intersection. That was the only hospital for Plant City. It would be the early 50s before a hospital was established at its present location. Dr. Alsobrook served the community faithfully as our doctor and surgeon for some forty years, from the horse and buggy days through the end of World War II. A city street was named in his honor.

One other time, we had a family doctor make a house call. In the late 40s, my parents had a doctor make a house call for me as I lay in bed with an extreme stomach illness. He gave me some medicine and I recovered quickly. That was the last time I remember a doctor house call for me. Treatment would always be either iodine or castor oil.

As we can imagine, compared to our culture today, it is very obvious our father at age 41 and mother at age 36 had their hands full with one fast growing 14 year old teenaged girl and six energized boys ranging from age 9 to a new born baby. If we take a few minutes to realize our parents had just survived the Great Depression and struggled to make ends meet on a farm during a world war, we cannot comprehend how they did it.

Without question, teenaged Mary became more of a mother, rather than a sister to us six boys, especially for me as a new born baby. We all had to pitch in to take care of the farm chores as our father worked full time at the Tampa shipyard as an electrician. I still wonder how we managed to sleep seven children and two adults in three bedrooms.

Roy Lott's father was two years younger than our father. Roy was the only boy in his family with three older sisters; Lauramae, Vonzeel and Ruby. At the time, they were ages 15, 14 and 12, respectively. Between our families, we had more than an ample supply of playmates. Our two families became close neighbors and friends. Two other neighbors included the families of Earnest Williamson and Alvin Simmons.

Roy's detailed memory recalled our lifestyle as if it happened yesterday. He remembered Dad Weldon Road being a dirt road. Most of the time, the boys would go bare foot at home, and quite often to school. Roy's father farmed fulltime. Our father worked fulltime as an electrician by trade while operating a farm with the help of our family and farm workers living nearby as necessary.

We purchased a sizable farm of 30 acres with a frame house. The property was located at the northwest corner of the Dad Weldon and Walden Sheffield Road intersection. A residential development called "High Country Acres" is located in the area now.

Farmers also utilized "sharecroppers." They were families that did the labor work while the land owner would provide a tenant house, necessary equipment, monies for the expenses needed to raise the crop, and land needed to grow the crop. The two families would split the profits with the percentages agreed upon by both parties (usually 50/50). Our father had two families that worked for us at times through this farming arrangement. Overall, I don't think that method of farming was very successful for either of the two parties.

Roy recalled families having milk and beef cows, chickens, and hogs. We also had strawberries during the winter months and vegetables for spring and fall crops. Vegetables included such foods as squash, pole beans (grown on a string trellis), black eyed peas, okra, eggplant, tomatoes, bell pepper, carrots, turnip greens, mustard, onions, watermelons and cantaloupes.

We would always hope for spring and fall rains and no frosty temperatures until after the fall harvest, usually in November. Vegetables were sold at the farmer's market along with a good supply of the produce being "canned" for food during the winter and summer months. Later, this process was changed to freezing foodstuffs in free standing electric freezers.

Roy's father had a five acre strawberry field. That was considered a large family owned patch at the time. I believe our family strawberry farm was larger than five acres. Parents and children, along with neighborhood children working when needed to do so, were used to pick and pack the strawberries for selling at the farmer's market in Plant City.

During the 40s and 50s, the wages for picking ranged from a few pennies up to ten cents per quart basket. Women would work in the shade of the tin packing shed, usually opened on three sides. The berries had to be washed in a barrel of clean water to remove the sand from them, graded to remove rotten and green berries, placed into pint containers, and then carefully capped with the largest available berries. They would then be hauled to the farmer's market to be auctioned off to the highest distributing company bidder.

Neighboring families would help each other harvest the berries. This tradition was very favorable to us kids as we would be paid like an employed worker. We would have money for ourselves that we could use for fun times like the movie theater, state fair, the strawberry festival, skating, etc. One of our better treats would be to buy a 6 oz. ice cold bottle of RC Cola and a Moon Pie (or Baby Ruth candy bar) at the country store and ice house in beautiful downtown Dover, at the intersection of State Highway 574 and Dover Road.

We had two varieties of plants, Missionary and Florida 90. The missionary was the oldest variety. It was a small berry but very juicy and sweet. The Florida 90 was developed and became very popular because it produced large berries, but they were not as sweet and juicy. They did look pretty.

About the time plastic was used to cover the strawberry beds, the processing system changed to leaving the picked berries in the quart containers to be shipped directly from the picking step. The washing, grading and capping steps were eliminated completely.

During the summer months, strawberry plant nursery beds were grown in order to produce enough plants needed to plant for the upcoming year in September. Farmers would usually purchase plants from a nursery in another state. Strawberry Schools were in full swing during that time. Students went to school from to mid-December with students being off from school during the strawberry harvesting time from mid-December through March.

We went to Dover Elementary School for the 1st through 6th grades, Turkey Creek Junior High School for the 7th through 9th grades, and Turkey Creek Senior High School for the 10th through 12th grades. Strawberry Schools would be discontinued about twelve years later due to the rapid changing culture in Hillsborough County.

Our father worked fulltime at the Tampa shipyard during the war. He was an electrician wiring war ships at the shipyard. He would car pool to work as items like gasoline and tires were being rationed. We needed them for our country's war efforts. Considering the time, he was being paid a good wage. This work experience also would help him to qualify as a construction union electrician after the war.

He would spend about fifteen or so years from the post war era through the early 60's working on large construction projects as an electrician in various large northern cities. That period of work travels would last throughout my school years, consequentially leaving our family much of the time without our father being at home with us.

Our Dover farm house was a typical Florida "cracker" house built with wood timber and boards with a tin roof and front porch set on 3 foot high brick piers. It had a nice size front porch, a combination living and family room, three bed rooms, a kitchen with a small back porch area, and the wooden outhouse some distance from the house.

We would have one light bulb in each room and maybe an electrical receptacle in each room. Some interior ceilings were constructed of strips of finished wood. There was no insulation in the ceiling or exterior walls.

The roof would leak water which we caught in pots and pans. Air was circulated by opening the windows and doors, making sure the screens always had holes patched to keep out mosquitoes and insects. The houses were almost always painted white, or quite often in need of painting.

We had a kerosene burning heater for heat on cold days in the living area and a stove in the kitchen. A primer hand pump with a shallow well jetted down into the ground some 40 foot deep or so and was installed at the back porch for water. We took our baths and washed our clothes in a galvanized tub on the back porch using warm water heated up on the stove.

Actually, these houses were also built in towns throughout the state, such as Ybor City and West Tampa. They were called "shot gun" houses as a person could shoot a shotgun through the house interior hallway and not hit any of the structure. They were built from the 1880s through the 40s.

Roy talked about playing softball with neighboring kids including our clan in their pasture, swimming in Moore Lake and Robinson Pool, (and roller skating at their rink), going to the movies at the Capital and State theaters in Plant City, fishing in nearby lakes and the Hillsborough River, catching blue gill and shell crackers. He remembers gasoline prices of fifteen cents per gallon, theater tickets ten cents each, and a bottle of ice cold Coca Cola could be purchased for a nickel.

I do have one story that our sister Mary shared with the family over the years. One day Mary and her friend were given the chore of feeding our family cows. I wonder if her friend was one of Roy Lott's sisters. They poured mole cricket bait into the trough for the cows instead of grain. Within a short time, the cows were dead.

Mary thought they selected the grain. Looking for empathy in this horrible error, the bait did resemble grain somewhat. Needless to say, we never had another cow in the family from that day on. The best I can determine, we moved to our Dover farm in 1942 as our father was planning to work at the shipyard, within that year.

As the war ended, manufacturing of war ships was abruptly discontinued. As our father became unemployed, we were forced to sell the farm and move back to Wauchula in hope. Tragically, one of the memories Roy shared with me was the day his father-in-law, a welder, was electrocuted in one of the ships being built. His father moved to Plant City after the war was over. Roy raised a family of three daughters and a son.

Later in life during the 70s I would drive by the old house quite often being aware of the fact that I was born in that very house. I did not remember a single thing about the place. I did take pictures of the house for the sake of memories. I have misplaced them since then. Sadly, years later, the house burned completely to the ground.

Fire may have destroyed the house, but fond memories are still there for us. I am very thankful that Roy Lott was instrumental in restoring and confirming so many of these memories of our families during one of our nation's most tested times in history, WW II.

President Franklin D. Roosevelt died on April 12, 1945, at Warm Springs, Georgia. We mourned with the world as his body was transported back to Washington D.C. on a train for his funeral service. Less than one month later, Germany surrendered unconditionally on May 8, 1945, and Japan surrendered unconditionally on August 15. We celebrated and thanked God as nations around the world could be free again.

I highly recommend a visit to the FDR Little White House in that southwestern Georgia town. In the same day, I also recommend a visit to the infamous Confederate prison camp for the War Between the States in Andersonville. It is about fifty miles south of the Little White House. A few miles south of Andersonville is Plains, the hometown of President Jimmy Carter. All three historical sites can be reasonably visited in one day.

After WW II, tax payers paid off the war debt within the next decade or so. That paid in full debt freed up new tax dollars needed to construct the nation's inter-state highway system and so many other needs at the time. President Eisenhower got the highway system ideal during the war when he saw the system Germany had built within their country for efficient and fast traveling. He convinced Congress to construct a similar designed highway system in our country. I think he would say "WOW" if he saw it today.

Our local first leg of Interstate I-4 from Tampa to Orlando was opened to public use in 1958. When we lived in Youmans, I remember seeing that interstate link opened for traffic with very few cars and trucks traveling on it. We would walk across the highway in our exploring the area north of the interstate. It had very little traffic at the time. That all changed as our population of people and vehicles increased tremendously since then. There is no way a person can cross any Interstates today without risking their lives in the endeavor.

I believe our regional cultures lost their local flavor as the "Mom and Pop" businesses on the old two lane highways going from town to town across the USA closed their doors, one by one for lack of business.

Today, the retail areas of our cities look the same all over the country. In their place, interstate highways zip us to our destinations as we choose between which chain we want to stop for our next "fast food meal on the go".

Gone forever is the service station attendant filling up our gas tank, washing the windshields and checking the tires pressure. Most of our engine troubles could be traced back to a broken belt to be replaced. Howard Johnson and Holiday Inn were our favorites in the day.

"…A time of war, and a time of peace." (Ecclesiastes 3:8b)

Front row, Lt to Rt: Pauline, Hattie Stevens Davis, Hugh, Mary Jane Rogers Stevens (Hattie's mother). Back row: Pearl, Earl, Bernice, Ammer.
Hugh Davis was Karen's father. Karen's Grandfather, Charlie Boyd Davis, died after moving to Florida in 1902. Hattie Davis raised her three sons and three daughters as a widow. Notice their attire, the wood fence and ladder with some of their cleared land in the background. The photograph was taken circa 1905 in the backyard of their typical "Florida Cracker" house.

Center: Father and Mother. Left to right and oldest to the youngest: Mary, Charles, Robert, Lloyd, Philip, Harry, Jerry, Michael, Donald.
Photograph was taken on Christmas Day 1962.
Next Generation nephews Bobby and Allan included up front.
This photo is the only one we have of all 11 of us together.

Mary and Harry 1965

Heritage & Hope

————— • —————

Chapter 11

Moving Again

As I started writing <u>Heritage & Hope</u>, the first family fact that struck me the most was the number of times our parents moved throughout their thirty nine years of marriage. All my life, I would be in awe of families that I knew moving so often, especially those serving in the military. And all the time, our family was one of those frequent movers, right within our midst.

Our father dropped out of school after the 8th grade and worked during his teenage years at various employments in Greene County, North Carolina. Those opportunities were most likely involved in the agricultural sector. At about age 20, he made his first major move in life by traveling to Florida in 1922 with his father and brother Johnnie. They placed Woodrow and Richard Lee in a children's home in Macon, Georgia. Their mother kept 1 year old Aunt Janie. They started a produce business in the Arcadia area.

In 1925, they abandoned that venture. Our grandfather and Uncle Johnnie picked up Woodrow and Richard Lee from the children's home and moved back to their Green County home where they joined our grandmother and Aunt Janie. He would eventually live with care giving relatives. Our father stayed in Florida as he became employed by the Phoenix Power Company, as a linesman installing new power lines in the area. That company was purchased by Florida Power and Light and now by Duke Energy.

At times, I believe he would stay at a boarding house in Punta Gorda, owned by the parents of Frances Caroline Blazer. Her family had moved down from Point Pleasant, West Virginia, around 1910 for her mother's health reasons and built a boarding house as a family business venture in this small fishing village. He had a business in land dealing. He would help his oldest son to establish and operate a prosperous manufacturing business in Nocatee, a small town on US Highway 17 a few miles south of Arcadia and twenty miles north of Punta Gorda. I believe they fabricated orange boxes and pallets for the agricultural and citrus industries in the area. He also served as a Justice of Peace.

Mother only moved two times before she married and left her cozy family home at age 21. Her family moved down from West Virginia to the Kissimmee, Florida area when she was 3 and then moved a year later to Punta Gorda. After enjoying a very stable and comfortable childhood throughout her twelve years of schooling in a small town, she married our father in Punta Gorda on September 21, 1928.

I tend to think it had traces of a fairy tale wedding. I believe our father had a venturesome spirit for new opportunities mixed with travel. Evidentially, Mother wanted to experience the same even if it was so different than the culture she grew up in till her wedding day. The family was all set for her to attend Florida Southern College in Lakeland until she heard wedding bells ringing.

I was amazed to discover that just four days prior to their wedding day, the 1928 Okeechobee hurricane devastated the Okeechobee lake area with some 2,500 people drowning. The hurricane went northward from the lake area. Life went on in spite of this nearby disaster which occurred only fifty five miles east of her hometown of Punta Gorda.

During that hurricane and the Florida land boom crash, their moving days started with their first move to Tampa, where our one and only sister, Mary, was born in June, 1929. In October, 1929, the Roaring Twenties economy "Bubble Boom" was collapsing followed by the Stock Market Crash. Was their first year of marriage a fore shadow of their next three decades? The state and national economy did not look good at all after their first year of marriage.

From their first residence in Tampa to their last home together in Plant City, they moved at least seventeen times within a thirty two year span, based on the known information we have. From the late 40s to the early 60s, our father would work as a union construction electrician mostly in northern cities away from home. What I find so incredible is the fact that over a period of eighteen years after our sister was the family's first child, Mother would then give birth to ten boys. I cannot stop wondering how she endured all that happened in those eighteen years.

The houses that we moved into for every move were almost identical. They would be built with wood framing and clapboard siding, set on brick piers with pitched tin roofs. Some would have wood strip ceilings, while some may have open attic space. Almost all of them had screens for the windows and doors, although some were torn.

A hand water pump with a sink was located on the back porch. Our water source was a 1" galvanized pipe that was jetted down into the ground about thirty to forty feet or so. They were called 'shallow wells" because the water level was close to the ground surface. Those wells were our basic water source until the late 50s as the water table dropped significantly. The house would have a tin roof front porch, and no landscape nor grass. They always came with an outhouse and family garbage land field. There was no telephone, television, books, hot showers, two car garages, nor high tech gadgets.

We took our baths in a portable galvanized tub with hot water heated on the kitchen stove. Since we did not have air conditioning; we just had to sweat it out, 24/7. During heat wave nights, we would lay in a bed of wet sheets from our body heat. Sleep would always sneak up on us as we gave up struggling with that nightly misery. We thought battling mosquitos, ants, fleas, nates, roaches, spiders, mice, and occasional rats and snakes was just part of life in Florida.

I will never forget collecting rain water leaking through a tin roof in pots and pans. The dripping water would produce a musical sound that was entertaining in a weird way. Since we never listened to the radio except for night programs like The Lone Ranger, Superman, Roy Rodgers and Jack Benny; the dripping sounds became a major source of music.

We were a one car family in those years. It was only by the grace of God that we endured through it all as a family. But still, I feel my heart strings tug as I think back on what my parents would reflect through them as they went through life one day at a time. They were giving us the confidence that everything would somehow turn out all right in time.

Every time we moved to a new location, we were always super excited to check out our surroundings as soon as we could. After sizing up the house, we would explore the surrounding wooded areas and check out the bay heads at its water edge (always looking for snakes), scrubs, pastures, creeks and ponds. And also the neighboring boyhood.

Florida had open range for cattle until a state law was established in 1949 requiring all owners of cattle and horses to fence their livestock. Many times we would end up crossing barbed wire fences while thinking that the fence was there to keep their animals in, not to keep us out.

It was a way of life for our family moving again and again to new experiences in a new community which most always welcomed us as a new neighbor. We would develop new friends even as the friendships would become short lived. We never carried a house key as we always left the front door unlocked as we went to and fro, day and night. We were indeed blessed!

Today, I think of childhood experiences that we enjoyed that are now gone forever. Activities that were supervised only by the oldest boy present included swimming in creeks and ponds, catching and releasing lighting bugs, swinging on vines, eating wild huckleberries and blackberries, smelling the fragrance of orange blossoms, and eating sweet juicy oranges and grapefruit from the tree. And yes, some of us did occasionally swim with our "birth suit" in the creeks, always a good distance from the nearest road.

Other special treats included a car load of us sharing in the cost of gas to go swimming at the Hillsborough River State Park, Lithia Springs or Crystal Springs. With an average gas price of twenty cents per gallon, we could always manage to pay for the swimming trip. Gas wars would always cut a few more pennies. After the Hillsborough River became polluted from agricultural enterprises and gators took it over as their domain, swimming was abruptly prohibited at the state park, except for the shallow above ground plastic pool.

The best experience of all was watching for shooting stars on a beautiful clear night with the sky flooded with stars so bright that you felt like you could reach up and touch them. If you viewed the sky in an open field without trees, the stars covered the sky from horizon to horizon. During a typical day, we had a clear blue sky with snow white clouds and beautiful sun rises and sun sets. The best part of this natural beauty to behold was that it was free, with all glory and honor to our God.

Another favorite past time was strolling or riding our bikes down the two lane gravel county roads past family farms and groves. Each one was a family enterprise, just like each store or business in town was family owned and operated. The groves were healthy and beautiful, especially in the spring as the trees were loaded with blooms and their fragrance filled the air for miles. Another sight to see was in the winter as the oranges and strawberries ripened for harvesting. We saw all types of trees in our neighbor's yards loaded with lemons, limes, guavas, persimmons, and kumquats. Central Florida was blessed abundantly during the 40s and 50s with beautiful farms and groves.

Since the 60s, due to a progression of housing developments, severe freezes and the greening disease, orange groves have become substantial extinct in Hillsborough County. We have to travel south towards Avon Park to find lush orange groves. Grove owners are desperately fighting to save their groves from the continuing menace of a greening disease. It is still progressing unchecked toward destroying all of the state's orange trees. The industry research teams are working frantically to find a solution to stop the disease from spreading out of control. The Sunshine State will not be the same if we do not have oranges.

Our parents lived in at least twelve locations from their wedding in 1928 till their last child was born in 1947. It is most likely they lived in additional locations during those nineteen years of childbearing. We especially believe they lived in other locations during the eight years of 1929 through 1937, when they were constantly moving back and forth between North Carolina and Florida. Mother gave birth to five children during those eight newlywed years.

During 1938, they lived in Moore Haven where Lloyd was born. Then they moved to Wauchula where Philip and Harry were born in 1939 and 1940, respectively. Harry was born on Christmas Day. Sometime early in the war years, our father bought a farm in Dover where I was born in 1943. I was the only child in our family that can be called a "WWII Baby". After the war was over, we lost the farm and moved briefly to Plant City where Michael was born in 1946, and then back to Wauchula where Donald was born in 1947.

Sadly, none of us thought to keep written documentation of every family location we lived in, even though our parents would frequently share with us about our many residences and then casually rate them as to how much they enjoyed living at each one. We had to rely on our memory for this history. No one in the family kept a diary. Donald determined our residences for the years from 1928 through 1947 through recorded birth and death certificates. We believe the family most likely lived in additional locations during this period of time. I listed a town residence summary below.

We moved from Wauchula to a typical cracker house on Clay Turner Road in the Springhead community. We lived there about one year in 1948. We lived across the dirt road from the Alderman family. I remember they had a big red barn. It was in that house mother's brother, Sandford Blazer Sr., gave us a surprise visit one afternoon. He took a snap shot of us standing in a strawberry field near sunset, with dirty faces, bare feet, and coveralls. I was age 5. Since it is one of only a few photos of my childhood, it is a classic.

In 1949, we moved to another cracker house on a dirt road near Knights Griffen Road and Highway 39. At that time, Knights Station Elementary was a two story brick building at the northwest corner of the two roads. Although my brothers were enrolled in "strawberry schools" my parents enrolled me in the first grade at Knights Elementary, with a regular school period from September to June. So, I went to school during the harvesting period in the winter of 50.

Like all of my brothers, none of us had pre-school care, pre-kindergarten, or kindergarten. Our formal schooling started with first grade with all of us attending "strawberry schools" from March to December. However, I was the exception for my first grade schooling.

For some reason, we moved to a house in the Cork community near Cork Elementary School during the winter of 50. My parents were allowed to enroll me in the second grade at the start of the Cork Elementary "strawberry school" in March, 1950. I skipped my first grade months of March through June. In 1951, we moved to a house with exterior rock walls in Cork. It was a unique house that always looked out of place in that rural landscape. I completed the third grade at Cork Elementary while living there.

In 1952, we moved to a house on Rice Road about a half mile east of Wiggins Road. Mildred Green's family lived across the road from us. Five years advanced, she would become Mrs. Mildred Humphrey as she married Lloyd on October 7, 1957. I completed the "strawberry school" fourth grade at Springhead Elementary from March to December 52.

1953 was a milestone year for us as we purchased a twenty acre farm with a house and barn. The property was on the south side of Trapnell Road about a half mile east of Trapnell Elementary School. I completed the fifth and sixth grades at this 'strawberry school" in the years of 53 and 54 respectively. I was able to walk to school until I got a brand new bicycle for Christmas in 53.

After finishing elementary school in December 54 at Trapnell Elementary, I went to Turkey Creek Junior High School for seventh grade from March to December, 1955. In March, 56, I started eighth grade at Turkey Creek Junior High. During that summer, the Hillsborough County School Board closed down all "strawberry schools".

During this time period, we sold our Trapnell farm and moved to a rental house with about ten acres of farmland in Youmans on the north side of Highway 92, about a quarter mile west of the County Line Road. We lived at this location during four of my teenaged years, 13 - 16. My life changed in experiencing regular schools along with still working on a family farm like we did at Trapnell during my preteen years of 9 to 12. In my senior high school years, I had one foot in rural culture and the other foot in urban culture. I was also active in Future Farmers of America (FFA) during my senior high school years.

Although our house in Youmans was a typical cracker house, it was quite different than the ones we had lived in. The house had a fireplace with a chimney, a large front porch that wrapped around the front, west side and back side of the house. The west side porch had been renovated into one large bedroom and a small bedroom. A bathroom was added on the back porch just before we moved into the house. I was a 13 year old ninth grader before we had our first indoor bathroom. Even though we had eight people using one bathroom, we were still thrilled to have indoor plumbing for the first time in our lives. The living room and master bedroom had the walls and ceilings finished with decorative strips of wood. You had to go out the house back door and into another exterior door to the porch bathroom.

We think that house could have been the house of the Winston pioneer family that was later moved to this location. The property was a few hundred yards from the highway. It had a one lane dirt drive with drainage ditches on both sides of the drive, similar to the drive we had at the Trapnell Compound.

We would use a sling blade to cut down the weeds that would grow in those two ditches. When we let the weeds grow too tall before cutting, it became very difficult to cut the brush. Today, that work chore reminded me of the movie "Cool Hand Luke", which played in the theaters years later. Paul Newman played World War II hero Luke Jackson. He was arrested and sentenced to two years in a Florida prison for cutting heads off parking meters after drinking too much one night. Throughout his prison time, he experienced a battle of wills with his guards. The conflict finally escalated into a tragic ending. I can never forget the Warden, played by Strother Martin, telling Luke during one of their confrontations, *"What we've got here is a failure to communicate."* The quotation was listed as number eleven on the American Film Institute's list of the one hundred most memorable movie lines. The movie was released in 1967, the year Karen and I married.

Chain Gangs, comprised of jail prisoners, would work on roads cutting the weeds and brush from the road ditches throughout the counties. This was a standard practice in our county along with other counties within our state, as well as in other Southern states. Every time we would drive by a chain gang working on a road side, we would feel sorry for the convicts. We would never, ever make eye contact.

The yard also had a section of real grass which was nice to play on, but a pain to keep mowed. We had the old hand pushed rotary blade mower. The blades were always dull, so we had to mow the grass over and over in order to cut it.

The farm soil was not as good for growing strawberries as other locations we had lived in previously. However, there was a huge beautiful orange grove directly behind our house. The property did have great woodlands to the north of our house that we enjoyed for exploring and hunting. This house was the best one we had lived in until we moved to a house we purchased in Plant City, after I graduated in 1960.

Interstate I-4 was just being completed between Tampa and Lakeland. When it was opened for public use, we would see a few cars and trucks driving on it in the beginning months. Who would have dreamed the volume of traffic it would receive over time? And who would dream of the constant nonstop construction required to provide for the needs resulting from the ever increasing traffic volume?

My school for our new Youmans residence was Springhead Junior High School. We were given an option of advancing to the next grade in September if we wish or we could stay back one year. I chose to advance. So in August 56, I finished eighth grade and advanced to the ninth grade at Springhead Junior High School in September 56. I graduated from the Springhead Junior High School ninth grade in June, 57. I transferred to Plant City Senior High School to start the tenth grade in September 57. I graduated from senior high school in June, 1960, at age 16.

While living at Youmans, my neighbor, Lonnie Norris, became a close friend in those four years. Early in his adulthood, he was called to pastor a congregation. During my school years, we lived in five different locations. They included rural areas all around the city. During those years, we all accumulated acquaintances and friends for each of our family siblings. Later in life, many of them would know me from their friendship with an older brother; even though I did not know them at that time of friendship.

Throughout our school years during the 50s, we had to wear lots and lots of "hand me down" clothing. Our family of eight consecutive boys made it an ideal method of providing clothing for us. Oh how I hated "hand me downs", especially when they had patches that were visible. But sad to say it was a way of life for us seven youngest boys. Does that mean Charles always got all new clothes? But what can you say. You do what you have to do and learn to get over it. Today, people pay top dollar for design clothing that has a worn and patched appearance.

About one year later, we bought our first family television. We were all so excited, even if we could only receive the three main networks of NBC, CBS and ABC. The volume dial and channel switching dial was on the television consol. We would take turns being the "go to" man. I remember some of our favorite programs such as *I Love Lucy, Red Skelton, The Ed Sullivan Show, Kids say the Funniest Things, Queen for a Day, Gunsmoke, The Twilight Zone, etc.* Rotating the exterior antenna to obtain fine tuning was an ongoing dreadful chore.

Another vivid impacting memory I had of the 50s was during our Springhead Junior High School 9th grade graduation. A classmate's mother was filming the event with a hand held video camera. I thought it was amazing to see someone taking motion pictures that could be viewed later like a regular movie. We didn't even take still photographs as we never had a family camera. Prior to 1960, I think we had only one photograph of our family; which at the time included our parents, Lloyd, Philip, Harry, Michael, Donald and me. It was taken by a relative in 1957. Mary was living in Ohio. Charles and Robert were married.

Regarding additional residences over the years, I do have fond memories of living in another typical frame house in the northwest section of Plant City for a brief time. The house was near Wilson Elementary, a few blocks west of Highway 39. We would roam the neighborhood and downtown streets. It was a different experience compared to living on a country dirt road with few neighbors. It was during 1948 and I was 5 years old, one year from starting school. It's hard to believe that we had eight boys ranging from age 1 through 14, plus our parents, living in that house. Although this residence was short, it was a fun time for us.

Charles visited us one day during our very last year of farming. He came down to the field where we were working to see how our strawberry crop was going. He teased me as he said, *"You're going to be a farmer one day"* I guess you could say his prophesy sort of came true. Later in life, I did enjoy a hobby of landscaping our home over the years. Actual, Lloyd was the brother to really enjoy growing stuff as a hobby.

Oh yes, I cannot close this chapter on our family heritage until I share some on a Southern past time – nick naming children. Our father had a thing about nicknames. He gave each of us a nickname of which we all used to address each other at home.

When we went to school, we would use our given names in addressing each other. This system worked fine for everyone until we had friends over after school as playmates. We would immediately go into a habit of using our nicknames.

We soon discovered it was very amusing for us to watch how troubled our classmates and neighbors were in trying to keep up with conversations as we interjected our nicknames. Our friends had to learn two sets of names for each child in order to communicate with us. If you take in account all of our siblings, they would have twenty names to remember.

As we graduated from high school and went our separate ways, we left all of our bitter sweet names behind us forever along with other quaint family culture. Those names are now locked in our imaginative heritage chest and the key was mysteriously thrown away many decades ago.

Dad with Kimberly at 3 months in 1977.

Our Humphrey Family

Parents
1902 Allan Rufus Humphrey, Sr., Hookerton, North Carolina
   August 2, 1902 – January 13, 1967 (Age 65)

1907 Frances Caroline Blazer, Point Pleasant, West Virginia
   December 29, 1907 – November 29, 1969 (Age 62)

1928 Punta Gorda
   Parents' Wedding - September 21, 1928

One Sister and Ten Brothers
1929 Tampa
   Mary Elizabeth, June 20, 1929 – February 17, 2013 (Age 83)
1930 Punta Gorda
   Allan Rufus Jr., December 16, 1930- October 21, 1932 (Age 1)
1933 Seffner
   Unnamed baby, January 23, 1933 (a few minutes)
1934 Winterville, North Carolina
   Charles Benton, August 25, 1934 – Dec. 19, 1975 (Age 41)
1937 Punta Gorda
   Robert Lee Sr., January 16, 1937 – March 22, 2013 (Age 76)
1938 Moore Haven
   Lloyd Allan, Sr., March 13, 1938 – February 25, 2017 (Age 78)
1939 Wauchula
   Philip Eugene Sr., September 24 1939 – Jan. 30, 2017 (Age 77)
1940 Wauchula
   Harry Blazer, December, 25, 1940 – June 26, 1996 (Age 55)
1943 Dover
   Jerry Ernest, September 16, 1943 -
1946 Plant City
   Michael James, May 8, 1946 – July 15, 2009 (Age 63)
1947 Wauchula
   Donald Patrick, April 14, 1947 -

My Schooling History

I have listed below the schools that I attended for each school year along with the name of the community we were living in. I completed my formal schooling within a total complete time period of ten years and ten months. I started my schooling at age 5 and graduated at age 16. I attended Grades 2 through 8 in five strawberry schools. I attended six schools in seven separate enrollments.

We didn't have child day care, head start, pre-schooling, pre-Kindergarten, Kindergarten, special tutoring, or free meals. We had no formal education prior to starting first grade. We did not watch any educational programs as we didn't have a television. We had very few books at home. In spite of all that, I believe I obtained an acceptable education during all of my moving and constant changing within the school systems.

Father visited Mary at her home in Ashtabula, Ohio in the late 50s. The town is located on Lake Erie, a few miles west of Pennsylvania. She taught school in Ohio and in Florida after moving back to Tampa in the 70s. One year, she was chosen Teacher of the Year for Ohio. She married Dwight McPherson of Ohio. They had a daughter, Diane. She went full circle to Ohio and back to Florida.

Schools and Residences

Grade	School / Year	Residence
1	Knights Elementary 9/49–3/50	Knights Station
2	Cork Elementary 3/50-12/50	Cork 1
3	Cork Elementary 3/51- 12/51	Cork 2
4	Springhead Elementary 3/52-12/52	Springhead
5	Trapnell Elementary 3/53-12/53	Trapnell
6	Trapnell Elementary 3/54-12/54	Trapnell
7	Turkey Creek Junior High 3/55-12/55	Trapnell
8	Turkey Creek Junior High 3/56-8/56	Trapnell
9	Springhead Junior High 9/56-6/57	Youmans
10	Plant City Senior High 9/57-6/58	Youmans
11	Plant City Senior High 9/58-6/59	Youmans
12	Plant City Senior High 9/59-6/60	Youmans

Lt to Rt: Mary, Charles, Robert, Lloyd, Philip, Harry, Jerry, Michael, Donald
Photo taken Thanksgiving Day 1973. Only one we have of us nine together.

Front row: Michael, Jerry, Lloyd
Middle row: Philip, Donald
Back row: Harry, Robert, Charles
Photograph taken circa 1963.

A 1968 photo of our house at 1610 West Ball Street in Plant City. We lived there during the 60s. Purchased in the summer of 1960, it was our last family home. Donald landscaped the property while he was attending USF.

Lt to Rt: Mary, Robert, Lloyd, Philip, Jerry, Michael and Donald. (1996).

Heritage & Hope

———•———

Chapter 12

Springhead / Bealsville / Coronet

Springhead community is located a few miles southeast of Plant City. It is an agricultural area located between Highways 60, 39, 92 and County Line Road. The name was selected for a spring in the middle of a bay head.

This community was instrumental in my life for many reasons. I attended fourth grade there when we lived on Rice Road in 1952. And later, I attended eighth and ninth grades at the school when we lived on Highway 92 in the neighboring community of Youmans. We always rode a bus to and from school. And most instrumental was my marriage to a native Springhead resident, Karen Davis. At age 10 in 1953, Springhead Methodist Church became our family church. I was active in the youth fellowship until I left for my boot camp training in February, 1962.

Karen and I were married at that church on June 9, 1967. We had our wedding reception at her parent's house with family and friends hosting our reception. The wedding party dinner was held at Johnson's Family Restaurant on Highway 39. Buddy and Freddy Johnson grew up at the restaurant learning to cook Southern cuisine so well. I think everyone knew Mr. Johnson. Naturally, Bill Friend was our wedding photographer.

While a few families settled in the area between the Indian Wars and the War Between the States, most of our settlers moved in after 1865. As soon as Henry Plant completed a railroad from Florida's east coast to Tampa in 1886, families steadily moved into the area, well into the 20th century. Early pioneers included George Hamilton, Joseph Howell, W. M. Clemons, and William English. They were followed by the Morgan, Harrell, Blanton, Bryant and DeVane families.

Raising open range cattle was always a way of livelihood until the 1949 state law requiring cattle and livestock to be fenced. The cattle would be driven on "cattle drives" to Fort Myers and Tampa for shipments to northern and Cuba markets. Growing oranges was also introduced as a cash crop for the area until they were destroyed in the disastrous 1895 freeze.

In the early 1900s, truck farming was being ushered into the area with the development of better roads for hauling produce to the Plant City train station. The strawberries would be transported to markets in northern cities via trains. As the Springhead area, along with the land surrounding Plant City, had excellent soil for growing strawberries; more and more families started growing them as a cash crop after the great freeze of 1895.

In spite of losing their orange groves to that freeze, many farmers planted new orange groves again with a hope that they would not have another hard freeze any time soon. Actually, the farmers that gambled on beating the freezing temperatures would win out as groves prospered into the early 1960s before being killed off again by freezing cold fronts and decades later by the dreadful "greening" disease.

I remember seeing beautiful family owned groves thriving in East Hillsborough County during the 40s and 50s. Developers began to buy groves and land to build houses and for increased strawberry farming in the 60s and 70s. This trend would steadily increase through the next four decades into our present. Today, groves in our area are "no more".

Karen's father, Charlie Hugh Davis, at the age of 1, traveled with his parents, Grandmother, and siblings from Mayfield, Kentucky to Springhead in 1902. They purchased 80 acres at the south side of the intersection of Clemons and Trapnell Roads from Tom Clemons. The previous owner, Cornelius Howell bought the property from the government in 1895.

Hugh's parents were Charlie Boyd Davis (1863-1903) and Hattie Mae Stevens Davis (1870-1937). The family had three sons and three daughters: Bernice Charles Davis (1890-1971), Ammer Davis Tomberlin (1894-1960), Pearl Davis Howard (1897-1978), Earl Neville Davis (1897-1965), Pauline Davis Colson (1899-1976), and Charlie Hugh Davis (1901-1970).

Pearl and Earl were twins. All six children were born on holidays. Bernice on Christmas Day, Ammer on Washington's birthday, Pearl and Earl on Easter, Pauline on July 4 and Hugh on Inauguration Day at that time.

Hattie Mae Stevens Davis' mother, Mary Jane Rodgers Stevens (1836-1919) moved down from Kentucky to Florida, to live with them the rest of her days on earth. She would experience growing up in western Kentucky during frontier days; living through the War Between the States during her young adult years of 25-29; the harsh War post reconstruction period; becoming a 49 year old widow with a 15 year old daughter in 1885; the Spanish American War of 1898; witnessing the nation changing from an agricultural society to an industrial country with electricity, telephones, automobiles and airplanes; repeating a life style of conquering a new frontier, this time in the "Cracker Country" of Florida.

She would live to see her daughter become a 33 year old widow with three boys and three girls between the ages of 13 and 2 while moving to the wilderness of Florida and helping to start a new homestead in the backwoods of that state with no other relatives to lean on; and last but not least, World War I. Both widows, Mary Jane Rodgers Stevens and Hattie Mae Stevens Davis, would remain widows.

Mary Jane Rodgers Stevens did live to see us win WW I including a peace treaty and the Panama Canal construction. In her last few years here, she also experienced all six grandchildren growing up into responsible young adults in a fairly stable, prosperous community. And she saw her daughter, Hattie Mae, help in the establishment of Springhead Baptist Church. She would see her granddaughter, Pauline, dedicate a new two-story brick school building for Springhead School in 1914.

This narrative is only a glimpse into a life that could make a best seller if it would ever be written. It is an amazing story waiting to be told. Eighty three years of persistent living and working in faith and hope.

She married Thomas Burris Stevens (1835-1885) and they had a daughter, Hattie Mae Stevens in 1870. Mary Jane Rodgers Stevens became a 49 year old widow in Mayfield, Kentucky with a 15 year old daughter, Hattie Mae Stevens when her husband died at age 50 in 1885. The daughter would marry Charlie Boyd Davis and they had their first son, Bernice in 1890, when she was 20. Mary Jane Rodgers Stevens husband died at age 50 in 1885, and her son-in-law, Charlie Boyd Davis died in 1903 at age 40.

When the family moved to Florida; Bernice was 11, Ammer 8, earl and Earl 5, Pauline 3, and Hugh 1. Charlie Boyd Davis moved south for health reasons. Immediately, he began to farm the land on the previously owned homestead. Within a year or so, he died suddenly from a heart failure in 1903. Hattie Mae stayed on the farm after his death and raised her six children as a widow. Her mother, Mary Jane Rodgers Stevens, helped in the house work and cooking. Bernice would have to take charge as the "Man of the House" at the young age of 12. Hugh was a 2 year old toddler.

Charlie Boyd Davis was a teacher and farmer, along with being an accomplished violinist. Prior to marriage, Hattie Mae Stevens was a teacher in Hickory, Kentucky, five miles north of Mayfield. The town is in the extreme western end of Kentucky, situated east of Arkansas and Missouri, south of Illinois, and north of Tennessee.

The family traveled south approximately 700 miles to their new homestead in Springhead. They made this trip via a passenger train. The father traveled with their furniture and animals on a freight train. He was delayed two weeks due to floods. They bought a horse and wagon for their new location transportation. While in Kentucky, they were teased about moving to alligator infested Florida. When the family arrived in Plant City, Pearl asked, *"Where are the alligators?"* I think it's no longer a teasing matter as alligators seem to be everywhere you find lakes and rivers.

With a desire to see the community children attend a local Sunday school, Hattie Mae Stevens Davis helped to establish Springhead Baptist Church in 1905. Although she was already an active member of Plant City First Methodist Church, she wanted to help start a local church in the Springhead community. Springhead Methodist would be established much later in 1939 at the intersection of Sparkman Road and Clemons Road. A few additional churches would be established as the 20th century population growth increased.

The six children would inherit 13.3 acres each. Hugh Davis inherited the tract of land that had the old framed homestead. In that house, he and Ethel Johnson Davis raised their family of two boys; Gordon and Gerald along with four daughters; Joan, Dale, Dorothy and Karen (my bride to be). His mother and Grandmother lived in that house also, along with his six children; similar to the Walton family in a popular television series about the depression days in Virginia.

Electricity became available for homes and farms around 1925. Also, with good roads leading to towns along with families owning automobiles and trucks, they could enjoy country living with the accommodations of nearby towns like Plant City.

Both generations were a typical family living on the land over the sixty to seventy some years as Hattie Mae Stevens Davis raised her six children as a widow and Hugh and Ethel Davis raised their six children with his prolonged health conditions. He worked at the Coronet Mine in addition to working the farm with his children. Their farm included an orange grove, orange tree nursery, vegetable crops along with domestic animals for meat, milk and eggs. In 1959, he had a ranch style home built in front of the old wood frame house, which was demolished as soon as they moved into the new house. The old house, built around 1900, served two generations plus the previous owners well.

In 1945, Lois Lenski, wrote the book, Strawberry Girl published by Dell Publishing Co. Inc. She wrote about fictional families based on families that were moving down mostly from the southern states of Georgia, Alabama and the Carolinas. The best I can tell by reading the book, I believe the story's location and time was in the Kathleen area (a small community northwest of Lakeland) around 1903.

Her book was based on extensive research of the area and included a very informative introduction of the people settling in central western Florida around 1900. The story is written in the local "Southern Cracker" dialect and culture of that time. I would think with the Davis family moving down from western Kentucky, they arrived in Springhead with a unique mid western accent and culture.

I find it fascinating that she accurately identified and wrote the story of the generation living in our strawberry farming world during the first decade of the 1900s. At that very same time, the Charlie Hugh Davis family with six children also was moving into their new Springhead homestead about fifteen miles due South of Kathleen as the crow flies. And our mother's family had moved from West Virginia to Kissimmee in 1910, and then a year later to Punta Gorda.

As you read Strawberry Girl, you will see how our ancestors lived during the first decade of the 20th century in colorful detail. The book is available in paperback from Amazon. I recommend it be added to everyone's "must read" list. The fictitious family owned and operated a small family farm with their six children helping with the household and farm chores along with attending what may have been an early version of "strawberry schools." The book gives a terrific insight into a small back woods Florida community of small family farms as our state entered the 1900s.

The story includes the Boyer family with six children moving from the Carolinas into a homestead deserted after the big freeze of 1895. Their neighbors were the Slater family with children about the same age as the Boyer family. Without question, the children would work the farm chores along with their family adults. Growing strawberries was a vital money crop. Our family settled into this agricultural area some thirty years later. One day in the early 1970s, Karen and I were visiting her mother, Ethel Davis. One of Karen's aunts, Pauline, stopped by with her husband, Clyde Colson, for a visit with Mrs. Davis. They reminisced about the "good old days" for some time. One of the stories Clyde shared was their family tradition of going via wagon to camp for a week or so on Tampa Bay at the Big Bend area. They would go fishing and crabbing everyday making sure they had plenty to eat, especially mullet. Obviously, in that time, around 1915 or so, they did not have nearby "handy dandy" convenience stores and restaurants.

Then Aunt Pauline talked about giving a dedication speech in 1914 for the new Springhead School two story brick school building. She mentioned she still had copies of her speech. Later, she gave me a copy as I had shown a keen interest in the memories she was sharing with us during her visit.

Somehow I managed to keep that copy without losing it for the next forty years or so in my files. As I was writing Heritage and Hope, I realized that I had to include her speech in its entirety without editing by me. She had hand written her speech notes on paper in cursive. Sadly, the 1914 brick school building was recently demolished; in spite of a public outcry to preserve the historic building.

The speech is a "must read" not only for history buffs, but for everyone in order to enjoy the flavor of a typical Florida pioneer community like Springhead. She covers the school's history from its beginning in 1875 through 1914, the year of the new modern two story brick school building dedication. The document was written as notes for her dedication message, so she may not have been too concerned about grammar and spelling in her speech notes.

It makes for a fascinating read. For some perspective of timing, she gave me a copy forty years ago and she gave the dedication speech some sixty years prior to our visit with her. It has been one hundred four years since the 1914 dedication ceremony. She was a 15 year old teenage junior high school student at the time. I have included her speech notes in this chapter. Note Miss Pearl Davis, at age 14, was listed as a Teacher Assistant in the year 1911. Pearl was Pauline's older sister and Karen's aunt. She was 17 at the 1914 dedication.

Pauline's closing statement over one hundred years ago touches on the identical intent I want Heritage and Hope to reflect. She noted, *"The past is interesting, now wish with me that the future may be more so."* I would like to think that our generation can close our book in history with a statement as promising in hope for our future generations. She makes another statement that we all need to seriously take heed to and just do it, *"be acquainted early with the history of our community."*

Bealsville. Another interesting slice of the area's history occurred in the adjacent community of Bealsville; located in an area of land with boundaries south of the Springhead community to the north, County Line Road to the east, Highway 60 to the south and Jap Tucker- Cowart Road to the east.

Bealsville, originally called Howell's Creek, was founded after the War Between the States by twelve slaves that had worked on plantations in surrounding communities including Knights, Plant City, Hopewell and others. The 1866 Southern Homestead Act provided a means for freed slaves to obtain tracts of property ranging from 40 to 160 acres. To retain title, the new owners had to develop homes, clear land, and demonstrate that they possessed the equipment to farm that land. A local plantation owner, Sarah Hopewell, helped them in starting their farms.

Through the years they would establish a school, farms, churches, a market place, cemetery, and a community center. Bealsville also had an active spring of water called Boiling Springs, very similar to Crystal Springs and Lithia Springs. The spring was a popular swimming hole for everyone until it eventually became inactive in the 1960's. I didn't know the spring existed until it was almost closed.

At that time, we lived in a totally segregated society. We existed in two separate worlds. Like it or not, that was the way it was.

Implementation and enforcement of The Civil Rights Act of 1964 started the gradual changes for an integrated society. Ironically, Bealsville's Boiling Springs was an integrated swimming place. I cannot think of any other local public swimming location integrated at that time.

As the former slaves were settling into their farms in the post war decade, the neighboring community of Springhead was building their first school building of hewed logs in 1875. Interesting, about the same time in Bealsville; a two room school was built around 1873, on land donated by Alfred Beal. That school, with first through fifth grades, was called Jamison School The school was renamed William Glover School and became a "strawberry school". Generations of African Americans received their first through ninth grades education at Glover School. Five school campus buildings, constructed between 1933 and 1949, are listed on the National Register of Historic Places. The school was closed in 1980. Since then, the school was changed into a community center.

Coronet community was very unusual in that a phosphate company built a self-supporting village for its employees. When Hugh Davis was 7 years old in 1908, Coronet Phosphate Company started a mining operation on the north side of the Coronet Road and Clemons Road intersection. The mining complex would eventually include a community center, company operated grocery store, and housing for the company employees. They also built a beautiful hospitality house with a swimming pool for the company's out of state home office staff lodging for their business trips to the plant.

In the southwest section of the intersection, the company built a village of about seventy five Cracker style houses for company employees wanting to live in the village. One huge fringe benefit was the employees missed out on rush hour traffic. They simply walked across the road to work. During his years of employment at the mine, Hugh Davis had a commute distance of less than two miles from his home at Clemons and Trapnell Roads. My brother, Robert, worked for a brief period of time at the mine also. Local men had an option of becoming farmers or going to work at the Coronet Mine.

I have fond memories of visiting the village during the 1950s on weekends and playing touch, and most often tackle, football with school friends living in the village. I remember attending various parties at the community center. Village friends included Billy Barker and John Kelly. It appeared the families were content with the village living conditions. The swimming pool was off limits to non-residents.

Around 1960, the village was closed down and the families had to move elsewhere. Many of the houses were purchased and relocated throughout the area, but some were also demolished. That unique village only lasted for about fifty years until it abruptly became history. In my memories, I still see the village of yesterday as if it existed today. Phosphate mining continues in Florida, but no longer in Coronet. In spite of young adults leaving the area along with the pollution and closing of Coronet Mine, life in these solid communities continues. Throughout the past 150 years or more since 1865, these local communities prospered as we toiled - always with hope for a better tomorrow – especially for our future generations.

1914 Springhead School Building Dedication Speech
(Speech notes written and presented by Pauline Davis)

"Ever (Every)* lady loves a story; were (where)* a little child can often understand a hard fact if it can be explained by a story.

This love of story inherets in every life as is amply proven by the number and variety of story books for little folks; books for boys and girls and even story books for the aged and the great. Ever living thing has its story - of birth – of life and of death. If it lives it must live in time as well as space.

Nations, peoples, states, communities and individuals have each their story.

We love and study history because it shows us life; life in action.

What we are is manifest by what we do. The study of history like "Charity" should begin at home; but too often we attempt to study and understand Ancient History or the Rise and Fall of the Holy Roman Empire before we have the home elements of History so necessary for interpreting the larger life.

For this reason we should be acquainted early with the history of our community.

As this year marks a distinctive period in our school community in that we have erected a splendid school building and have for the 1st time in the history of the school a Graduating Class; our minds naturally turn with questions of the past.

The first Spring Head school was established about 1875 about one mile north from the present site.

The school houses as well as the other buildings at that time were very rude; this one was built of logs; and the seats were also made hewed cedar logs and the teachers desk of the same material.

The terms of school then were only three months and the teachers were paid by the patrons; so that only the most prosperous were able to send their children to school.

Many people have often asked where Spring Head got its original name; this school was called Spring Head from the fact that all the water used was carried from a spring being in a Bay Head near by.

After only a few terms the school was moved to a more convenient place and several terms were taught by Prof's Hollingsworth, Belton, Deshong. Serauton, Procter, Ohipps, Watkins and Ellis; by this time more people had settled near by and it became necessary for a better and larger building which was built where this one now stands in 1902.

The teachers salary was now being paid by the county and at that time the first assist was employeed; the terms being taught by Mr A. L. English; Prin and Miss Ruby Harrell assist; who were both students of Spring Head School.

The Prin of the year 1903 was Prof Jiur Robinson of P. C. with Miss Gerlie Guaze of Tarpon Springs as assist.

The Prin of 1904 was Prof, Bill Howell one of Spring Head noted teachers with Miss Laura Robinson assist.also of S. H.

The year 1905 as the school funds were low we had only one teacher Mr. Salter Blanton who taught 6 weeks followed by Mr. James Herold Flye of Winter Park who finished the term.

The Prin of the year 1906 was a lady teacher of Tampa Mrs J. H. McCelland with Miss Sallie Howell as assist another one of S. H. teachers.

The Prin of 1907 was Miss Mattie Regester of P. C. with Miss Sallie Howell assist again.

During this time the school was progressing Rapilly ; one of our former teachers Mr. J. H. Flye had sent the school a collection of discarded books about 250 in number from Yale University which were prized very much and the Book case we have now was bought for them at this time the rooms ere ceiled and lamps and stoves were bought.

The Prin of the year 1908 was Miss Ida Blanton of S. H. with Miss Lilian Swdley of P. C. assist.

1909 and 1910 the Prin was Prof Jim Robinson assisted by his wife Mrs Robinson who taught a successful school.

1911 a third room was added and during this time Merle Perry 1st assist who taught 2 months followed by Miss Eva Smith of Clearwater with Miss Ida Blanton as teacher of the Primary grades.

Rev. Snipes taught two terms during which high school work was organized and close to the closing of this term the Prin was Prof C. W. Miller Assisted by Miss Avis Smith, Miss Miller and Miss Pearl Davis as assist's this year.

The increase in number of pupils and the advanced work in high School. together with the growing interest of our community in better facilities of Education; demanded a better school building and as a sequel to the urge we have today in place of our old antiequate wooden building; this beautiful Modern brick building for which we are justly proud.

We are not only proud of our building we are more proud of our school

Next term will demand 4 rooms; where better grading may be had and well organiz classes of the 9th and 10th grades of high school   The past is interesting now wish with me that the future may be more so." Pauline Davis

Footnotes
Pauline's closing statement tells us of our parent's generation regarding their heritage and hope in the year 1914. We celebrated the one hundred year anniversary in 2014. We continue to appreciate our heritage as we look to the future in the same hope they had.
* Spelling for speech notes edited for convenience of reading.

Our June 9, 1967 wedding was held at Springhead Methodist Church with a reception at Karen's home given by family and friends. Israel won their historic providential six day war during the same week of our wedding.
We are blessed. May we be a blessing.

600,000 Promise Keepers Stand in the Gap at the Washington D.C. National Mall October 4, 1997. Lt to Rt: Justin Wilson, Greg Humphrey, Shad Fitzpatrick, Jerry Humphrey, David Fitzpatrick and Randy Rhodes.

Three generations of our family include Karen, Kim and Carter. 2013.
We have six generations from mother's grandfather to our Grandson Carter.
Our heritage is through family and country with our hope being in Christ.

Heritage & Hope

————— • —————

Chapter 13

Trapnell / The Compound

In 1975, our niece Cheryl (Lloyd and Mildred's first child) married Billy Trapnell of the pioneer Trapnell family. They have a son, Thad and daughter, Theresa, plus six grandchildren. After graduating from the University of Florida with a major in elementary education, Karen's first assignment would be the sixth grade teacher for the Trapnell Elementary School 1965-1966 school year. Karen and I married as she finished her second year in June, 1967. In that first year, Billy Trapnell was one of the students in her sixth grade class. I attended the fifth and sixth grades at that very same school with the same wood framed classrooms twelve years previously.

The community of Trapnell was established, grew and prospered about the same timeline as the adjacent communities of Springhead on the east side and Turkey Creek on the west side. One of the pioneering families in these three communities was the Trapnell family. Over a period of time, the road, school and community were all named after the family. The community runs along the north and south sides of Trapnell Road from County Line Road to Turkey Creek Road south of Plant City for about a distance of seven miles.

In 1868, Billy Trapnell's Great Great Grandfather, Elijah Trapnell and Great Grandfather, William Trapnell along with other family members, moved from Georgia to the Keystone area. William served under Robert E. Lee in the War Between the States. About the same year, the fictional family of Penny and Orry Baxter with son Jody in The Yearling settled in an area north of Ocala. Penny was a Confederate Veteran also. After reading that book, I wonder about how many encounters the Trapnells had with bears and rattlesnakes in their day.

In 1900, Billy's Great Granduncle, Rodolphus, Great Grand Aunt Rose Trapnell, and family moved into the area. One year later she served as the School Teacher in her home after Trapnell School was established on Trapnell Road just east of Highway 39. She had five students with a five month school year. The next year, the community had a new building with a county employed teacher. Billy's parents were Bill and Eunice Trapnell. His Grandparents were Charlie and Julia Trapnell.

About the same year, Karen's grandparents with their children were moving into their eighty acre homestead, only a couple of miles due east on Trapnell Road. About that time also, children of the fictional families in the novel <u>Strawberry Girl</u> were struggling with their farm chores and schooling in an area about ten miles northeast of Trapnell. Our mother's parents and two brothers moved from West Virginia to Punta Gorda in 1911. Eight years earlier, our father was born in North Carolina, destined to move to Florida in 1922 with his father. Eventually, Father would stay in this area.

In 1930, the school was moved to its present location on Trapnell Road, one mile west of Highway 39. A new wooden building was constructed in 1935 with plenty of large wooden windows, installed for cross ventilation. As the school was a "strawberry school", the hot humid summer heat was an extreme determent to our learning process. I know this all too well. A lunch room building was added in 1944. Both buildings were demolished and replaced.

My fondest childhood memories were from the time we lived on what I now consider "The Compound" during a three year period from 1953-1956. Our father purchased a twenty acre farm with a three bedroom frame house on Trapnell Road, east of Trapnell Elementary School. It was located on the south side of the road.

Today, it has an upscale housing development, "Little Alafia Creek Reserve", built on the very land that we once owned as a family. At age 51, while working out of town as an electrician on construction projects, I believe he felt like he had finally achieved his American Dream in that purchase.

As I look back at all the places we lived, this property had by far the best memories for me. It was the best of times for our family in 1953, as all eight surviving brothers were enrolled in school during the same year. We ranged from our youngest brother, Donald, being a first grader at Trapnell Elementary to our oldest brother, Charles being a senior at Turkey Creek Senior High School. My four years at "The Compound" included my last three years as a preteen and then a teenager. It was indeed a very special year in our boyhood.

Mary had already graduated from high school and college in preparing for a teaching career. Ironically in 1950, she married a Michigan *"Wolverine"*, Dwight McPherson, and they settled in Ashtabula, Ohio; the very state that our mother's ancestors had lived in the 1800s (a full circle of life over one hundred fifty years). In 1951, they had our family's first niece, Diane. It would be another seven years, in 1958, when Robert and Donna would have our first nephew, Robert Jr. We would be blessed with an abundance of nephews and nieces.

We moved onto our Trapnell farm in 1953 when I was 10 years old. Forty one years prior in 1912, our father was a 10 year old growing up in the tobacco country of Greene County, North Carolina. Our father's time then was twenty four years removed from the time Grandfather John Council Humphrey was 10 years old in 1888 in the same area. Our great grandfather, Rufus Humphrey was 10 years old in 1863, only twenty five years removed from his father's time. Rufus had two older half-brothers die during The War Between the States; not from battle, but illnesses. While roaming his paradise, I believe he was always looking over his shoulder for Yankee soldiers in addition to the regular dangers of snakes and bears to watch out for during his boyhood.

Then we had our Great Great Grandfather, Hiram Humphrey, being 10 years old in 1811. We gained our complete freedom from England after winning The War of 1812. About that time, in 1819, Abraham Lincoln was a 10 year old living in southern Indiana. Great Great Great Grandfather Lewis was 10 in 1782. Every one of our listed ancestors was reared within the surrounding area of Green County, North Carolina. They lived in small neighboring towns such as Farmville, Winterville, Fountain, Hookerton, Walstonburg and Greenville.

The innocent age of 10 (1953) for me, my father Allan Rufus (1912), Grandfather John Council (1888) Great Grandfather Rufus A. (1863) Great Great Grandfather Hiram (1811) and Great Great Great Grandfather Lewis (1782) occurred only six times for those one hundred seventy one years of our history.

Always wanting "elbow room", Daniel Boone would keep moving Westward from civilization in North Carolina and Kentucky, eventually settling down in the last home of his life west of St Louis, Missouri. His moving west was in contrast to our family staying in Carolina until 1922, when our grandfather and father went south to Florida. Actually, Daniel Boone's desire at one time was to settle in Florida. It seems like only yesterday they would look forward in hope. We are living that future now. I believe all of our previous generations would wonder what the future held for their future generations as eternal time kept moving onward.

In the fictional novel, The Yearling, Jody Baxter was about 10 in the 1870s when his family settled in an area north of Ocala. Our Great Grandfather, Rufus, was close in age to Jody when he was 10. One was growing up in the scrub land of Lake Orange. And I can only imagine that as our Great Grandfather was growing up in the tobacco farms of North Carolina, he enjoyed plenty of woodlands, creeks and ponds to spend idle days dreaming about his tomorrows. And he would always be wondering when their real nightmare of war would ever end.

During the three decades following The War Between the States, many families settled in rural communities throughout the state with community names such as Dover, Turkey Creek, Trapnell, Springhead, etc. They were all hoping to prosper in their new venture. With railroads being completed throughout the state during the 1880s, a floodgate was opened for people to move economically to this area as settlers.

Plant City was renamed after H.B. Plant, the man who built the railroad from the Atlantic coast to the Gulf Coast in Clearwater. He built the rail road through the small town of Plant City. In 1892, he completed the construction of a winter resort hotel in Tampa. The beautiful architectural masterpiece is now a historic building on The University of Tampa campus. It is a "must see" for tourists as well as our local residents. Other beautiful architectural masterpieces built twenty two years later include the Tampa City Hall and the 1914 Plant City Senior High School, both beautiful historical buildings. They all had brick exterior walls.

As I recalled my memories of our Trapnell farm, I thought it would be good to give it a name after all these years. At this time, I wish to call it "The Compound". It's regrettable that we were not able to keep the property in the family. Hopefully, you will see why as you read through this chapter of history in our family life.

A beautiful meandering creek, called "Little Alafia Creek", ran through our property on the west side from north to south. It was a shallow creek, flowing southward; always full of active frogs, spiders, snakes and occasional fish. It was like a waterway straight out of the novel The Yearling. Like Jody in the book. I would go down to the creek and play along the water's edge. The stream ran through the woodland filled with a beautiful landscape of pines, oaks, grass, and wild flowers.

That small portion of God's creation had remained untouched with maybe the exception of native Indians stopping for a drink of fresh clear water from the creek as they traveled through the area going from coast to coast. It had flourished untouched for centuries. Words are hard to find to describe the beauty of this tropical paradise, especially on sunny days filled with the bright sunlight flooding through the trees from a blue sky. It was like entering into a garden of paradise. It would be priceless to have an opportunity to see that landscape in its untouched surroundings once again.

It has only been sixty five years for me since those days. If we go back another forty years or so from our move to the compound in 1953, we would be at the time my father would be 10 years old most likely spending free time at a local creek near his North Carolina tobacco farm. If we look once more at a time period from 1912 to the 1870s, we have another forty year span from our father to Jody's fictional time. My time at Little Alafia Creek was only two forty year generations removed from Jody's time. Every day on earth has value.

Without any doubt, my most cherished memory of all as a youth would be me standing in an open field on a clear night seeing the pitch black sky overflowing with bright stars from all four horizons. That view reminded me of the time God told Abraham about the stars in heaven and the sand on the seashore. As recorded in Genesis 22:17-18, God told Abraham, *"in blessing I will bless you, and in multiplying I will multiply your descendants as the stars of the heaven and as the sand which is on the seashore: and your descendants shall possess the gates of their enemies. In your seed all the nations of the earth shall be blessed, because you have obeyed My voice."*

Hallelujah! God is blessing America because of Abraham. This is the sky we both looked upon, some 4,000 years apart. He was in our heritage land of Israel at that time and I was on our Trapnell, Florida homestead having a time span filled with thousands upon thousands of books on mankind's history. Also, in the few times we went swimming at Clearwater Beach, I would think on God's Word regarding the sand on the seashore.

The stars were always so bright. Except for one or two sixty wattage light bulbs burning inside our scattered farm houses, night lights were non-existent. Today I am deeply saddened by the reality that we cannot now see those same stars at night as we could then. I hate for this to be a reality for our present and future generations. We have simply flooded our urban and rural landscape with way too much night lighting.

Other vivid night memories included catching lightening bugs by cupping them in our hands and then releasing them, watching swarms of bats fly just above our heads as if they were jet fighters strafing us in battle, large owls hooting from large live oaks, animals (like a wildcat) crying out in the dark night, and seeing red eyes looking back at us as we would shine a flashlight into the wilderness. These common night experiences lessened as each decade came and went until now they are basically non-existent in this area.

We bought The Compound from a Hungarian family. Our neighbor to the east was a bachelor from Hungary also. He had a close relationship with the previous owners. He worked in a bakery in Plant City and would drive to work early in the mornings, like at 4 A.M. or so. Our farm house and barn were built on an acre of land in the center of the property with a one lane dirt drive going to the house. The house compound was about two hundred yards from the road. Our neighbor told us they had migrated from Hungary during the 30s and built their houses at that time.

What was so very unusual about that property was the fact that the previous owner had Australian pines planted in straight rows along each side of the drive and around all four sides of the house with a one acre yard. The dirt entrance road had three foot deep ditches on both sides of a single lane drive, and then the pines. This unique layout of pines for the drive and house compound boundaries reminded me of farm villas in Europe. I thought the tree planting arrangement was very stately looking. Wind blowing through the trees would produce a peaceful whispering musical sound. We would see these pines throughout the state, especially along some of the Gulf Coast beaches. Today, they are slowly being removed as they are now considered invasive trees.

The house was a typical wood structure built in the early 1930s. It was a typical one story frame house constructed on brick piers. The house had a small back porch, kitchen, combination living and dining room, and three bedrooms. I think it had less than 1,000 square foot of living area. A small third bedroom was added onto the back porch.

The house did have one very unusual feature. It did not have a front door or front porch. I had never seen a house like this before or ever since. Our father always talked about adding a porch and front door to the house, but it never happened.

We had a shallow 1 1/2" diameter pipe well with a self-priming hand pump on the back porch for our house hold water source. We had to keep a full bucket of water near the pump in order to prime it with water until it was then hand pumped out of the ground. Since the well was not very deep, we always had sand to deal with. The sand would always settle at the bottom of the water container. We always thought a little bit of sand wouldn't hurt a "feller". The outhouse was behind the barn. The barn included a horse stall for the horse that came with the property sale. We had a huge mulberry tree south of the house and east of the barn.

Our household landfill was in an area east of the yard tree line. We had a 50 gal drum for burning garbage that was combustible. We would dig a 5' foot deep hole about 10' x 10' to bury the non-combustible wet garbage items. Over a period of time, we would keep moving the landfill as each pit would fill up. We would top the full landfill with about a foot of dirt. At the time, we didn't have garbage pickup service, so we did what we had to do with what we had available to us. This waste management method was the only way families got rid of their waste. It was a common practice for everyone in the countryside.

Local towns had similar large open landfills on a larger scale called "The City Dump" for their citizens. Most of those dumps were allowed to be stacked up into one huge open mountain of stinking garbage at the outskirts of the city limits. Yes, those dumps did present an unpleasant appearance and odor, let along serious rodent problems. As we entered the 60s, the garbage disposal industry was gradually being established in the use of incinerators and improved landfills. Yet once again, we saw another way of living like the city dump and individual farmhouse landfills vanish without any fanfare.

During that time, outhouses were in the process of being replaced with in house bath rooms including a toilet fixture and waste piping to a septic tank and drain field. Our family would not experience that change over until the next residence we would move into three years later, in 1956.

Our Trapnell compound had land cleared on all four sides of the house for farming with some wooded areas along the west and south property lines. A large untouched wooded area also existed to the south of our property. Our creek ran through the west woodland. Neighboring farms were scattered on the north and south sides of Trapnell Road.

As we settled into our farm compound, Mary had already graduated from school and college, married, and moved to Ohio. That year, Charles graduated and enlisted in the Marine Corp for four years. Soon afterwards, Robert would marry Donna Crofton and at about the same time enlist in the Air Force for four years.

Our father was working in large northern cities as a construction union electrician and would travel home for a few weeks at a time between project assignments. The rest of us, six boys ranging from 8 years old to 17, were all intact at home and went about running the farm as the best we could at the time. The oldest brother living at home would always be our straw boss in the absence of our father.

It was during our first year of farming at Trapnell in 1953, that we witnessed farming methods that would simply disappear right before our eyes. And we would barely acknowledge it had become a forever bygone time. Our family farming methods suddenly changed from horse and buggy days to the use of modern farm equipment.

I have vivid memories of using a horse for our plowing needs. I remember seeing our father and older brothers plowing away behind our horse. I even had one experience of turning the land with our horse pulling a turning plow. Needless to say, it was a very slow process, but it served its purpose of preparing the soil for planting a new crop. We would hire a tractor contractor to disc the fields for the final planting preparation.

After one year at the compound, we managed to purchase a brand new Farmall tractor and an irrigation pump with aluminum watering pipe. The best I know; we were one of the last, if not the last, farm family to plow with a horse and water crops by hand with buckets of water. Around 1955, that era for us became history with good riddance on our part.

In the spring we would plant strawberry plants about 12 inches apart in nursery rows. During the summer months to follow we would weed the beds and place the plant runners close together so they would grow out new plants and we would work them down into the dirt so they could sprout roots quickly for each plant. Strawberry nursery plants grew and spread just like St Augustine grass runners. They spread runners producing new grass sprouts with roots.

We would hoe and weed the nursery beds along with bunching the runners close together. The process included constant man hours of monotonous labor. As soon as we finished weeding the nursery beds, then we would have to start over again as a new crop of weeds were taking over the beds. Since we were in school during the summer months, we would have to do the weeding after school hours and on Saturdays. We usually didn't work on Sundays unless we had to play catch up.

I found it quite amusing and a little questionably that some sixty five years later, I am still pulling weeds. Instead of strawberry plant nursery beds, it is for our home landscape. It is the same tedious chore. One big difference was the fact that the nursery beds were out in an open farm area where you were in the direct sun light all day long with no relief from the hot sun except to head for the compound Australian pines refreshing shade. Remember, this was before air conditioning. Mosquitos and nates were a constant nuisance also. There is no more horrible feeling than having a nate fly up your nose. Now, I follow the shade cover with my weeding and use a lot of mosquito spray.

As we worked the nursey beds, I would spend a lot of time daydreaming about all of the exotic places I had read about in the world that I wanted to visit someday such as the Statue of Liberty, Empire State Building, Israel, Westminster Abbey, Eiffel Tower, etc. Today as I weed our garden, I find myself reflecting on my childhood experiences as cherished memories. It makes for a full circle.

We would do those nursery chores throughout the summer. In September we would dig up the nursey plants with a potato rake and break each plant from its runner vine so we could plant each nursery plant in beds prepared to place the strawberry plants about a foot on center. While most farmers planted double rows, we would always stay with single rows.

Lloyd was our oldest brother living at home around that time and he became our straw boss. He was also our planter as we would drop plants ahead of him as he would plant each plant with a hand trowel. He was quick and efficient at this task. Whether they wanted to or not, each oldest brother would be required to be our lead planter along with being the straw boss. Philip and Harry would also work as planters. We only raised nursery plants for a few years. It was more economical to buy the plants from nursery suppliers. One year we also experimented with selling nursery plants to the public. As the business venture was not profitable for us, we abandoned it.

Somehow, within a couple of weeks or so, we would always end up getting acres of strawberry plants in the ground ready for them to grow into full foliage with strawberries by January. We would end up with strawberries fields on all four sides of our farm compound. From October through December, we would have to hoe the beds for weeds at the same time taking care not to cut the plants, which would severally stunt the plant growth (reducing the production of berries) with our hoe.

By January, we would have our first strawberries of the season ready to be picked, packed and hauled to the farmer's market. The strawberries were auctioned off to the highest bidding distribution company. Those companies would take the auctioned strawberries and ship them to large cities in the North, like New York City. It was a special treat to ride along to the market where we could hear the auctioneer sing the bids out and then declaring the winning bid amount, "Sold at 35 cents". The strawberries would be harvested through March and sometimes into April.

Robins and more robins! At times, robins would flock into our field like locust to eat the strawberries as soon as they started turning red. As scarecrows were worthless, we had to take turns at "minding" the field everyday as best we could. We would chase them out of one section of the field while they flew to other sections. There was no pattern to their visitations. We used a 410 shotgun to help chase the birds out. Tourist driving by on the road would see us shooting at the birds and give us stern stares as they thought it was horrible that we would harm a bird as beautiful as a robin. Actually, we would shoot close to them to make them fly away and not want to return.

At that time, we planted either Missionary or Florida 90 strawberry varieties. The Missionary strawberries were small, but very sweet and juicy. The Florida 90s, a relative newly developed strawberry at that time, were a lot larger, but not as sweet and juicy. As time progressed, newer varieties were developed as improvements in regards to volume, taste and appearance; for example, the Sweet Charlie. Recently, the

Sweet Sensations variety was developed as an improved marketing strawberry. Now, we also have the BB1 21 species, a really sweet and juicy strawberry.

In the 50s, creative farmers would plant two rows of plants per bed. Later, they began to install black plastic on the earth formed beds to prevent weeds and also to keep chemicals and nutrients in the soil for the plants growth. Many farmers installed galvanized pipe on top of post to irrigate their crops. That system was replaced by on ground movable aluminum pipe. Finally, the irrigation system was changed to underground piping with sprinkler heads located close enough to achieve full coverage watering. On today's large strawberry fields, a large heavy duty pumping system is necessary to meet the watering needs. This is the same irrigation system used for our residential and commercial irrigation systems.

Prior to having an irrigation system for watering our crops, we would fill a 50 gal drum with water that we bucketed out of the creek. As we did not have a tractor, we would use our horse to pull a sled with the drum of water on it up to the strawberry field and water each plant with water bucketed out of the barrel. And that was how we watered our freshly planted strawberry plants. It was a truly a "horse and buggy" process. As we would say, *It's not rocket science*. Needless to say, we would pray for rain every day as we usually had very small amounts of rain in late September and October.

The next year, out of the clear blue sky, our father bought a brand new Farmall tractor. I know it is hard to believe today, but our family fell in love with that brand new tractor like it was a new car. The monetary valve of our horse fell like a rock. I seized the opportunity to drive the tractor at about age 12. I would even drive it down the two lane county gravel road to the nearby general country store at the intersection of Highway 39. As the oldest brother at home, Lloyd became our official Tractor Operation and Maintenance Man.

And as a double surprise, our father also bought an above ground water pump and aluminum piping for our existing farm well to irrigate our crops. Everything seemed to go along fine until we started having trouble with sand filling the irrigation pipe water spray outlets. That problem created dry spots at random areas of the water spray coverage. It was a consistent problem as we would keep going around cleaning out the stopped up openings. The problem was that our well was a shallow well and too much sand was being pumped out of the ground with the well water.

The solution would be to drill at least a four inch well one hundred feet deep or more. The cost for this solution prohibited us from correcting our problem. Instead, we would keep on cleaning the stopped up nozzles. It became a game for us to dodge the sprays of water as we opened the clogged openings. On warm days it was fine, but not so fine on chilly days.

Our neighboring family to the west had two boys near my age and we would play together often. I would have to cross our creek, walk through a small wooded area, cross a barbed wire fence (for our horse) and then walk to their house. Their father was a carpenter and they were one of the first families in our neighborhood to buy a television. As I had never seen a television before, I was memorized as I stared at the shows being shown during my first Saturday morning visit to watch their television. The program basically included cartoons with a Moderator named Jungle Jim (or something like that). It was like having a movie theater right in your home. I was totally blown away with watching it. It would be another four years before our family would buy a television.

Television was catching on like wildfire in the early 50's with antennas going up on houses constantly. No one cared that there were only three channels and that you had to work the volume and channel selection on the TV console. Remote control devices were decades later. We had to rotate the antenna pole until we got the best image possible, and then we had to keep adjusting it frequently.

In 1954, the U.S. Supreme Court ruled that quiz shows were not a form of gambling. Television broadcasting companies increased the production of those type programs. The prizes given out for the shows were extremely enticing. The *$64,000 Question* became one of the first big money quiz shows. I remember going home one night and telling my mother about the *$64,000 Question* show and how someone was about to have a chance to win that large sum of money.

Although we would wonder, we didn't know those programs would be exposed. In 1956, the show *"Twenty One"* featured contestants Herbert Stempel and Charles Van Doren competing with staged questions. Two years later, the scandal was brought before Congressional hearings and corrections were implemented. The *"Twenty One"* scandal was portrayed in the 1994 movie, *"Quiz Show"*.

For our communication from the outside world, we had a radio of which we primarily listened to comedies and adventure series after dinner. Although we didn't have books in our home, except for our school textbooks, we did subscribe to the Tampa Tribune. We also subscribed to the Tampa Times that was issued in the afternoons. The Tribune Times closed after television networks began to present the evening local and national news on a daily basis. I always enjoyed reading the daily question and answer columns that Billy Graham and Ann Landers wrote, along with some of the comic strips. I also followed the Pro-baseball Grapefruit League each spring.

Ironically, The St Pete Times parent company bought The Tampa Tribune in June, 2016. That was one more local beacon of light that existed since 1895, for one hundred twenty one years. With very little fanfare, the Tampa Tribune was all of a sudden no more. I am trying hard to overlook liberal editorials and articles that are consistently being published in the Tampa Bay Times newspaper that we subscribe to now. In addition to our family subscribing to the Tampa Tribune during my elementary school years, I have also subscribed to the Tribune faithfully since 1970. It will be almost impossible to stop now after a life time subscription.

Our father also subscribed to the ever increasing liberal Time and Newsweek magazines of which I would read somewhat. Although our father was an eighth grade school dropout, he read the newspaper and these magazines so he would be able to discuss and debate current issues with his coworkers during his work days.

He was a strong union member. Like many union workers, he became a loyal Democrat. He would share his thoughts and opinions with his captive family audience at the dinner table when he was home on leave from his northern work assignments. I believe that over time the Democratic Party convinced unions it was for the working class more so than the Republican Party. Charles, Philip, Harry and Michael were union members in their respective construction work trades. I believe under this present administration, the Republican Party is doing more for the construction workers.

Our parents would discuss politics and different Presidents with each other as we listened to their current events that would later become history. They would compare the different Presidents we had during the 20th century such as Woodrow Wilson, Franklin Roosevelt, and Harry Truman. During these dinner conversations, they would also discuss which famous movie stars they liked or disliked. They talked about how sad it was when Charles Lindbergh's son was murdered and when Presidents Wilson and Roosevelt died. On a side note, our father would tell us about the time his father took his family to a Billy Sunday crusade in North Carolina.

It was at The Compound that we had our very first telephone installed in our home. It was sort of funny in a way. We didn't have any one to call especially. We did have Mary, Charles and Robert all living away from home. The long distance calling fees prohibited our parents from calling them except in case of an emergency. So we had a phone that we hardly ever used.

At the time, we had to share the phone with a few of our neighbors. That telephone calling arrangement was called a "Party Line". When we picked up the phone to make a call, we had to listen to see if anyone else was already talking. We had to wait on them to finish their phone call before we could dial the number we wanted to call. So when you had long winded neighbors on the phone, you may have to wait long periods of time just to make a brief call. Also, a person could ease drop on conversations just by picking up the phone and listening to any conversation that was going on. To say the least, party lines were extremely unpopular. Soon afterwards, that telephone calling system became history.

I started looking for ways to make some spending money. One day I responded to an ad to become a delivery boy for *Grit Newspaper*. That national company would arrange for people to become local distributors of their newspaper. So one year I signed up to be a distributor for our local community of Trapnell. True to form, I received the number of newspapers that I committed to sell. So off I went from door to door trying to sell a subscription to every household in our community.

There were only about twenty households within a one mile radius of my home to work with as potential customers. Needless to say, that experience was an eye opener for me at my 5th grade age. I actually got some neighbors to faithfully subscribe to the newspaper and actually pay me the dime or so price. I think I made about a nickel per newspaper.

The Grit was actually a good newspaper with a little bit of everything in it. I would read it also and thought it was interesting and informative. However, my base of customers started to slip away one by one as time went by until I finally discontinued the business. Looking back at my short experience, I realized I did gain some valuable business lessons early in life, like how to sale someone a product when they may not want to buy into it. I learned to deal with the rejection if they would say, "No thank you". And I learned how to tactical follow up on "slow pay" customers. Yes, slow payers were healthy and thriving even back in the day. And some would end up as "No pay".

Another business venture I undertook was to sell mulberries from the huge tree in our back yard. My first customer was my father's insurance policy premiums collection agent as he visited us to collect the couple of dollars premium cost. I picked two quarts of the best looking ripe mulberries. As he was leaving, I asked him if he wanted to buy some mulberries as I showed him the berries. Without any hesitance, he told me "No thank you". I got the same response from the ice delivery man also. Since I hated rejection, I shut down that business venture. Maybe I just needed better marketing.

Once a week, usually on Monday mornings, the ice delivery man drove up to the house and read the sign next to our back door on how many pounds of ice we wanted for that week. We used either 25 or 50 pound blocks of ice for our ice box upper compartment. We left the ice in one big block so it would not melt as fast as broken up ice. The use of ice blocks was a very crude method of keeping refrigerated food chilled enough to eat. We could not use our ice box to freeze food. Eventually we bought a freezer /chiller refrigerator.

Wash day was like an early 20th century chore. We had a wash tub with a washing blade and a hand operated crank wringer attachment with a rinsing tub located on the back porch. We would take one piece of clothing at a time from the washer and wring out the water for each piece of clothing as we rolled it through the wringer. We would then take each washed and wringed piece and hang it on the clothes line to be dried by the sun light. And we would pray that they dried before a fast moving thunderstorm soaked everything wet again. We would then have to leave everything on the line to be dried through the next day. In extreme drought weather, we would have to be careful that dust wouldn't blow on the washed items as they dried on the clothes line.

On occasional Sundays, we would have fried chicken for Dinner (Lunch). I remember the last time we killed, plucked, cleaned and cooked a chicken in a frying pan. We would take turns on pulling the wishbone under the table with each other. The tradition of butchering a home grown chicken and pulling the wishbone soon afterwards became extinct in the 50s.

Breakfast usually included scrambled eggs, grits and biscuits. Sometimes, we would have bacon. Dinner (Lunch) included cornpone mix bread fried in a pan and cut into small pie shaped pieces, potatoes cut into small chunks and boiled in water, and great northern beans. This meal was also quite often provided at Supper (Dinner) also. Our father would tell us that the Army fed their troops potatoes and the Navy fed their sailors great northern beans. So he figured we would be getting the better of two worlds with a combination of potatoes and beans. Very seldom we had a dessert.

As a toddler, one thing that I hated more than anything was drinking milk in a bottle made from condensed milk. Water would be mixed with it and then served at room temperature. I still remember it having a horribly taste. To this day I will not drink milk, no matter how good the quality. Snacks of potato chips or cookies were a special treat. Whatever snacks we had were few, and far in between. One time our father brought us a bag of chips to us as we were working in the field. It was gone in a matter of minutes as we shared it between five brothers. Our drink with that treat was the fresh water from our hand pump and shallow well.

A short lived Christmas tradition on the compound included our sister Mary shipping a box of mini size candy bars to us as her gift to our family. She did this for a few years in a row. She was living in Ashtabula, Ohio as a suburban mom. This was the best treat ever for me. I told her about this a few years ago and she did not remember it at all. I found it very strange that I had such a vivid memory of that and she didn't. Could it be that it was just another gift to her and it could have been just another gift for us brothers except for the fact it was indeed a treasured experience. I know it was for me.

A phenomenon that was prevalent during that time was hitch-hiking a ride with someone driving in the same direction you were traveling. We found it very commonplace in our rural communities then. Looking back at hitch-hiking, I would think it started as soon as people started buying and driving auto vehicles in the early 1900's. It became more common during the depression (as many would even hitch rides on freight trains). Johnny Cash made a hit record, "*Orange Blossom Special*", about hitching a ride on a train to Florida.

I learned at a very young age of 10, if I would stick out my right hand thumb, people (especially if they knew you) would stop and offer you a ride, as long as you were going in their direction. My first hitching ride that I remember was when we lived on Rice Road and a family friend picked Harry and me up and gave us a ride into town. We thought that was easy.

I would hitch hike countless trips to the two country stores at the next east and west Trapnell Road intersections (Highway 39 and Mud Lake Road). Unfortunately, I had to tolerate forever re-occurring comments such as, "*For a nickel more, you could have gotten red hair. I bet you curl it every night.*" I had fire engine deep red curly hair. As I grew to 6'-2', people would also say to me "*How's the weather up there?*"

I would continue to hitch hike throughout my school and college years until I married. Early on I guess I was too young to realize the potential danger in this way of life. I would hitch-hike in Florida, Alabama, Georgia and North Carolina. I hitched to and from Auburn University quite often.

Later on, well into the 60s, I started to notice suspicious behavior patterns with some of the people giving me rides and I became more concerned about the serious risk I was taking. News reports on criminal acts involving hitchhiking increased during the next decade until now hitching a ride is, for all practical purposes, extinct. At times I got into cars when I couldn't wait to get out of them as fast I could. No doubt about it, I had ministering angels.

In every residence, we had everything needed for a self- sufficient life without leaving our immediate area. We had family farms and groves, commercial and industrial businesses within a short driving range. We had local family stores at each nearby intersection, we had a drive-in theater, a family owned and operated drive in restaurant (although we could never afford to purchase a hamburger and coke treat), family owned and operated grocery store of which all were on Highway 39 south of the city limits.

Mr. Johnson had just opened his family operated restaurant on 39 South also. His sons would later open a restaurant they named Buddy

Freddys. The Wilson family owned and operated the drive-in restaurant on South 39, next to The Starlite Drive-In Theater. The Zambito family owned and operated a grocery store across from the drive in theater. Their oldest son, Pat, was a classmate. Our local radio station, WPLA, was on the west side of Highway 39.

My mother bought our groceries at the Zambitos when we lived at the compound. Mother would end up shopping there the rest of her life, even after we had moved to Youmans and then moved again into a house located on West Ball Street in the southwest section of town. That relationship would extend over sixteen years of time. As I look back, I now wonder if that arrangement was one of Mother's best social times. Along with *"Customer Loyalty"*, shopping was a pleasure at Zambitos also.

We had two air conditioned theaters, the Capital and the State, in town along with businesses selling necessities for living. We had other family owned businesses like McGinnes Lumber, Hooker's Department Store, White's Pharmacy, Crouse Service Station, Fleming Paint, jewelry stores, and many more.

We also had a Five and Dime Store (todays' Walmart) managed by a local manager, but owned by a corporation. The store was always a treat to visit whenever we made a trip downtown. This is where Santa would always get his gifts for us kids on the night before Christmas. It was real convenient as our parents only had to make a one stop shopping trip for our gifts. The Manager's son was a classmate also. The store was loaded with aisle after aisle of very inexpensive practical household and toy items along with just plain "stuff".

If you lived in Plant City during the 50s, you could never forget the Robinson Swimming Pool and Roller Skating Rink. It was located a couple of miles west of the city on Highway 92. It was extremely popular within our area as it was the only public swimming pool available. I don't ever remember seeing a pool in anyone's back yard during that time period.

Anyhow, a car load of us brothers would pile into our family car and drive over to the pool for a Saturday swim. This was a huge treat for me. After all of those steaming humid hot days in the fields, swimming in this clean cool pool of water was like a heavenly experience. The entry cost was about a quarter. Even so, each trip we made was so special to me. In all I think we only went to the pool no more times than you can count on one hand. It was a typical pool with a big diving board on the deep end and a shallow area on the opposite pool end. I would swim in the shallow end and stayed away from the diving board.

One day when we were swimming, the life guard and manager told everyone to get out of the water and stand next to the pool. Then they told us they had a treat for us as they explained the rules for the "money grab" game that they were going to let us play. They scattered loose coins (pennies, nickels, dimes and quarters around in the pool and then told us to dive in and collect as many coins as we could grab until all of the coins were taken by someone. This experience proved a reason to have a bathing suit with a pocket. Although I didn't collect a fortune, I did collect quite a bit of loose change. I have always held a fond memory of that one time event.

The roller skate ring experience was totally different as we always went at night and there would always be couples and singles skating together. Roller skating was an on the job training experience with me primarily being my own instructor.

I watched the experienced ones skating with speed and confidence, as they would roll backwards and make figure eights. Some couples showed off their skating style together. Skating contest were always being called during the night. Now that I think about it, this roller skating entertainment reflected quite a bit of what the old barn yard square dancing events were like. Just like the swimming pool visits, I could count the fingers on one hand for the times I went skating.

During the 50s, we would gather together a car load of brothers and neighborhood friends; pitch in a couple of nickels each for the family car gasoline cost and head out to one of our favorite swimming holes. The oldest brother would be the designated driver and the next older one always rode as "shotgun". Our favorite places included Lithia Springs or Hillsborough State Park. Robinson Pool was a very special favorite also, except for the entry cost. We only went to the gulf beach on very special occasions as it was too far to drive. Close by creeks were popular also, especially after a heavy rain. We could walk or ride to them on our bicycles.

Swimming experiences included nearby creeks after heavy rains raised the water level to a desirable swimming depth, phosphate pits (very dangerous), Lithia Springs (a special treat), the gulf beach (a triple treat) and the Hillsborough River State Park (before the water became polluted and gators took over the river for themselves).

Crystal Springs, on Highway 39 south of Zephyrhills, was another local swimming hole. However, the spring bank always looked like it was a natural hiding place for snakes and spiders. It would only take one miserable experiences with getting our foot cut on a broken beer bottle near a bridge before we stopped swimming within throwing distances from bridges. At that time, Lithia Springs was a private owned property with a single lane dirt road running to it from Lithia Pinecrest Road. There was an old dead tree with a swing rope at the edge of the spring for swinging off the tree into the water. A trip to the springs was a special treat also as we would go in a car loaded with boys. Gas prices of 20 cents a gallon made it a very reasonable trip as we shared the cost.

Old framed houses were scattered among pastures, orange groves with grapefruit trees, and farms with majestic woodlands in the distant background. Memories of seeing a blend of countryside beauty is now only a small note in the history of East Hillsborough County. It is sad to know future generations will never be able to see the beauty we saw. At the time, we all took it for granted.

That blessed abundance came crashing down during the 60s as hard freezes killed off those beautiful lush groves. It seems like everything north of Highway 60 and some points southward were totally wiped out by hard freezing temperatures. Some grove owners started over with new trees in these areas but were to meet the same fate again as we experienced more freezes that once again killed off the new trees.

We have known of orange groves as far north as the Ocala area. Marjorie Rawlings had an orange grove during the 30s. She described in detail how they had to fire up the groves in order to save the trees and oranges from freezing when the temperature dropped below 30 degrees. Some of her trees are still struggling to live, even though in a weaken condition.

During the last forty years or so, land being purchased and converted to housing developments replaced a lot of those pastures, farms and groves. Recently, the greening disease finished off just about any other orange trees in our area that managed to survive the harsh weather. Today, a person has to drive south toward Sebring to find heathy orange groves.

As of this date, the greening disease is not under control. To make matters even worse, experts are predicting the disease will destroy all of the orange trees in our state if it is not stopped somehow within the very near future.

Considering a lighter item of state history, Florida was an early tour for Elvis Presley. As his popularity spread rapidly during his first year of being discovered, even our father picked up on the phenomenon. One day he pulled his car up near us as we were finishing up a day's work in the field. We listened to Elvis finish singing one of his hit songs "Hound Dog" and then the car radio DJ announced that Elvis Presley would be performing at a concert in Tampa. It was 1956, and sure enough, Elvis was going to be one of several recording artists scheduled to sing at the Amory in Tampa.

Of course we all knew none of us would be going. It was out of the question because of the cost involved and the fact that our father didn't really care that much for Elvis anyhow. Presley's tour through Florida was instrumental in helping him to become established as a superstar rock and roll performer.

The tour became part of Tampa's history as rock and roll music was being birthed across the nation. Elvis Presley's Manager, Colonel Tom Parker, was Dog Catcher for Hillsborough County before he became his Manager. Throughout his life, Elvis would keep Colonel Parker as his Manager.

Elvis returned to Florida in the summer of 1961 to star in the movie "Follow That Dream". It was released in 62. I think the opening scene shows his family driving over the original 1924 Gandy Bridge. The bridge had only two lanes with no emergency lanes. The 1912 Citrus County Courthouse in Inverness was featured in the film also.

As for The Compound, the next owners demolished the house, barn and our beloved Australian pines. They built a new home in the northeast acre and planted an orange grove on the rest. Recently, the property was sold again and developed with upscale designed homes. Adventurous children living there may still be enjoying Little Alafia Creek. However, the creek is still a straight ditch full of weeds.

Lord, our Lord, How excellent is Your name in all the earth, You who set Your glory above the heavens! (Psalm 8:1)

Existing "Cracker" house very similar to the one I was born in September 16, 1943, during WWII. We owned a farm on Dad Weldon Road. The house burned down some forty years later. Some of the houses had a fireplace with a brick chimney.

Heritage & Hope

———•———

Chapter 14

Turkey Creek / Football / History

Turkey Creek is located next to Dover and Sydney to the west, Interstate I-4 to the north, Plant City and Trapnell to the east, and Highway 60 to the south. The name was based on a large population of turkey and deer living along a creek, appropriately named Turkey Creek, running through the area from north to south. Landmark Beatty's Corner is located at the intersection of Turkey Creek and Trapnell Roads.

Similar to adjacent rural communities in Hillsborough County, pioneers moved into the area gradually. A saw mill was established to meet the demand for lumber. Population growth was slow. The community, growing from a population of one hundred in 1911 to two hundred in 1925, included a Baptist church, a public school and two general stores.

The first school was a one room log cabin built in 1873, near the intersection of Turkey Creek and Trapnell Roads. That was about the same time a school was being established in Springhead. Various Turkey Creek schools were built at different locations through a period of time until 1908, when a two story frame building was built at the present location of the Turkey Creek and Connell Roads intersection.

A new two story brick building was built in 1927 to replace the wooden building for a construction cost of $19,800. That was the same building along with the one story brick building where we attended high school in the 50s. The school continued to operate as a strawberry school until 1956. Both buildings are still serving as a middle school. About that same time, a new agriculture building was constructed for the Future Farmers of America (FFA) educational program.

To help refresh memories of my strawberry schools 7th and 8th grades at Turkey Creek Junior High School in 1955 and 1956, I traveled down memory lane looking through Mildred Green Humphrey's and Vivian Green Brewer's five school annuals ("*El Pavo*") for the school years of

1952 through 1956. During visits in recent years or so with Donna, Mildred, Lloyd and Philip, we would recall many childhood memories together. I have included them in <u>Heritage & Hope</u>. In December 1956, Mildred and Lloyd graduated together in the very last graduating class for the strawberry schools. They married about a year after graduating from high school.

The Hillsborough County School System included Elementary School Grades 1 – 6, Junior High School Grades 7, 8 and 9 (Freshmen), and Senior High School Grades 10 (Sophomores) 11 (Juniors) and 12 (Seniors). The school had forty teachers and 1,028 students in the 1952 school year. The teacher pupil ratio was a high average of twenty five students per teacher.

In March 1951, 153 students were in the Turkey Creek Senior High School 10th grade. Those students came from Cork, Dover, Springhead and Turkey Creek Junior High Schools 9th grades. Only 124 students returned for the 11th grade March 1952 class. Then, a dismal seventy five students returned for the 12th grade March 1953 class; of which seventy had their senior photos taken and were expected to graduate in December 1953. Charles was one of the students in that graduation class. Afterwards, he joined the Marines.

In the annual, I noticed the clothing attire for boys wearing cuffed trousers and rolled up short sleeved shirts. Girls wore long petty coat dresses. A few daring older boys carried a pack of cigarettes in their rolled up sleeves. That habit plus combing back oiled slicked hair was the fad. Crew cuts were also the rage for some. Rock and roll music was introduced into our bland world of the 50s. And then Dick Clark and the American Bandstand appeared on the TV scene.

I saw plenty of barefoot boys in the elementary school grades one thru six class photographs. It reminded me of the days I went to elementary school barefoot. That life style had pros and cons. We always felt cooler and more carefree when going barefoot. However, we were exposed to the dangers of cutting our feet, dirt stained skin, athlete's feet, and sandspurs tearing into our feet; all of which I had personally experienced at one time or another during my childhood. Going barefoot at home was pleasant, only if you were blessed with tough skin and a "Daniel Boone spirit".

As I studied the photographs of the administration, faculty, lunch room staff, custodians, bus drivers, and students, I did not see any minorities.

Living in a total segregated society was the norm for everyone. It was a society and culture established through the ruling authority of local states, counties and municipalities after the southern states Reconstruction Era from 1865 - 1877 was dismantled. State and local Jim Crow laws and mandates were used in enforcing racial segregation in the South.

The laws mandated the segregation of public schools, public places, and public transportation, restrooms, restaurants, and drinking fountains for African Americans. The U.S. military and governmental workplaces were also segregated. Enacted after the Reconstruction period, these laws and mandates continued to be enforced until 1964. Starting in 1877, the Democratic Party gained power in the Southern legislatures. They disrupted the Republican Party and ran Republican officeholders out of town. They intimidated African Americans to suppress their voting. Extensive voter fraud was present also. The Democratic Party was instrumental in establishing and implementing evil Jim Crow laws and mandates throughout that eighty seven year time period till 1964.

The Republican Party evolved from several fractions over several decades into one united party by 1854. The first Republican President elected was Abraham Lincoln serving from 1861 until he was assassinated in 1865. The Democratic Party was established about 1828 by supporters of Andrew Jackson. He was the first Democratic President. We have had 18 Republican Presidents and 13 Democratic Presidents.

By 1900, a new racial system was deeply embedded in the South, including Florida, with a disenfranchisement of African Americans voters, and a rigid society of racial segregation. African Americans were restricted basically to low wage agricultural and domestic employment. Anyone challenging the order was punished by legal maneuvering and/or violence.

In the 50s, I vividly remember the Plant City Greyhound Bus Station having separate waiting lounges and "Colored" signs for separate bus station entrance doors, restrooms and drinking fountains. That arrangement would be the same for all other businesses also, with signs everywhere. They could only order take-out food from restaurants through the back doors.

"Dixiecrats" opposed integration and wanted to retain Jim Crow laws and white supremacy to oppose possible federal intervention.

After the 1948 election, its leaders returned to the Democratic Party. They were referred to as "Dixiecrats" (Southern and Democrat). The term "Dixiecrat" was sometimes used by Northern Democrats to refer to conservative Southern Democrats from the 1940s to the 1980s. Integration was achieved in spite of the resistance.

I don't remember any personal interactions with a minority until my Marine Corp boot camp training in 1962, at age 19. It was only because the camp was a federal controlled entity and facility. It would be the mid 60s before our education system and society were integrated. The Jim Crow laws were overruled by the Civil Rights Act of 1964 and the Voting Rights Act of 1965. Those drastic changes were implemented mostly peacefully through court challenges and at times forcefully.

Obviously, our parent's generation had the most difficulty in dealing with "the Old South" changing into "the New South". My generation along with my parent's generation dealt with the challenge in our own ways. Our two generations are a part of American history that experienced the end of a tragic eighty seven year southern culture. That way of life lasted from 1877 through 1964. We experienced the end of "The Old South" and a birthing of the "The New South" beginning in 1964. It was a very big deal for everyone. At the time, I was a 21 year old focused 100% on obtaining a college degree. Like so many others, we were just making ends meet.

It took a decade plus more of time to fully implement the changes. Somehow, we survived the integration process and moved on with our lives, each in our own fashion. Since then, volumes have been written on this transformation in the South. Even so, that era was a large portion of our heritage, whether we like it or not. Through God's amazing grace, we are still experiencing restoration through His love and peace.

In deeper reflection, I was amazed with the class dedications that were included in the annuals. They included a common thread of the Judeo-Christian ethic values and work ethic, American exceptionalism, the American dream, and spreading liberty and the gospel of Jesus Christ to the nations. They reflected the purpose and destiny that God has for each of us. We were established in a great heritage with hope and faith. And oh yes, the school had a Bible Club with some 60 students.

The 52 annual was dedicated "...*that this nation should be known and honored throughout the world, as one whose foundation is built upon*

Christianity…" and also to *"…to our country and to the Saviour for whose Kingdom it stands…"* The 53 annual was dedicated to two classmates, *"…Madie and Katie Taylor, who were suddenly taken from our midst".*

The 54 annual centered on the Television Channel 54 TCHS-TV with a Foreword opening statement, *"Several years ago the seniors of today, just as Television, were unheard of."* Television was the baby step for the high tech gadgets soon to grip humanity. The 55 annual was dedicated to the marketplace business enterprises for their support of the school activities such as the school yearbook.

The 56 annual had a full page with a dedication to our churches complete with the picture of a church and a Holy Bible opened for reading. I believe it will be permissible to share the dedication statement in its entirety for our reflection, *"To the divine institutions commissioned by our Creator, differing in form, but alike in the common desire to promote the spiritual welfare of all, to minister to mankind and prepare him for life eternal, to these institutions that have had such an important part in guiding our lives through these informative years, we solemnly and reverently dedicate the El Pavo of 1956 to,,, OUR CHURCHES."* We need to think on what has happened to us, the people, since 1956 (sixty two years ago).

Throughout our school years, we rode the big yellow bus to and from school. Those rides were filled with small chatter mixed with times of riding in silence, day dreaming about our future. Our school atmosphere was lively, cheerful and sort of laid back as we were always trying to cool off as there was no air conditioning. We were in school throughout those hot humid Florida summer months. The windows were always in the open position.

Cooling afternoon thunder storms were always cheerfully received as we scrambled to close windows. We stayed wet from sweating all the time throughout the days and nights in our homes, cars and schools. We did indeed live life at a slower pace, even in our driving, as we can see in the lawful speed limits of that time period. The 56 annual had a Driver Education Handbook Cover citing lawful day light speed limits of 60 mph and 50 at night. Today, we are past in the dust by vehicles going 80 mph.

During the 1955 world series between the New York Yankees and Brooklyn Dodgers, one of our teachers let us listen to some of the afternoon games on his radio. They played each other in four of the five World Series between 1952 and 1956. The Yankees won three of the series while the Dodgers won one series (and that was the series we listen to on the radio). As everybody likes the underdog, most of us cheered for the Dodgers to win, and they did win four games of seven. Although I didn't remember much of his math teaching, I did remember those baseball games. Regardless, I never did develop a personal interest in baseball.

General courses of study included English, Math, Science, History, and elective courses such as Band, FFA or FHA. Our teachers were always held in high regard, having total authority over their students. Teachers like Isabel Preacher, Henry Potter, Leroy Alderman, Jacqueline Colson, Elton Hinson, etc. were regarded with high respect. I remember learning about art for the first time in my life in Harvey McCollum's art class. In one annual, Elton Hinton was listed as a graduate from Auburn College with a degree in Agriculture. I think the name should have been written as Auburn University, where I would eventually graduate in 1968.

One of our math teachers, Joseph Hafer, would tell us about the time he was a POW during World War II. He would describe the horrible food and living conditions. He said that as the war was winding down, they had to eat horse meat and watered down soup just to survive from starvation. He along with my Sunday school teacher, Ernest Brunson, and my Uncle Johnnie were the only three men that I remember telling me stories about their war experiences in WW II.

One heart wrenching story I heard about the war included a Springhead School friend telling me that his Marine father was killed in action in one the Pacific islands battles. I had the opportunity to meet his mother one day. She was still youthful looking and still a widow. It was about ten years removed from the war till my meeting her. As I look back on that very day I met her, I can only imagine the tears she shed and the hardships she endured during those years raising her son as a single mom.

As I write this chapter in our family heritage; I would be horrible to not mention Turkey Creek High School Gobblers most beloved sport, football. Our family was introduced to the game of football through this school. Since then, I think it has always been our favorite sport.

My first memory of football was the time we lived at Trapnell. Our oldest brother, Charles, was playing on the Turkey Creek High School football team. The team mascot was named Gobblers (a male turkey).

Although he played football in high school through his graduation in December 1953, I do not remember ever going to a game to see him play. Regardless, the state of Texas did not have the corner on *"Friday Night Lights"* as our small rural community was making history with powerful football teams playing under Friday night lights in the 40s and 50s, rain or shine.

Herb Bonar was coach. You had to be tough to survive playing on his team. Herb Bonar is rated # 40 in the most wins record coaches in Hillsborough County with a record of 46-12-4 at Turkey Creek from 1947-1953. He had a respective 74% win record including 4 ties. In a 53 El Pavo tribute, we learn that he excelled in West Virginia high school football plus he excelled in college football, baseball and basketball. He was a U.S. Navy Lieutenant (Senior Grade) from 1943-1946. *"He has led Turkey Creek High School into being a well known school all over the state. We are very grateful to Coach Herb Bonar for his great leadership in Turkey Creek."*

From the 1950 through 1952 years, his team won 26 consecutive games without a tie or defeat. They were 9 – 0, 9-0, and 8-1 for the years 50, 51 and 52, respectively. They were undefeated through all three years until they lost their last game in the 52 season to Pasco High. At that time, they set a new state record with 26 straight wins.

The team experienced a heartbreaker when they lost their last game of the 52 season, breaking their winning streak along with losing the Tampa Bay Conference Championship game to Pasco High 20-6. The three years that Charles played as an end on Coach Bonar's team, he experienced the thrill of winning 24 games while only losing 3 during his three years of Turkey Creek football. In the years 50 through 52, Coach Bonar had 26 straight wins along with the last game of the season loss.

The 53 team had 7 wins and 2 losses. In that last year for Bonar and Charles, the team beat Wimauma, St. Paul, Brewster, O. L. P. H., Admiral Farragut, Brandon, and Dade City. They lost to Pinecrest and Largo.

The 54 team had a respective record of 7 wins and 3 losses under their new coach, John Blizotes, as Lloyd played his first year of "A" squad football. He played an end position. The next season of 55, the team would finally win the elusive Tampa Bay Conference Championship.

Coach Blizotes is rated # 44 in the most wins record in Hillsborough County 44-38-2 (Wimauma 1950-1953, and Turkey Creek 1954-1958).

The 55 team won the Tampa Bay Conference Championship with a 9-1 record. They lost their first game to Dade City 14-0 and then won their next 9 straight games.

'55 Championship Team Record

TC   0   Dade City 14
TC 13   Wimauma 6
TC 39   St. Paul 0
TC 14   Pinecrest 0
TC 20   Brandon 6
TC 49   Admiral Farragut 0
TC 46   Brewster 0
TC 31   Largo 0
TC 20   Tarpon Springs 6
TC 32   Plant City 9

They scored a mind boggling 260 points to 41 points against their ten opponents with an average game score of 26 to 4.

Jim Reed followed Blizotes as the team coach in 1958. He is # 11 with the most wins record of 100-72-7 (Pinecrest 1954-1958, and Turkey Creek 1959-1971). I had the privilege of meeting him in 2015. One of our Physical Education Teachers, Holland Aplin, would become a successful coach at two schools in Tampa. He is rated #15 with most wins record of 79-55-3 (Brewster Tech 1955-1958, Robinson 1959-1967).

Another notably high school sport accomplishment included the 53 school baseball team winning the Tampa Bay Conference Championship for the second straight year. No other conference team had won back to back championships. They beat Dade City 6-3 to win the championship. Dan McMullen was my Physical Education Teacher in the 7th and 8th grades. He was also the Junior Varsity football team coach. He was admired for playing professional football with the Chicago Bears.

I was surprised to learn about the many extra curriculum activities Charles was involved in high school. At that time, we lived on Rice Road in the Springhead area and then at our farm in Trapnell. In addition to playing football, he participated in baseball, FFA, Cotillion Club, track, swimming, Letterman's Club and softball during his senior year. He was also class Treasurer in his junior year.

Somehow Charles managed to get our parent's reluctant permission to stay after school for his participation in sports. After Mary left home, he was our family farm "Straw Boss" whether he wanted to be or not. I assume he hitched rides home after practice sessions with his team mates. I remember noticing he was not at home much during his high school years. He would rather be playing football or hunting with friends like Olin Shephard and Junior Varnum, along with others. After Charles and Robert left home, Lloyd became our "Straw Boss".

The school was a strawberry school with a school year of March through December. After Charles graduated in December 1953, Lloyd played on the school team till he graduated in December 1956. Robert attended Plant City High School with Donna Crofton. Soon afterwards, Robert and Donna married and he joined the Air Force. Charles joined the Marine Corp after graduating from high school. He played on the Marine Corp football team at Camp Lejeune.

At the time, we didn't have television so we never actually saw a football game on television until 1957 when we finally purchased a TV. Also, I was able to attend a few high school games during my senior high school years.

I actually played on the Plant City High School junior varsity team in the 10th grade. I believe we lost almost every game we played. That was the extent of my football playing career. The next year I tried out for the track team. Charles and Lloyd were the only high school football players in our family. However, that did not stop us from playing with neighboring friends every chance we could team up for a quick back yard fun game.

My Plant City High School 10th grade driving class teacher was Tilrow Morrison. He was the football coach for Plant City from 1954-1956 with yearly records of 8-2-1, 6-3-1 and 9-1-0 respectively. In 1954, Plant City beat Turkey Creek 14-0 in the Charity Bowl. Lloyd played in that game. Coach Morrison was one of few coaches leaving the sport as a winner. He had an outstanding 74% win record for those three years.

Television broadcasting of professional football games with teams like the Cleveland Browns and Detroit Lions were gaining more and more popularity each year during the 50s. College football was beginning to be televised and was becoming increasingly popular. We would identify with well-known coaches and teams such as "Bear" Byrant of Alabama, "Bud" Wilkerson of Oklahoma, "Woody" Hayes of Ohio State and the most beloved coach of all, "Shug" Jordan of Auburn.

All we needed was a minimum of four players on each team to make a good go of it. We always thought we were scoring the winning touchdown for our favorite college or professional team like star players such as Cleveland Browns running back Jim Brown and quarterback Otto Graham. We felt like we were "the #1 quarterback" whenever we threw a long down and out completion for a game changing momentum touchdown.

Classmates that I sort of hung around with at times included Kenneth Lawson, Alex Szanyi, Sam Shepherd, Kenneth Sellers, Jessie Nichols, Allen Lightsey, Eddie Lee and Kenny Wynn. As our family moved so often (a total of six locations) it was difficult to develop lasting friendships during our school years. Quite often later in adulthood, we would always run into acquaintances of the family.

In 1946, a Tampa Tribune Reporter, Jock Murray, wrote a newspaper series exposing "strawberry schools" as an antiquated practice. In 1950 he wrote another series of articles challenging the practice. Despite the outcry that resulted from these articles, there was no immediate change in the established "strawberry school" schedule. The debate became more contentious resulting in an open panel discussion with the County School Superintendent and other school board representatives in December 1954.

When the school session began in March 1955, there were only four schools remaining as "strawberry schools"; Dover, Cork, Trapnell, and Turkey Creek (three elementary schools and one Junior & Senior High School). On July 25, 1956, approximately 1,000 people attended a meeting called by the Hillsborough County School Superintendent in the school auditorium to announce the closing of "strawberry schools". A public protest was spear headed by the community residents.

Despite the public outcry, a special meeting was called by the school board the following night to pass a unanimous board vote to end the "strawberry school" system at the close of the school day on July 27, 1956. All county schools would be operated on a single calendar known as "The Winter Calendar". Superintendent Crockett Farnell stated "*The school board action was the greatest step the Board had ever taken toward improving the welfare of the children of Hillsborough County."*

As a very interesting note on our county football history, Crockett Farnell was the football coach for Hillsborough High School from 1942-1948. He was # 27 for his most wins record of 61-8-0. He had an outstanding 88% win record for his short six years of coaching during the 40s.

Father was one of those crying out against the county school board for their horrible action to close down the "strawberry schools". He was known on his construction projects for always being involved in growing strawberries every year, in addition to his working full time as a construction electrician.

July 27, 1956 was a historic date for eastern Hillsborough County as strawberry farmers would not have child labor available to pick strawberries in the winter months anymore. This labor source void was replaced with migrant workers from outside the community.

I was personally relieved to hear the "strawberry schools" were closing. I felt like I was being set free from the work required throughout the year from vegetables in the spring and summer along with raising and harvesting strawberry crops in the fall and winter months. For our father, along with many other strawberry farming parents, the ruling was like watching their world collapse around them in addition to their children growing up and leaving home in search of individual dreams.

During the summer of 1956, Father sold our Trapnell farm and we moved into a rental house with farm land in Youmans. He half heartily had us grow some acreage for old time sake of having a strawberry field. I guess it would be like *"Strawberry Fields Forever"* if for no other reason. He had us work the farm for another four years. After I graduated from high school in June, 1960, we never turned over another clod of dirt on strawberry land. It was the end for us.

Mary, Charles and Robert were no longer at home at that time. Mary was married and teaching elementary school in Ashtabula, Ohio. One year she was selected Teacher of the Year for Ohio. Charles was serving four years in the Marine Corp while Robert married and joined the Air Force. He served in England.

Lloyd started his career with the Florida State Road Department after his graduation. He ended up with our family Farmall tractor as he would develop a hobby of growing vegetables. For some reason, strawberries were not included. I can only wonder why?

Within the next three years, Philip and Harry graduated with Philip becoming full time employed with a Lakeland ceramic tile company and Harry joined the Army for two years. He served in Germany. Philip and Harry would eventually become journeyman electricians for the IBEW Local Union 915. In 1969, Philip became the Director of the Union Apprenticeship School. He retired thirty years later.

As we flashback to 59; Michael, Donald and I were left at home to tend the farm. The three of us did the best we could during our last year of farming. At age 15, I found myself as the oldest brother at home with the three of us running the farm. Ready or not, I became the family farm "Straw Boss", even though it was only for one "closing shop" year. During the 60s, Donald and Michael each became "Honorary Straw Boss" of the landscaping and grass for our home in Robinson Airport Subdivision.

In a short period of time, our family strawberry world dramatically crumbled into extinction. By September 1960, as I enrolled in the University of South Florida, we sold our farm equipment and bought a small masonry house in a southwest Plant City subdivision. Large enterprises like Wishnatzki and Nathel filled the void as most small family farms became extinct.

Without any fan fair, that historic year of 1960 sealed the end of our family farming tradition. Going all the way back to the American Revolution era, I believe our family was always somehow involved in living off the land along with hunting and fishing for food throughout the generations.

The 50s had to be a difficult decade for our father as he dealt with the loss of a tradition that was comfortable to him. That lifestyle was now gone at the same time his children were leaving home to start our own families and careers in the market place. Child farm labor became history.

In 2017, we had some 100 strawberry farmers in eastern Hillsborough County producing some 11,000 acres of strawberries every year. This industry requires a tremendous source of labor. These average farms of 110 acres are a far cry larger than the old family farms of five to ten acres or so.

As our family siblings married and started individual families, we would meet for a Thanksgiving meal always topped off with a traditional family football game. As the family grew, we were able to have plenty of youthful talent to have eleven plus on each team and for more than one game.

What would start out as a friendly two hand touch game would progress to a "down and out must win attitude" in full speed tackle football until someone was hurt. Actually, we did go easier on our preteen youth.

My backyard football career ended abruptly when I was about 35 and nephew Bobby almost sent me to the emergency room when we collided at full speed as he accidentally gave me a block against my throat. It took a few weeks for my voice to sound normal again.

Later in life as I watched documentary films of the Kennedy family playing football at their Cape Cod compound, I realized we were having the exact same kind of fun as they were having in the simple game of backyard football. However, the older we got, the more we appreciated playing gentler sports such as volleyball and horseshoes at our family gatherings.

Construction of the "New Plant City Hospital" was started in the early 50s but was halted for financial reasons after the structural steel framing was erected. The project was fenced and abandoned for a period of time. One day, a preteen boy was killed when he was playing on the steel structure and fell. Soon afterward, the project construction was finished. The facility became South Florida Baptist Hospital.

I include some advertising classics from various El Pavos that brought back fond memories of yesterday. Note the three numbered phone numbers like 509, the promotion of air conditioning, and catchy promotional wordings.

Publix Super Market's 53 El Pavo promotion *"Shop and Save at Publix Super Market"* was changed to the 54 annual slogan *"Publix … Where Shopping Is a Pleasure…"* The promotion included a photograph of the newly built Publix on Collins Street. It was one the first Publix's to be built as the grocery store was established in neighboring Polk County. Their slogan has not changed since 1954.

That new slogan has served the company very well over these past sixty four years. And they always made sure the public knew that their stores were air-conditioned. That was a huge selling point for shoppers living a life in a world of no air-conditioning. And we can still weigh ourselves free at any Publix store.

"Compliments of your Air-Conditioned Capital Theatre
Phone 205 Plant City, Florida

Robinson Roller Rink "For Health's Sake, Roller Skate"
Plant City, Florida

Congratulations from Starlite Drive-In
Plant City, Florida

Shop and Save at Publix Super Market
S. Collins Street, Plant City, Florida

Compliments of Strawberry Drive-In
Plant City, Florida

Compliments of University of Tampa
Thinking of College? Send for Catalog

Browns Prescription Across from the New Hospital
Phone 509   Plant City, Florida

WPLA - Music, News, Sports, Special Features

Heritage & Hope

———•———

Chapter 15

The End of Strawberry Schools

A Culture Lost Forever

Sixty two years ago, I attended my last strawberry school year. It seems like only yesterday. The area of land in eastern Hillsborough County, Florida, was created with a rich soil suitable for agriculture, especially excellent for growing strawberries. Also, favorable temperatures helped the process of producing plentiful sweet berries. That small strip of land includes an area west to east from Dover and Turkey Creek to Youmans and Springhead, north to south from Knights Station and Cork to Trapnell and Pinecrest.

Strawberries in the winter months became the king crop. Most of my education was forged in what was called "strawberry schools". The original strawberry school buildings were built with lumber set on piers with plenty of windows to compensate for the lack of air-conditioning. The walls, floors and ceilings were all wood. The buildings were constructed mainly during the 20s and 30s.

We would open the windows to circulate the air. The summer heat worked an extreme toil on our learning advancement pace. The constant heat during the school sessions made us feel washed out and created a tired feeling which was detrimental to our learning progress during "heat wave" days. We were always looking forward to afternoon thunder showers with cooling winds. Some of the elementary students would often attend school bare foot.

Our school year would run from March to mid-December. That schedule allowed school children time off during the strawberry season to help pick them during the harvesting period from late December through March. These strawberry farms were family owned and operated. The school board operated two separate school systems. I believe they knew they could save on operating cost with only one.

Elementary strawberry schools included Springhead, Trapnell, Pinecrest, Dover, and Cork. Turkey Creek and Pinecrest had junior high (7th thru 9th) and senior high schools (10th thru 12th) along with elementary grades. Bealsville had a strawberry school. Although the name was "strawberry schools"; we also called them "summer schools".

The strawberry schools system had justified itself as long as everyone felt there was a need for child labor. It was a workable and acceptable system when I believe it was started at the turn of the century, and ended in 1956. The era lasted about fifty six years, more or less.

The post-World War II years brought about changes in our life styles. By the 1950s, society and culture begin to drastically change. As the economy grew and expanded, the family farms started to fall by the wayside. People had so many better opportunities to earn income than working the family farm from generation to generation.

Social pressures and economical feasibilities hastened the closing of the strawberry schools. There was resistance, mostly from families that still needed to use child labor. Some adults, whom had grown up in the schools, wanted them to be continued as a cultural tradition.

After holding public hearings on the matter, the Hillsborough County School Board voted to discontinue strawberry schools. There was no small amount of outcry from the public. However, the decision was quickly enforced. In September, 1956, I went from the 8th grade summer school to the 9th grade winter school. Strawberry schools were over forever.

"I and My Father are one." (John 10:30)

"At that day you will know that I am in My Father, and you in Me, and I in you." (John 14:20)

Heritage & Hope

―――――・―――――

Chapter 16

Migrant Work

The year 1948 was very special for God's Kingdom on earth. After some 2,000 years of being dispersed and scattered around the world, the nation of Israel was re-established in their original land with the same name and language that God had given them. British control of Palestine ended on May 14, 1948. David Ben-Gurion, Executive Head of the Zionist Organization and President of the Jewish Agency for Palestine at that time in their history, declared the establishment of Israel. God said He will bless those that bless Israel and curse those that curse Israel. As for me and my household, we bless Israel always, unconditionally.

In 1948, President Harry S. Truman (Democrat) won re-election in spite of a wide expectation that he would lose. He campaigned hard, appealing to the people with his directness on the election issues. He also gained increased popularity during his "Whistle stop" campaign tour of the country. We can never forget the photograph of a smiling Truman holding up a newspaper headline proclaiming, "Dewey Defeats Truman."

President Truman held working vacation retreats at a naval base residence in Key West. It became a functioning Winter White House from 1946 through 1952. Future Presidents Eisenhower, Kennedy, Carter and Clinton would also use it for brief vacations.

Today, it only reflects fading memories. The Harry S. Truman Little White House in Key West is one of Florida's most unassuming historical sites. The furnishings are original and were used by President Truman. It was also used by Thomas Edison, for about six months as he worked to improve new weapons being developed for the Navy in WW I. Also, make time to take the house tour to learn more about this outstanding president, whom I admire deeply.

Picking Cherries in Michigan. In 1948, our parents would be celebrating their 20th anniversary. Their last child of eleven births would be 1 year old. One of my earliest memories in life was about our family trip to Michigan in the summer of 48. I was almost 5 years old when our parents packed a small boxed truck with seven brothers ranging in age from 1 to 11. Mary and Charles did not go with us as I believe she was living with a relative in Punta Gorda and Charles stayed home with friends.

We filled the truck bed with a layer of Wauchula water melons that we would sell as we traveled through Georgia. We placed a layer of cardboard on top of the melons and then a thick layer of hay as a cushioned floor. A barricade/gate kept us secured safely in the truck.

Today as we consider the absolutely ridiculous political correctness that we have had forced upon us during these past eight years, our father would probably be arrested and jailed. The cell key would be thrown away, and we would be placed in foster homes. It was my first and only childhood out of state trip until we worked on a Long Island, New York farm in the summer of 60, at age 16.

Father started traveling to large northern cities to work as a union construction electrician after World War II was over. At that time he worked in large cities like Kansas City, Cleveland, and Detroit. I believe he made arrangements for our family to work in the cherry orchards as he was working in Detroit. The land along Lake Michigan in the Lower Peninsular is one of the most productive fruit growing belts in North America. Michigan leads the country in production of cherries.

We traveled the 1,000 miles or so to Michigan on two lane highways, averaging 45 to 50 miles per hour over a three day or so trip. I have no idea how we handled the necessities of life in that era while traveling that distance as a large family. Father allowed a man to ride with us. After we woke up from our first night's sleep, he was gone. To this day we do not know if he got off the truck at one of our stops because it was too uncomfortable for him or what. I remember the dreary foggy morning. I think he went looking for a softer ride.

I always had a genuine empathy for the "Oakies" traveling westward on Highway 66 from Oklahoma to California in the Great Depression Dust Bowl days of the 30s. They were fleeing from their foreclosed farms in their stacked high flatbed trucks. We got the same disdainful looks that they had to endure on their trip. We would half heartily forgive their ignorant looks as we kept on trucking down the highway.

We did make it to our destiny in due time. We settled into a large cabin tent that was one of many tents provided at the harvesting labor compound. We would harvest red and black cherries. The orchards were full of large cherry trees loaded with big beautiful cherries. The following morning we immediately went to work picking the fruit. They were very juicy and sweet tasting. After a short time of sampling the delicious fruit, all desire to eat them faded away quickly as the sun got hotter during the morning. What was fun earlier now became what I quickly learned to call work. We also picked raspberries and strawberries during that summer.

One night, I remember my father commenting about my contribution to the family's cherry picking income. I remember his comment vividly, *"Puddin, you make our egg money by working on the ground picking up the cherries and by picking the cherries at the bottom of the trees."* Those few words of encouragement made it a lot easier for me to stay in the orchards doing my assigned task of gathering the lower tree fruit along with good cherries off the ground. Those few spoken words would stay with me through my adult years. And yes, Puddin was my nickname. As Michael was 2 years old and Donald was 1, they stayed back at the tent with our mother.

The harvesting labor force portable tent compound was located on the edge of Lake Michigan. We would bathe in the lake close to sunset. The water was painfully cold. It made for a quick "bird bath". We were spoiled by a lot warmer water temperature back home in Florida. Mother would cook inside the tent. One night, we had a stove fire, but it was quickly extinguished by our parents. Another scary incident was the day 10 year old Lloyd fell off his ladder as he stretched a little too far from his ladder for the cherries. He was known to stretch his limits.

Another memory of this experience included the day my older brothers got into a heated scrabble with some other teens within the compound. Our father was holding "court" with us that night on a who did what to whom type inquiry. Like most teenaged flare ups; the next day, life at the compound went on as if nothing happened.

During that year, we lived on Clay Turner Road and my older brothers were attending the Springhead strawberry school with the March through mid-December school sessions. We were gone for a long period of time during that summer. Upon our return home, Father decided it wasn't worth my brothers' time to return to school for the remaining school year. Immediately afterwards, a Truant Officer showed up at our door. In spite of a lively discussion, my brothers went back to school in due time.

I don't have any other recollections of that trip. Even though it was short lived and was no fun at the time, it became a blessing in disguise for me as I fondly look back at it, almost seventy years later. It was all about family. With being forced into such close quarters, it had to be family. We lived that life for a short period of time. Migrants live this life style year in and year out, as they travel to different states around the country.

Picking Strawberries in Florida. During our out of school winter months in our "strawberry schools" calendar year, we picked our family farm strawberries without any payment to us. We would also pick at neighboring farms with pay on an "as needed basis".

We would be paid to pick at a pay scale of five to ten cents a cup. We would put our identification ticket in the bottom of each quart basket (we called them cups) so the total daily number of cups could be counted for each individual worker. On good days, a worker could pick over one hundred cups. The money earned would be used to help the family budget in providing for our personal fun time events such as attending the state fair and the strawberry festival.

This work system probably started around the early 1900s as strawberry family farms increased in the area. This way of life ended abruptly in 1956 when "strawberry schools" were discontinued. Four years later, we sold our farming equipment and moved into a house that we purchased in the city. Strawberry farming became big business and migrant workers had to provide the labor force.

Today the local strawberry growing production ranges from 8,000 to 10,000 acres per year. The need for farm laborers today is huge. I worked in strawberry fields every year during my school years till graduation. As I reflect on my experience, I was personally involved in history making. We were one of the last families with the children being the labor force.

It had always been that way since the area's first strawberries farms in the late 1880s. I believe pioneer families were already growing strawberries by 1890. School attendance was enforced lightly in the early 1900s. I think the "strawberry schools" were officially established in the 1920s. As of 1956, we were the last child labor force generation. As we know, migrants have harvested the strawberries since those days.

Picking Oranges in Florida. One winter in the late 50s, we tried earning some extra money by picking oranges during our two week Christmas and New Year holidays. At the time, I was a young teenager and we were living on Highway 92 in Youmans, a community between Plant City and Lakeland. We had to rise early in the morning and drive to a maintenance shop near Mulberry where we would board an old bus that was a county school bus at one time. Other workers joined us for a ride to the orange grove we would be picking in that day.

The ride was not a pleasant experience as we rode quite a distance, mostly in silence. The bus was usually cold and noisy along with the bench seats being hard and uncomfortable. We would almost bounce off the seat with each bump we drove over. There was very little conversation as everyone was trying to be as comfortable as possible and getting a few more minutes of sleep or simply chain smoking cigarettes in solitary.

Finally, we would pull up to a spot in the middle of "nowhere" with orange trees in every direction we looked, all loaded with fruit. Ladders and crates were quickly distributed from a "goat" to each of us to work with. This particular "goat" was a "convertible" flatbed truck cut down from an old school bus. It served the purpose of hauling materials, ladders, boxes of oranges, etc.

We were assigned a row of trees to pick for each of us and then off we went to work picking. I was strong enough to manage the picking and carrying of a loaded bag of oranges down the ladder and fill them into the wooden crates. However, I had to have an older brother move my heavy wooden ladder every time to my next tree.

As we arrived at the site, the air was still cold and frosty like. As the sun climbed higher during the day, it would become hotter. By two o'clock, it would become uncomfortably hot. We could only hope for a slight breeze to help cool us off. Some of the more talkative workers would chatter about "much to do about nothing". Others would break out in various types of songs such as spiritual or Rhythm & Blues. Some did not want to socialize and were painfully quiet throughout the day. Then it would be time to take the bus trip back to the shop and on to home in our cars for the night.

With night, came dawn. Then we would repeat the previous day again. Each work day was similar to Bill Murray's days in "Groundhog Day". And remember, our nights of sleep were in houses that did not have air conditioning. I don't remember the pay scale, but it wasn't anything to write home about. We did this work for about two weeks. Then we were back in school with the miles and miles of groves with bright oranges quickly fading "out of sight and out of mind".

However, I do have an original Adams Company wooden orange crate keepsake from that era. It is the old two compartment box built with wood slats and three solid box walls with handle openings. We use it on our back porch as a stand for flowers. I would guess it was manufactured in the early 50s. I found the box at a flea market. Later, they were replaced with huge plastic tubs for quicker loading.

Picking Strawberries in New York. My last experience with working as a migrant was on Long Island during the summer of 60. Our father was working in New York City and had arranged for us to work on a Long Island farm. We had an agreement for our family to work on the farm for room and board. Although the venture was not profitable, money wise; it was an experience that included lifetime memories for me. The work basically included us picking and selling strawberries. It reminded me of our farm life back home. Our encounters during the trip are presented in Chapter 20.

The farmer, Mr. Ralph Moreland, had small travel trailers set up on his farm for workers to stay in during the harvesting. Mother stayed in the farm house and we stayed in a trailer along with some others staying in trailers also. He had workers from Porto Rico and Quebec.

Migrant Life Exposed. On November 25, 1960, the day after Thanksgiving, CBS News showed *"Harvest of Shame"*, the Edward Murrow television documentary exposing the horrific conditions of America's migrant workers.

Coincidently, that documentary was broadcasted about six months after we worked in Commack, Long Island during the summer of 60. Florida farms surrounding Lake Okeechobee were featured in the documentary. Although the documentary was filmed in Florida, the issue concerned migrant work throughout the country including California, not just Florida. I remember it.

Fifty years later in 2010, CBS News network's National correspondent Byron Pitts, went into the fields to produce a progress report on the working conditions at that time. He reported some improvements in the lives of the workers. However, he also reported terrible conditions that had also existed during Murrow's visits; the same life of brutal work, deplorable conditions, and the treatment of workers unable to defend their own interest. As needed, involved parties continue to find agreeable solutions for ongoing challenges.

For various reasons, this chapter was very hard for me to write. Our family experienced only a few fleeting glimpses of migrant life. The topic is a concern that most of us prefer to act as if it doesn't exist. Obviously we do not hunt or gather our food on an individual basis anymore. However in the USA alone, we have over 320 million people needing our daily bread.

Equipment and technology play a big role in farming, but the labor force is the most valuable role. We need legal workers willing to endure the harsh agricultural work. As child labor was finally dis-continued in the 50s, the need for workers was filled quickly with farmers using migrant workers from where ever they could legally obtain them at competitive wages. In that labor market atmosphere, I believe serious problems arose that were not addressed by politicians, in both parties, mainly because they feared losing votes at the polls.

Immigration Correction is Needed Now. Illegal immigration was swept under the rug as many politicians (and most of us) looked the other way. Now, over sixty years later, our country is being forced to deal with the problem as realistically as possible. I believe this is a major problem for our country that has to be corrected now. We need to stop kicking this can down the road like we are doing with our "very soon to be" twenty trillion dollar national debt as it continues to increase daily. First, I believe we need to use correct terminology. People entering our country illegally are "Illegal Aliens". They are not "Undocumented Immigrants" as described by the politically correct language that our previous federal governmental administration was using incorrectly. An "Alien" is defined as a foreign-born resident who has not been naturalized and is still a subject or citizen of a foreign country. An "Immigrant" is a person who comes to a country to take up permanent residence. As needed, and for whatever reason, some requesting citizenship may not be accepted. A "Migrant" is a person who moves regularly in order to find work, especially in harvesting crops. Without question, this is a harsh life. I know firsthand that it is a cruel life with little or no appreciation.

Next, we need to simply enforce the immigration laws that we have already legislated. We need a system of Immigrants applying for American citizenship as always in the past – going through the "Ellis Island" front door. Ellis Island, in Upper New York Bay, was the door for over twelve million immigrants during some sixty years from 1892 through 1954. Its closing was about the same time child labor became history. Those twelve million got in line and went by the rules to become American citizens.

During the sixty four years since 1954, we have another estimated twelve million plus "Illegal Aliens" basically walking into our country, hoping they will eventually be given citizenship just because they now live here. For comparison purposes, the count was three million in 1990. The estimated count is now between seventeen to twenty two million. Most likely we will never determine the exact count. Walking over an open border does not automatically give someone a "free pass" to become an American citizen. They are trespassing.

We also have to stop the terrorist, drug cartels, gangs, human trafficking, and assorted criminals from entering into our midst. Over time, we may not survive as a nation as long as we have wide open borders for anyone and everyone. We need effective and fair legislation for our immigration process along with a wall.

At the same time, Immigrants may apply for citizenship through our entrance door and legal process. After they may possibly obtain their legal citizenship, they are then officially an America citizen. As we move forward with these concerns in compassion and empathy, we must maintain a "Rule of Law" for everyone.

"and also that every man should eat and drink and enjoy the good of all his labor- it is the gift of God." (Ecclesiastes 3:13)

Heritage & Hope

——————•——————

Chapter 17

Keystone Cops and Whatever More

A family history cannot be written without including a chapter on a few episodes of "Keystone Cops and Whatever More". I present "not so funny at the time", short stories from my past.

Green Hair for a Day. One vivid memory comes to mind when I was approximately 4 years old experiencing life on a farm in the late 1940s. One of my older brothers was painting the trim on our house with a thick deep green exterior paint (with of course, an oil base). That was the time when paint was real paint. He had a can with paint setting on the top step.

Just like any unwatched child, I walked right under that ladder; and I must have bumped the step ladder quite forcefully. All I know is that I was enjoying life to the fullest as a curious 4 year old in the midst of a new interesting action scene. In a matter of seconds, I quickly changed into looking like the creature from the black lagoon.

You could say this was an early version of the distant future television sliming craze. I was instantly covered in thick green paint from the top of my head to my shoulders along with thick splotches of paint on my shirt and trousers. I had gained the full attention of half dozen brothers and my mother. They were beside themselves on how to get the paint off me as they entered into an excited discussion on how to best clean me up.

Like always, Mother took control of the situation by cutting off all of my curly red (green) hair with a pair of scissors. Then she carefully cleaned the paint off my face and head. Somehow, I managed to recover without any serious damage to my head and face. In a few weeks, my hair grew back to normal; all to my mother's delight. To this day, I paint with no more than one inch of paint in my painting cans, and I keep toddlers (and adults) away from my ladders whenever I paint.

"You'll shoot your eye out!" BB guns were the rage for our family and friends in the 50s. We hold memories of that discouraging line everyone, including Santa, told 9 year old Ralphie Parker in the 1983 classic movie, *A Christmas Story*, when he asked for a Red Ryder Carbine Action 200-shot Range Model air rifle for a Christmas gift during the 1940s.

Just like Ralphie, I think almost every boy would get some sort of a BB gun at one time or another in the 40s and 50s. As young teens in the 50s, we often played Cowboys and Indians, GI Joe Combat Soldiers, or Cops and Robbers. Without question, those games would all be politically incorrect today. The aggressive brothers and friends would end up shooting at each other with their BB guns, always being careful to aim below the head.

As forewarned, in one gun battle, our brother Robert was hit in his eye with a shot. Fortunately, because it was from a long distance, he did not incur permanent eye damage. But our older brothers paid dearly for this "not so fun" play time. Eventually, he recovered with his eyesight intact.

Soda Pop – Not! Cold Drink – Yes! In the day, when we wanted a beverage, we would say *"I want a cold drink."* This meant we wanted our drink straight out of a country store ice water chest. So it was only logical to call them "cold drinks". Then we would proceed to identify the drink we wanted such as Coca Cola, Pepsi, RC Cola, etc. Our recently transplanted Northern friends would always say, *"I want a soda pop."* We responded with, *"What in the Sam hill is a soda pop? It's not a soda pop, it's a cold drink!"*

Then we all would laugh about our difference in such a trivial matter as ordering a beverage to drink. In the day, the cold drink would cost us a nickel. And we could buy a Baby Ruth candy bar for another nickel. That was indeed the ultimate treat on a hot summer Saturday afternoon, as we made the trip on our bikes.

Slow Down in Rain. Two near tragic family automobile accidents occurred in front of a family grocery store owned and operated by the Zambito family on Highway 39, a couple of miles south of Plant City. One Saturday afternoon during the mid 50s when we were living at the Trapnell compound, Robert was driving Lloyd, Philip, Harry, Michael,

Donald and me into town to see a movie while he would go out on a date.

Yes, if you count everybody, there were seven of us in the car. Three were in the front seat and four in the back seat. It was a rainy Saturday late in the afternoon as he hurried along the highway headed north to town as fast as he could go by testing the speed limit. Our father was home in between projects and he had let Robert drive his four door 1951 Buick for the trip to town. The car body was solid steel. But we did not have safety belts and the windows didn't have the tempered shatter designed glass for our safety.

As Robert started to pass a car, he suddenly skidded off the road sideways and hit a wooden power pole broad center of the car on the driver's side. The crash broke the pole into two separate pieces about half way up and it crushed the car inward, right at the center of the car' driver side. The power and telephone lines did not break and they were holding up the top piece of the broken pole.

The weight of the broken pole top made the line sag somewhat. I was setting in the back seat behind Robert. We all scrambled out the passenger's side of the car as fast as we could. I think Philip slightly broke his arm. Other than that injury, no one else was hurt.

The accident occurred directly in front of the Zambito family store. This is the very store our mother shopped for our groceries every week. They along with other bystanders that came to our aid were telling us how lucky we were to survive such a bad accident and that none of us was seriously hurt. I still remember slamming into the pole and getting out of the car seeing the bystanders and looking at the broken power pole as we all stood safely in front of the grocery store, about 40 feet from the broken pole and crushed car. The most startling fact on all of this is the "what if" question. What if the power line had broken? Then it was possible for the hot broken power line to fall on our car and electrocute all of us before we could have gotten out safely. What if another car was driving south at that same spot and time? Looking back at that day, I can only believe angels were definitely working for us that day big time!

I can only guess how our father was trying to come to grips with this nightmare. Being thankful no was seriously injured he still had to deal with replacing the family car. Even so, his fatherly patience that day was tested to the hilt. Like all accidents, it happened so fast, there was nothing anyone could do at those few spilt seconds. The car was sliding on a slick highway surface. Robert had no control of the very heavy car as it hydroplaned over the surface. But it also seemed to have happened in slow motion. It's as if your life is slowly moving in front of you and you are watching it all from a safe distance away. Every time I drive by that pole, I think of that particular accident that occurred some sixty four years ago.

Here Today, Gone Tomorrow. I remember another bad accident just as horrible. Some 10 years later, our family was involved in a major automobile accident at exactly the very same spot; directly in front of the Zambito Grocery Store. At the time, I had a "cream puff" car that I have always considered one of the best automobiles I had ever owned. It was a 4 door '57 Chevrolet two tone blue and white colors, with air conditioning. I had stayed out of college for a period of time in order to pay for the $1,800 cost, which I thought was a costly price. Like always, I had one coworker tell me I paid too much for the car. At the time I was working at a phosphate plant near Mulberry and I had one of those coworkers who thought they always made a better deal. Anyhow, I was thrilled with driving it, as well as my brothers and friends. It was a beauty, interior and exterior.

One day, my brother Michael and a couple of his friends had talked me into letting him drive it to the grocery store. A short time later, Michael called to tell me that he was involved in an accident in front of the store. He was making a left turn to park in front of the store and had misjudged the speed of an oncoming car driven by a young lady. Once again, it may have been due to his eyesight, even with glasses. She hit our car on the passenger side. No one was seriously hurt except for Michael breaking his arm. The car was totaled.

I was devastated as I was ready to resume college work at the University of Florida in a week or so. Our pastor helped by driving me to Gainesville for my entrance as a transfer student from USF. He had family in Webster so he used the trip to visit them on his way back home. He was pleasantly surprised when we loaded only a few suitcases and cardboard boxes of my personal items as luggage into his car. He was prepared to see me wanting him to haul a truck load of stuff for me.

For my car need, I eventually bought one of those space ship car designs that were so popular for a few years. It was a white 4 door 1958

Chevy Impala with wide space ship wings that went forever long and wide. You would keep wondering when you would be lifting off the ground like an airplane as you gained speed. It was just an awful looking car. Needless to say, ownership of that car was short lived. And, will we ever forget the 1958 Ford Edsel? Personally, I liked it.

Huckleberries and Rattlesnakes. The year was 1947 and the place was rural Wauchula. As the war ended, the Tampa Shipyard work of building warships was discontinued. Soon afterwards we lost the ownership of the Dover farm I was born on. Disappointingly, we moved to a rental farm house near Plant City where Michael was born in May 1946.

The next year, we ended up renting a farm house near Wauchula for about a year where Donald was born in April 1947. I was going on 4 years old. The fourth wave of brothers (Donald, Michael and me) ages 3, 1 and newborn was obviously homebound during that time. However, wave two (Charles, Robert and Lloyd) ages 13, 10, and 9 respectively and wave three (Philip and Harry) ages 8 and 7 had sort of an accepted freedom to roam our neighboring land as much as they dared to do so.

As a side note, Philip was born in Wauchula, September 1939, when we lived there for a year or so eight years earlier, before the war. One sunny day, all five brothers in waves 2 and 3 took a hiking trip through the woods, bay heads and open land, looking for blackberries and huckleberries. They all felt comfortably safe going deep into the woodlands in such a large group. Florida had open range at that time in our state's history. It would be another two years before a state law was established to fence all livestock.

About a mile into the wilderness, they earned their reward for hiking so far from home. They found their prize in a plentiful patch of wild huckleberries. Their joy of eating freshly picked ripe berries soon took a very frightful turn. Robert cried out a dreadful scream as he jumped back. He continued to scream at the top of his lungs as he hollowed, *"A rattlesnake bit me!"* As no one had a shotgun, they had to let the snake slither away. All they knew about a crisis like this was to get him home as fast as they could. They were not prepared to provide any treatment.

Charles started out by carrying Robert on his back. After he became exhausted, Lloyd and Philip would carry him. At times they would drag him for short distances. It was difficult carrying the 10 year old from so deep into the wilderness back home. Miraculously, they finally made it. After some delay, our father drove him to a doctor in Wauchula, where he was treated and released. Robert experienced a fast healing. Soon, everyone was back to playing in the woods as if nothing had happened. Like the cat fable, Robert had more than nine miracles during his journey on this earth with healings and trials.

Robert's near death reminded me of another rattlesnake episode that I had read about in Marjorie Rowling's book, <u>Cross Creek</u>. During the 30s, reluctantly at first, she went on a rattlesnake hunting trip to Arcadia with the famous rattlesnake expert, Ross Allen. Arcadia is twenty miles south of Wauchula and twenty five miles north of Punta Gorda, with all three towns being located on Highway US 17.

They drove a few miles outside of Arcadia for their hunting experience. Instead of shooting the snakes, they would catch as many as they could alive. He would take them to his Silver Springs tourist attraction in Ocala. The account of that trip in her book, <u>Cross Creek</u>, *was* like reading a horrible campfire nightmare story. Rattlesnakes were easy to find, but not always so easy to capture alive as she noted so vividly in her book. Ross had a special designed hook on the end of a long pole as the tool they would use to capture a snake without letting it bite them. She was brave enough to actually catch one with the homemade devise for herself. She wrote that the hunting trip helped her to overcome a fear of rattlesnakes. After that experience, now I know why she was able to write the heart pounding episode of Penny Baxter's rattlesnake bite with such passion in her book, <u>The Yearling</u>.

In 1929, Ross Allen founded the Reptile Institute at the Silver Springs tourist attraction at Ocala, Florida. He established the alligators and snakes facility for research, as well as education and entertainment. The center included reptile demonstrations, with alligator wrestling and rattlesnake milking. For decades, it was a very popular tourist attraction. During his career, he was bitten more than a dozen times. Like most of the original Florida tourist attractions, it faded into history as Disney World opened for business.

Wave four (Michael, Donald and me) would end up doing the very same thing; year after year, looking for blackberries and huckleberries during the 50s, in spite of our mother warning us about the dangers we could encounter in the wilderness. She would remember the snake bite incident a lot more vividly than we would as we continued our Tom Sawyer and Huckleberry Finn adventures right up to the summer of 60.

Actually, we did have a continuing respectful awareness of our surroundings, always listening for that eerie rattling sound in the brush. We would never, ever go within ten feet of palmettoes and gopher holes. A gopher is a burrowing edible land tortoise. During the depression years, gophers and possums were in demand as edible food. As economic times improved in the 40s, that demand vanished.

A gopher hole is about a foot in diameter and goes from a few feet to several feet deep on an incline, which makes for a good sleeping place for a gopher. Rattlesnakes love to take up residence in gopher holes after they become deserted. They also love to hang around inside large clumps of palmettoes. Wild blackberries and huckleberries are hard to find in Hillsborough County any longer as the land became more developed, and fenced in cattle ate them as snack food. Gophers and rattlesnakes are hard to find anymore also in populated areas of our county.

More Snake Stories. One dramatic rattlesnake experience for me occurred in the 70s as we were leaving a family picnic at a camping park on the Alafia River in Riverview. A healthy looking six foot rattlesnake was slithering slowly across the asphalt drive in front of me as we were leaving the park. I quickly drove over its head and then backed over it to make sure it was dead for good. Our sister Mary and brother-in law Mac were in the car behind us. As he was raised in Ohio towns, it was the first rattlesnake in nature he had ever seen in his life. Needless to say, he was astounded at his front row seat of seeing this episode unfold right before his eyes. I think he stayed away from nature more so after seeing such a huge rattler for the first time in his life.

As a preteen when we lived on Trapnell Road, I personally experienced a face to face encounter with a cottonmouth water moccasin. One hot summer day I rode my bike with a couple of neighborhood friends to swim in Holloway Creek near Mud Lake Road and Holloway Road. The swallow creek had white sand in an isolated area so we could see the sandy bottom through the crystal clear water. It was a small area of white sandy beach. We had been enjoying our swim for a period of time as we kept watch for spiders and snakes.

While standing on the creek bank, I looked up stream and saw this huge dark brown snake raise its head and then I saw a large mass of white as he opened his mouth. I hollowed *"Moccasin, Moccasin"* as we all scrabbled towards our bikes as fast as possible. The snake went in the opposite direction. Obviously, our swimming days in that spot were over forever.

Today, Florida has a very serious challenge to eliminate an invasion of pythons in the Everglades and South Florida. They have become invasive since the late 1900s, as people released pet pythons into the wild. With a population of 100,000 plus, they are reproducing rapidly as they eat a variety of small animals at an alarming rate. We are fighting a losing battle to control them. Also, will they migrate northward to Hillsborough County and other parts of the state?

Minding Robins Duty Gone Very Wrong. On our Youmans farm in the late 50s, Harry and a neighbor friend, Donald Bell, were minding the field on a quite Sunday morning. Donald had recently moved down with his family from Brooklyn, New York and he was learning about life on a strawberry farm. We were trying our best to train him on how not to speak like someone fresh out of Brooklyn as he would tease us on our accent.

An ongoing strawberry farm harvesting chore was to constantly chase robins away from the ripening strawberries. We would do this by shooting at them with a 12 gauge shotgun. The loud shot noise would scare them from one end of the field to the other end. The birds were beautiful with their red chest. We would shoot near them to shoo them away.

After finishing his turn shooting, Donald gave Harry the shotgun. He pulled the shotgun in a downward motion with the barrel pointing toward the ground. During that downward motion the gun accidently discharged, blasting the buck shot into his foot. With the gun barrel almost resting on his shoe, the ball of buckshot went clean through his shoe and foot as if he had been shot with a rifle bullet.

Our father was working out of the state at the time, so Mother, once again had to handle the situation all by herself. With the help of Donald's family, they managed to drive Harry to the hospital in Plant City for emergency treatment. This was before the "Dial 911" emergency system. You either drove yourself to the hospital or called for an ambulance. She was home alone with Harry as the rest of us had gone to church in the family car.

Since there were no cell phones, we did not hear about the accident until we arrived home from the worship service. We had to wait till she came home with Harry to hear about what happened that morning. She had the shoe he was wearing. It had a clean hole in the big toe area about the size of a quarter. I still have a clear image of that shoe. Mother was still stressed out with the whole ordeal of having to handle the emergency by herself, not knowing what the outcome would be like. Thankfully, he recovered completely without losing any toes or his natural balance to walk. In spite of everything, he enjoyed a complete recovery. He would even be accepted by the Army to serve two years in Germany. No, he didn't see Elvis.

Sugarcane. Growing a food staple like sugarcane in our area evaporated into thin air, about the same time as hand rolled cigars in Tampa. Throughout the area, some farmers would grow small patches of sugarcane as an extra cash crop and for their family consumption. Until the ground water table was lowered with drainage ditching, the soil conditions for growing sugarcane was fair.

When neighboring farmers would harvest the cane with machetes, they would give any children present, a few pieces of cane for their enjoyment. We would use our Jim Bowie knife to skim off the tough skin and then cut bite size chunks to chew on for the sweet juice. This was always a special treat. As our family never stayed in one location for very long, we never considered growing sugarcane.

The year we lived on Rice Road, we were enjoying one of those short stalks of cane to chew during a sugarcane harvesting celebration at a neighboring farm. In poor judgement, one of us gave Michael, a first grader at the time, a knife to use for himself. Unknowingly he had weak eyesight at the time. Immediately, he cut his left hand thumb so badly he had to be rushed to a doctor for stitches. Years later, after failing an eye examination in the fourth grade, he had to start wearing glosses for reading and distance.

For all practical purposes, growing sugarcane throughout our countryside and hand rolling cigars in Tampa cigar factories from the late 1880s to the 1950s, are now non-existent. Today, there is one cigar factory left in Tampa fighting federal regulations in order to stay in business.

Below Ground Hideouts. Many preteens and young teenagers built treehouses. Primarily due to a lack of money to purchase the necessary lumber, we would build underground hideouts in an open field that was not used for farming. We would dig a square hole about 6 x 6 and about 4 foot deep. We would then dig an entrance trench on one side. We placed old scrap lumber and pieces of rusted tin over the hole as a roof. This activity was popular for a short period of time in the 50s. I remember building them at our Trapnell and Youmans farms. Some very bold older teens would actually dig long tunnels under ground to their hideouts.

Sadly, we heard about an incident where an earth tunnel collapsed on a boy, smothering him before he could be rescued. The existing earth was basically sand with no clay to act as a bonding agent. It was a disaster waiting to happen. As the public became aware of the danger involved, that fun time activity was dis-continued. We also had the possibility of rattlesnakes sleeping in them.

Quicksand. During the 50s, the fear of quicksand was right up there with a fear of Invaders from Mars (a 1953 movie) and for an ever present potential atomic bomb war with Russia. We had a constant fear of walking into quicksand at any time in bay heads and swamps that had standing water.

In the rainy season, Florida had more standing surface water than we have today. This fear was engrained into us after watching low budget movies showing bad guys being sucked into quicksand until they disappeared below the surface. The good guys were always rescued at the very last second. Movies filmed in Florida made the fear that much more scary to us.

As the fear for this unknown was real, we took the precaution to have a buddy with us and to carry a long deadwood tree limb (as a weapon for snakes too). We would always walk cautiously and stay clear of suspicious areas just in case. In all of our exploring days, we never saw anything close to quicksand. It did make for a neat memory along with another swamp legend 1954 movie "The Creature from the Black Lagoon". The movie was filmed at water scenes in North Florida. Anyhow, we did keep hoping for that pot of gold at the end of a rainbow.

Alligators. Due to their loss of habitat plus the over hunting of alligators for their hide and meat, the alligator population was at an all-time low with only several thousand living in the state by the 1950s. They were in danger of extinction by illegal hide hunters. In 1967, they were added to the endangered species list. Within the next twenty years, the alligator was declared fully recovered, making it one of the first endangered species success stories. The protective efforts exceeded all expectations. By the year 2016, the state's alligator population exceeded 1.2 million alligators.

An Exploding Alligator Population Concern.
1950 population had 2.7 million people with 6,000 gators.
2016 population had 20.6 million people with 1.2 million gators.
People increased 7.6 times while gators increased 200 times.

Average gator increase for the state's sixty seven counties.
1950 total of 6,000 gators equaled 90 per county average.
2016 total of 1.2M gators equaled 17,900 per county average.

These statistics reveal some very disturbing information about a proportion of people to alligator populations. The state is holding limited alligator hunting to help control an over population of alligators. Today, about 8,000 gators are killed per year during the gator hunting season. We will need more serious alligator population controls very soon. Otherwise, the increasing face to face encounters between people and alligators will become totally unacceptable. How many gator encounters will be required before we take action?

As alligators are unpredictable and quick acting, children and pets should always be kept at a safe distance from them. During the 50s, we would swim in any of the local waterways with little concern. I remember only seeing a few gators during all of our countryside swimming days. Today, I would not walk close to any body of water in Florida without extreme caution of my surroundings.

"So then faith comes by hearing, and hearing by the Word of God."
(Romans 10:17)

178

Karen with Kimberly and Greg enjoying a cake party. (circa 1982).

Cousin Caroline and Kim partying with Greg in background. (circa 1983)

Heritage & Hope

_____·_____

Chapter 18

Birthdays / Holidays / Movies

Birthdays throughout the year came and went with only a slight acknowledgement of each one. That pattern of observation went on throughout our years living at home. Birthdays for each of us were usually verbally noted each year on the birthday. When possible, a cake would be shared at the nearest Sunday lunch for the one being recognized. There would be no party or gifts.

I remember wanting so much to have a real party with invited friends bringing gifts for my 12th (my last preteen year) and 16th birthdays. I spent weeks thinking about each one on what all I wanted to have included. As these two special birthdays finally arrived, nothing different happened. Both birthdays came and went like all of the others.

As the years went by, we learned to accept it as a way of life for our family and to move on with our lives. Looking back at it, I can realize the enormous cost that would have been involved if we have had just a basic party for each of us eight boys and one girl for our first eighteen years, plus parties for our parents also. We even thought it was odd to hear about people spending money on birthday parties.

Harry was the only exception to our family's no birthday celebration policy. Every Christmas day, we would remind him how fortunate he was in celebrating his birthday on Christmas day. Yes, he was born on December 25, 1940. Who was to say if at least one of his gifts on Christmas morning was for his birthday? We would sing _"Happy Birthday"_ to him as we gave him a cake. Our grandson Carter's birthday is on December 21, so he enjoys double blessings with gifts on his two special days four days apart.

Christmas was always celebrated with a decorated tree and limited gifts for each of us. Presents included cap pistols, BB rifles, red wagons, footballs, and always some clothing. We would be given a bike at least one time each during our childhood.

I remember my 5th grade Christmas the most of all. Our father mentioned that I was getting old enough to have a bicycle, but he teasingly said that I probably shouldn't get one as I was still young and might run off the road looking at the girls. When I heard this, I resigned to not getting one that year. I was completely taken by surprise on that Christmas morning; I got a brand new shiny bright red and white bicycle.

This was to be the best Christmas gift of all for me because of the surprise element. I never did see any girls on the road ways. However I did end up running off our home drive into the ditch and went flying over the handle bars at least one time. That bike became my means of traveling around the neighborhood and to town at my pleasure.

We never celebrated New Year's Eve and July 4th with fireworks, and certainly not with a party. We would see a few fireworks from neighboring homes. New Year's day was just another work day. College and pro football games were beginning to be shown live on television.

Valentine's Day was nonexistent and Labor Day was just another work day. We celebrated Thanksgiving Day with a turkey and trimmings. On Halloween night, we would go trick or treating around the neighborhood within walking distance.

We didn't wear costumes. Lights were out on many of the homes on that night. Treats were few and far between. As we grew older, we would team up with some older friends and we would drive around looking for porch lights burning at homes. We would stop to trick or treat those houses. The adults would comment on us being too big to trick or treat. But they would still give us candy anyhow. The next year we did stop doing it as we felt like we were committing a crime.

Halloween spending was projected to be 8.4 billion dollars in 2016. In comparison, our world's population today exceeds 7.5 billion. That amount of spending could have provided a copy of the New

Testament to 90% of our world's population. Food for thought as we continue on.

In and out of state vacation trips were nonexistent while day trips were few and far between. In addition to a few day trips to Clearwater Beach over the years, we made other day trips to see Bok Tower Gardens, Spook Hill, Manmade Mountain, Webb's City, Sunshine Skyway, Cypress Gardens, Weeki Wachee Springs, 301 Apex Rock House, and the original Busch Gardens attraction including a plant tour.

Until we purchased our first television in 1957, our entertainment consisted of going to the movies every chance we got, which was maybe a couple of times a month or so. I remember one Sunday afternoon when we lived on Trapnell Road, Harry pedaled my bike to town and back with me riding on the bike horizontal bars. It turned out to be a horrible, and dangerous, experience as we both agreed that we would never do that again.

I clearly remember it being a John Wayne movie "The High and Mighty". He was the pilot of a commercial airline having to make an emergency landing in the Pacific Ocean. An incident like that would be the real thing decades later on the Hudson River in New York City.

I believe the ticket price was about thirty cents, a lot less than the eleven dollars today. Robert would drop us off at either one of the two theaters we had in Plant City, the State Theater or Capital Theater. And then he would go out on a date.

When the movie was over, we had to vacate the theater. Most of the time, Robert would be another half hour or so before picking us up. It was very awkward for us to run into the local policeman walking his street patrol. He would give us the once over on why we would be out walking the streets at that late hour. Robert would eventually drive up and we would all climb in the car and take off leaving our policeman friend a happy man since we were now safe from our street walking as midnight approached.

Going to the movies in the 50s was always a special treat. On Saturdays, they showed B grade movies. They were mainly westerns, cops and robbers, and war movies with a cartoon and a short feature serial like Flash Jordon. Singing cowboys Roy Rodgers and Gene Autry were super stars. Tickets cost more on Sundays as hit movies were shown on Sunday, Monday and Tuesday. I remember going to State Theater one Sunday afternoon with my parents to see "Giant" starring Rock Hudson, Liz Taylor and James Dean. One time we saw "Love Me Tender" starring Elvis Presley in his first of many movies that he would make after his introductory role. Buying a candy bar and coke some of the time was a very special treat.

Another favorite outlet for movies in the day was the popular drive in theaters. We had the Starlite Drive In south of Plant City on Highway 39. It was only a few miles from our Trapnell house. During the four years we lived in Youmans, we would go to the Silver Moon on Highway 92 west of Lakeland. The movies were not the best, but the atmosphere was exciting and the cost was favorable. It was like watching television at home. You could chatter all you wanted to during the movies. We made fun on the bad upcoming previews. Sad to note, we witnessed another culture in our society becoming history. One by one, the drive in theaters closed without any fanfare. However, I think Ruskin still has a drive in theater.

Our parents literally grew up with movies from the very beginning of the industry. We listened as they talked about the stars of their childhood and young adult years. After 1928, they rarely went to the movies during the time they raised us over a thirty year period. A reality fact is that before we purchased our first television in 1957, we had no other visual medium entertainment except at local theaters.

"But the Helper, the Holy Spirit, whom the Father will send in My name, He will teach you all things, and bring to your remembrance all things that I said to you." (John 14:26)

Heritage & Hope

—————•—————

Chapter 19

A Hunting We Will Go

My 18 year old brother, Charles, hollered out, *"Let's go!"* He would lead two of his school friends plus tag along brothers Robert and Lloyd into our backyard forest in Cork as their blood hounds darted out on their own upon being released. Off the five hunting buddies went, with their head band lights burning brightly to see in the night even though moonlight was shining somewhat through the trees and underbrush. They ran in the direction of the roaring dogs. In other hunting adventures through the 50s, Philip and Harry would join the hunting parties every chance they could go.

All five looked larger than life to me, at age 9, and my two younger brothers, Michael, age 6 and Donald, age 5. The three of us had to share one small flashlight as we scampered out together trying to stay up with the "real hunters". They had real guns, and we had sticks. Before he bolted off with his friends, Charles had told us that we could not go with them. We had to stay at home until we were older.

In spite of his earlier instructions to us, we followed after them anyway. I felt like Jody in The Yearling chasing after his Pa, Penny Baxter, on a bear hunt, running through the underbrush and wetlands. After running about one hundred yards into the wilderness, we were so far behind, we decided to give up and head back home to our cozy beds that would be waiting for us. After realizing what a bad situation we were in, it didn't take long to make that decision. The barking and hollering faded into the night as they went one way and we started home in the opposite direction.

When I was about 21, I went on my last hunting trip with Charles. He drove me up to Northeast Florida for a weekend of deer hunting with some of his hunting friends. That trip finally convinced me that the hunting life was not for me! The trips included rising early in the mornings before sunrise with almost non-existent meals that were never close to being edible. The weather was always either too hot or too cold. You could always count on rain. Waiting for a buck deer to cross in front of your tree stand was painstakingly boring.

Charles was considered the real hunter in our family. I think Lloyd and Philip came in at a close second to him. All three continued their hunting and fishing passion throughout their active lives. Robert participated somewhat, but very little after meeting Donna. Harry seemed to enjoy it from time to time. I personally never did develop an interest in fishing, hunting or shooting guns for sport. Michael and Donald would develop very little interest in hunting also. For whatever reasons, our father never showed any interest in hunting or fishing. I guess I followed in his footsteps. In later years, a few of our nephews would develop into very respectable hunters in their adult life. During that time, I continued in life as a bookworm.

As a teenager in the late 40s, Charles was introduced to what I now call "Backyard Woodland Hunting" as he made friends with a few of his high school classmates. They also played on the Turkey Creek Senior High School football team together. A couple of the friend's families were adamant hunters as their fathers would take part in the hunts. They would go hunting in nearby open range woodlands.

From generation to generation throughout the state's history, this way of life was the norm for hunters. It was the same as the 1870's fictional families we read about in The Yearling. Through the years of history, pioneering men would hunt deer, turkeys, bears, wild hogs, and gators for meat. Charles was a teenager when hunting was still a good way to obtain meat as necessary food for families. This necessity of hunting for meat vanished as more and more of those men started working fulltime for wages in the 40s.

Charles and his friends were in the last generation to enjoy the Florida Cracker culture of open range hunting. As we approached the 50s, the state's population was exceeding two million people. Since then, we have watched it grow ten times over to twenty million plus. More and more of the hunters were beginning to hunt for the sport of it as families were not as desperate to hunt for meat to eat any more. At about the same time, governmental agencies were banning the killing of many wild animals due to their potential extinction.

In the early years of the 20th century, our state experienced one of the most disgraceful times in our history. Hunters shot exotic birds such as egrets in the Everglades in order to sell their feathers. Large cities like New York City and Boston placed a high demand on the feathers in making hats for women. That tragedy peaked circa 1902.

Manufacturing hats with bird feathers were finally banned in order to protect the bird population from devastation. Ten thousands upon ten thousands of birds were killed strictly for their feathers. The situation became so brutal that a US Marshall was murdered trying to protect birds from poachers. Few people know about this history.

Also during the 40s, accidents involving cars and trucks with cows walking onto country and city roads were becoming a serious problem. The increased population clashing with free roaming cattle resulted in our state establishing a law in 1949 that required all livestock to be fenced. The law stopped open range cattle drives.

Most of the drives came up from the Lake Okeechobee area to the Tampa shipyard. The cracking sound of the cowboy's cow whips working the cattle disappeared, except on cattle ranches throughout the state. Cowboys can now be seen cracking their whips during demonstrations at the Florida State Fair Cracker Country. The law did help land owners to keep people from trespassing. That action kept people from crossing over wire fences, shutting down good hunting grounds that had always been open for hunters.

As the law was implemented and enforced, hunters traveled to North Florida, Georgia and Alabama to hunt on large tracts of land with wildlife. In the 50s, hunting became a sport as it was no longer a necessity. The law was a death blow to our open range hunting and cattle drives. The law resulted in a culture lost forever; open range hunting in order to bring home desired meat for families to eat.

Robert's Boomerang Bullet - A Hunter's Nightmare. As a teenager, Robert was shot by a 22 rifle bullet while hunting with some friends. This story is hard to believe. He was minding his own business during a friendly outing when his buddy shot at a squirrel on a huge tree limb. The bullet ricocheted off the limb, then another tree limb, and ended up hitting Robert in his leg. With the trees softening the force of impact, his wound was superficial.

One day during my fifth grade at Trapnell, I was alone as I crossed through a three strand barbed wire fence for our pasture while I held onto a loaded 22 rife that I was carrying. Unexpectedly, a bullet discharged. Fortunately, I had the gun barrel pointed at the ground away from me. I was shocked at how quick it happened.

In Memory of Charles Benton Humphrey (1934-1975)

Charles was so much older than me that I looked up to him like a father. He was our admired fearless leader during the time we had together growing up as family. After returning to the area in 1970, I enjoyed spending holidays with him during the next five years.

Tragically at age 41, Charles was killed as he fell about thirty feet on a construction site six days before Christmas 1975. He was an excellent Connector fitting steel columns and beams into place, one piece at a time. He connected on large bridges and high rise buildings throughout the South such as the Skyway Bridge and the Tampa International Airport.

Thankfully, Mother did not have to experience that sad tragedy as she died six years previously. Charles had a daughter Desiree (DeeDee) and two sons, Mark and David. We hold fond memories of him being full of life and caring for others during his journey with us. We look forward in faith to a reunion in the family of God.

"But seek first the kingdom of God and His righteousness, and all these things shall be added to you." (Matthew 6:33)

Future NASCAR racer Carter Goins. 2012.

Heritage & Hope

———•———

Chapter 20

Summer of 60

The summer of 1960 started for me as June arrived. My first order of business was to graduate from Plant City High School in the first week of June. I was faithfully riding to school on the big yellow school bus from a Florida cracker house on a small tract of farm land we rented in the tiny community of Youmans. The property was located on the north side of Highway 92, a few hundred yards west of the Polk County line.

Next, we had to buy a used car to drive a round trip to New York. While our father was working in New York City, he made arrangements to have our mother, Michael, Donald and me to work on a farm in Commack, Long Island during the summer; harvesting strawberries and grains. He would fly home and we would drive the car to Commack (about forty miles east of the City). Long Island is about one hundred twenty miles long.

Charles offered to help me buy a used car. The shopping task didn't take long as we found a stylish four door 53 Chevrolet with a fluid drive automatic transmission. A price of $300 was quickly agreed upon. It was definitely an improvement to the old floor board manual gear shift transmission that I had learned how to drive in our old 39 four door Plymouth sedan. Our old car reminded me of the one Bonnie and Clyde were driving when they met their demise.

So off we went as owner of what I thought was a real beauty. Our father would later tell us that he was afraid we had bought a car that would not make the long trip to New York and back home before it would totally collapse. After all, it was seven years old and it was not his favorite automobile, a Buick. However, when he drove it for the first time, he was ok with the car, and thought maybe it would make the trip after all.

As I was finishing my last high school year at age 16, my application to attend the University of South Florida in Tampa was accepted. The educational institution was a brand new state university. It was years in the making during the 50s, before the opening date in September, 1960 for students to attend classes for the first time.

I was student number 259. I was given a beautiful medallion commemorating this very special occasion. I still have that medallion as a keepsake, hopefully for generations to follow.

When the university opened its doors for us, I believe there were only five buildings on the 1,800 acre campus. We had an administration building, a library, a couple of classroom buildings and a combination student union/classrooms building.

They were all connected with sidewalks. If you deviated from those sidewalks, you immediately entered the world of sand, weeds and wicked sandspurs at your own risk. Those original buildings and the campus entrance drive are still standing in the same location as they did on the opening date.

In that year, the entire campus consisted of sand, weeds, sandspurs, native scrub pines, oaks and palmettos compared to the immaculate landscaped grounds with big beautiful buildings that now have filled almost every square foot of the campus some fifty eight years later. Large areas of undisturbed native palmettos made for some good rattlesnake country.

As soon as I received my college acceptance letter, I bought a "USF" decal and put it on the back windshield. One of the few things that I remembered about our drive to New York was having a car pass us on 301 just north of Zephyrhills with a man driving a car with the same "USF" decal on his back windshield. I wondered if he was one of our professors.

The university would be known for having a high percentage of professors with advanced degrees from universities in Northern and Midwestern states. I believe they were eager to help guide us freshmen into a new age of educational enlightenment and culture. After all, we knew this would be a university for students wanting more from their education than just spending September through December concerned about making it into the top national football rankings. A successful football program at USF would be established decades later. With no dorms, we commuted from home.

As we packed for our trip, I have no idea how we got our luggage in the car trunk for the five of us. Our parents were in the front seat as we three boys sat in the back seat. So if we nodded off during the day, we would have to sleep in a sitting position. We did not have seat belts. At the time, 301 was the major highway everyone took for traveling north including our favorite traveling companions – the truckers. I remember many a time, following them for miles on end driving most of 301 with only two lanes for traffic.

We had one lane for north traffic and one lane for south traffic. The interstate highway system was still under construction. In Farmville, North Carolina, we visited Uncle Richard Lee and Aunt Janie's families in the afternoon with an overnight stay. The next day, we had a brief visit with Uncle Woodrow and Aunt Lucille in Norfolk, Virginia, as we continued on our trip.

I remember seeing so many farms and small towns as we drove through Georgia, South Carolina, North Carolina and Virginia on US 301. We crossed the huge Chesapeake Bay on a ferry. The hazy fog horizon was thick and chilling, being a distant difference to our Sunshine State's bright and clear sunlight. We stopped at a place with cottages in Maryland to spend the night. That was a time when we did not make reservations; we would just stop and ask if a room was available. It seemed like there would always be one.

The next thing I remember on our drive up was that we had engine trouble in New Jersey, just south of New York City. The garage we pulled into was next to a clay hillside. Being the first hill we had seen in our lifetime, we climbed on it regardless of getting clay all over us as it was still damp from a recent rain. As we had grown up in the flat lands of Florida, we thought this mountain climbing experience was something special. Mother scolded us for getting clay on our clothes. We had to spend quite a bit of time cleaning up the mess.

The car repair was completed quicker than we thought it would be. Father was afraid we would have to spend another night in a motel room as we waited on the repair work to be completed. He decided we could make it to Commack without staying another night. So off we went, determined to make it in a matter of a few more hours. By nightfall, everything went ok until we took a wrong turn somehow and became lost in the city. Our father finally got us back on track to find the Long Island Expressway and then we were less than a couple of hours from the farm.

We made it there later than everyone expected. The farmer, Ralph Moreland, and his wife were still up waiting on us to arrive. She actually had dinner prepared for us to eat upon our arrival.

Mr. Moreland had small used travel trailers set up on his farm for workers to live in during the harvesting time. Mother stayed in the farm house and we stayed in trailers along with others staying in them also. He had a family from Puerto Rico, and a couple of French Canadian women from Quebec.

The next morning, we went straight to the strawberry fields to work. I was very excited because I thought I would be paid so much a quart for each one I picked. I started right out picking aggressively. Father had told him about the experience we had in strawberries back home. He was very impressed with what he saw in our work. Well, I was rudely awakened from my dreams of getting rich quick as I found out that we were working for our room and board. Sad to say, after that enlightenment, I looked at our payment arrangement with quite a different perspective.

The strawberry plants filled the flat ground with runners. They did not grow plants in single or double rows like we did at home. After the harvesting period was over, we mowed the strawberry plants with a tractor mower. Later in the fall, they may put straw on top of the plants for protection from the winter temperatures. Once we finished picking the strawberries for the day, we would sell them. One way was at the fruit stand they had on the road side in front of their house. As the road was a major highway with heavy traffic, they were blessed with good sells during the day time hours. Mrs. Moreland and our mother ran the fruit stand sales. They also did the cooking and housekeeping work.

The other way of selling was to select a few of the workers to sell the strawberries on the roadside at different locations in the community of Commack and nearby areas. I was assigned a location on a major expressway with quite a bit of traffic. It had a large area of land to pull off the road safely and for parking. In addition to my stand, there was a man and woman team that drove up in their food truck daily and set up to sell hot dogs and cokes. We sort of became a combination calling card for traffic to pull over to buy strawberries and lunch.

I had to paint a big "Strawberries for Sale" sign while I sold strawberries at the same time. I finally finished the sign and proudly showed it to the couple and asked them what they thought, knowing they would say something like *"great job Jerry"*. Well, I was shocked when he, with a bit of hesitance, told me that it looked great except for one problem, I misspelled the word "strawberries". I think I left it spelled wrong. We all know this kind of thing has haunted mankind in years past and it will continue to do so. I think our misspelling of words increased more so after we entered the computer age.

I had already experienced this method of sales back home with strawberries we had raised on our farm. Our father would drive us up to Zephyrhills, the next town north of Plant City full of "snow birds" with extra spending money for luxuries like fresh strawberries. He would find a good location on main street (US 301) to set up a sales stand, usually in front of a service station. Remember, this would be in our world of the late 50s. He had us stand out near the street sidewalk with two containers capped with large strawberries so people driving by could see them being offered for sale.

I was not pleased with this method of marketing. Not to mention the looks you would get from adjacent business owners and local policemen that sort of thought I was doing something wrong, but they didn't want to be the bad guy and tell me that I should not be selling strawberries in this manner. We only did this method of marketing briefly.

Though I detested peddling strawberries as a street vender, Mr. Moreland boasted of my sales success to the other workers. He would keep egging all of us on with his exhortations. One day a big luxury car pulled up and two men dressed with white shirts and ties got out, ate a hot dog lunch and then came over to my stand. They checked out the strawberries and bought a couple of containers. I overheard one of the men tell his friend that I looked like Sal Mineo and he asked his friend if he thought so too. Mineo was popular at that time as he became an overnight star in the movies 'Rebel without a Cause" and "Exodus".

I felt excited as I wondered if I would be discovered for a movie audition, right there on the spot. The second man sluffed his shoulders with a weak *"Yea, yea, if you say so"*. To my dismay, they quickly got back into their car without saying another word to me as they sped off to, I assumed, the "Big Apple", My instant dream of Hollywood disappeared instantaneously after that flippant reply.

One farm duty I had was to drive the large flatbed farm truck that had floor board gear shifting which was ok, except this particular truck had to be doubled clutched every time to shift gears. It was a challenge to do this, especially on hilly countryside roads and in traffic. I don't know how I managed to do this without causing an accident or stripping the transmission gears. I also had to drive his Farmall tractor to his strawberry fields and mow them.

One of the most unforgettable characters I met at the farm was a local teenager named Ernie. He was about 18 years old and lived nearby. He had worked on the farm through his teen years and the Morelands treated him like their son. He was a dedicated worker.

His favorite past time was to race go carts at a track in neighboring Central Islip. He and the farm couple were always talking about going to the races every chance they could do so. Ernie would race go carts that he worked on. Also, he was the operator and maintenance man for the farmer's grain harvesting equipment. One day he was involved in a terrible accident as his hand was chewed up badly after it was caught in the harvester blades. The couple took the tragedy very hard. In time, his hand healed and he recovered most of his hand use. I remember him being full of energy with a competitive spirit in everything he undertook. Their relationship reminded me of Spencer Tracy portraying Father Flanagan with his orphan boys in the 1938 movie "Boy's Town".

Another unforgettable character I met on the farm was a 19 year old Jewish boy from Brooklyn as he worked with us for a brief time. He would tell me about the experiences he had the previous summer working on a Merchant Marine cargo ship. He was a member of the crew and he had to hold his own in the duties he was assigned. One day he bought a six pack of beer that was not chilled. He offered one to me. It was so warm tasting that I could not drink it. He drank his down with gusto. For the time we worked together, he was like a big brother to me as he was 19 and I was a mere 16.

Mr. Moreland was also definitely a most unforgettable character. He would always wear khaki trousers and long sleeve shirts along with his straw hat. He would chew on a stalk of grain as he spoke in a soft monotone voice. Some thirteen years later, after I married Karen and she started her career in teaching and I started mine in construction; we went on a vacation trip to DC, New York City, New England and Quebec in 1973.

Before leaving New York City, we drove out to Commack and actually found Mr. Moreland still living on his homestead. The house and stand looked the same as it did in 1960. He was very excited to see me and was amazed that I would actually take the time to visit him again. His wife had died and the area was rapidly becoming more developed. He talked about the changes that were taking place on Long Island, especially with housing developments taking up so much of the farmland. He told me that Ernie was doing fine. Our conversation was very sad as we talked about the changes. At the end of our brief visit, we took a couple of photos and said our goodbyes. That was the last time we would see each other.

Fifteen years later in 1988, we went on another vacation trip to the same areas with our daughter, Kim and son, Greg. Once again, we made the drive out to Commack. This time we could not find the farm house and fruit stand. Sad to write, we could not find Mr. Moreland either. We only saw new residential and commercial developments, streets and traffic with scattered farms. Long Island farming had been painfully reduced. The small beloved Moreland family farm along with neighboring farms, were sold for suburban development.

I thought back to the time a developer flew me to their home office in Long Island New York for an interview as I was graduating from Auburn University in March, 1968. The recruiter interviewing me boasted about all of the houses they were building on Long Island including near my beloved adopted town, Commack. He stressed the many houses they completed every day of the week, nonstop. They needed people with a construction management education and experience to keep that assembly line of houses going full steam.

I concluded their direction of growth was not compatible with the career desires I was seeking. I believe it was also the same company that started Levittown in the 50s. The way I saw it, Long Island and the Tampa Bay area faced similar crossroads in their unstoppable tidal wave of progress.

One weekend in that very special summer, Father drove us to Princeton, New Jersey to visit Aunt Annie. She was 61 and Father was 58. I included details of that intriguing visit previously in Chapter 3. One Sunday, our father drove us into New York City to sight-see. For the first time in our lives, we were real tourist, even if we didn't have a camera. In those days, Holiday Inn was starting to offer travelers nice economical motel rooms. Families started swarming the roads in the 70s to take those perfect vacation trips all over the USA.

First, he drove us by the apartment he was renting in Queens. He would rent an apartment where ever he traveled in his work as a union construction electrician in various large cities including New York City, Boston, Pittsburg, Cleveland, Baltimore, Kansas City and Newark. He lived that lifestyle from the late 40s till the early 60s. As Disney World and Cape Kennedy started up in full swing, along with a surge in the phosphate industry expansions, he was able to work at home during the 60s right up until his death on January 13, 1967.

Our next stop was the Empire State Building. I remember he parked the car at the street curb near the front door. I think we paid a few dimes for the parking meter. We got out of the car, walked into the building lobby and took an elevator to the top. We went out to the observation deck and viewed the city from all four sides of the building. Then we went back down. We didn't take any souvenirs or photographs. And there were no crowds either. It would never be like that today. In the tourist seasons; New York City, like Disney World and other major attractions, is flooded with multitudes of people from the USA and countries worldwide.

We didn't have a camera, so we couldn't be real tourists. As a matter of fact, we did not have a camera during my school and college years. I was married for a year or so before I bought my first camera.

The Empire State Building was completed in 1931. It was the world's tallest building for forty two years, until the World Trade Center Twin Towers were completed in 1973. It was still considered sort of a new building in 1960 at 29 years old. As one more trivia item, who hasn't seen the classic 1933 "King Kong" movie with fifty foot tall King Kong holding onto the peak of the Empire State Building with one hand while holding the screaming actress, Fay Wray, in the other?

Upon leaving the Empire State Building, we drove through the various boroughs of the city and ended up parking the car at the Bowery and taking a ferry to the Statue of liberty. When we got to the island we were free to roam anywhere we wanted to go as often as we wanted. It was thrilling to climb the stairs to the crown and look out to the city from that level. And we had only a small group of people touring the landmark.

We drove over the Brooklyn Bridge, George Washington Bridge and through the Lincoln Tunnel during our driving tour. Ellis Island was not open then, and the Twin Towers would be built years later. Twenty eight years later, Karen, Kim, Greg and I viewed the city from the top of one twin tower.

One night, Donald, Michael and I drove to the local Drive-In Theater to see the much talked about 1960 movie "Psycho" directed by Alfred Hitchcock with actor Tony Perkins and actress Janet Leigh. Needless to say, I had trouble for quite a few nights sleeping out in our tiny travel trailer with its flimsy door and windows. I avoided horror movies the rest of my life after seeing that one. Too many demons for me!

Our summer farm work quickly came to an end and it was time to say our goodbyes. On our trip home, I had to drive the distance as Mother did not drive and our father stayed in New York.

About all I remember of the trip home was one incident we had just south of Dade City on Highway 301. Michael was in the front seat with our mother and Donald in the back seat. All three of them were sleeping and I started dozing off. As I drifted off the road, I heard Michael scream at me to wake up as he grabbed the steering wheel to keep us on the road. He told me I almost hit a mailbox. I notice it was a few inches from our car as we flew by it. He woke up just in time to keep me from hitting it square on. Or was it my Guardian Angel again?

Soon after we arrived back home, Hurricane Donna hit Fort Myers, then moved north through Central Florida and across us as she headed towards Dayton Beach with sustained strong storm winds and rain. In reflection, it reminded me of the hurricane in the 1948 movie "Key Largo" staring Humphrey Bogart, Edward G. Robinson and Lauren Bacall. The storm also hit us as night fell. Mother, Donald, Michael and I spent the night with Philip and his newly wed wife Bonnie in their new home in Willow Oak. As we were experiencing our first hurricane, we didn't want to stay in our rental frame house.

I didn't think the wind and rain would ever stop. Phillip spent most of the night trying to calm Bonnie down as the rest of us kept watch for water leaks. While we hoped the wind would not rip off the roof shingles and plywood or blow out a window. The house survived the storm's fury without damages. Philip and Bonnie drove us back to our house in Youmans. During the drive, we saw pine trees broken off half way up and oaks blown over. We had damages to our rental house exterior.

We were in the process of moving into a three bedroom house we purchased in Robinson Subdivision located in southwest Plant City. The developed land was previously Hugh Robinson's airport. Our address was 1610 West Ball Street. The houses were constructed in the late 50s design. We bought the house for about $9,000 with a loan interest rate of 3%. We sold the house in 1970 to Realtor Jack Camp. Our mother enjoyed living in a comfortable residential home for ten years, her longest period of adult life for living in one house. It would be seven years for our father.

The house was built with exterior masonry walls on a concrete slab on grade with wood roof framing. It had a living room, kitchen, one bath room and three bedrooms. The one car carport had a small utility room and a concrete drive to the street. The architectural design was considered modern at the time. The houses were very basic and affordable to middle class families. The house lots were small but acceptable.

It was similar to another development east of Highway 39 near WPLA radio station. That development was constructed in the early 50s. Robert's in-law's family lived in that subdivision. The masonry and concrete floor construction made the typical cracker house built with wood framed floor and walls set on brick piers obsolete. Wood houses basically became history as concrete, masonry and stucco construction became the norm. Today, the median price of a house in Hillsborough County is about $235,000 (twenty five times the 50s pricing of about $10,000). After we had moved into our new home, I started my first day in college as a charter member of the first year of classes beginning at the University of South Florida in early September 1960.

The summer of 60 also brought our country a new political arena as we witnessed the Democratic Party nominate John F. Kennedy as their Presidential candidate to run against the Republican Party candidate, Richard Nixon. Who can forget the infamous TV debate between the two men as we experienced, as a nation, how much image plays in a person being elected President. Ever since that campaign, we would see that election factor much more so through the years.

Our age of superficial legalist innocence was starting to erode in the late 50s as we lived through the Presidential election in November, 1960. Chicago's politics, led by Mayor Richard Daley, made the headlines with a heated inquiry for possible voting ballots fraud. Claims by the Republican Party went out to deaf ears on the counting of votes. The election votes were so close; the ballets in question could have made a difference in whether Nixon would have won the Presidential election.

We had finished eight years (1952-1960) of conservative leadership under a Republican President, Dwight D. Eisenhower. He was a beloved war hero and a tremendous leader. He started our interstate highway system. He would be ecstatic to see how we accomplished the vision he had for America. I believe we also enjoyed seven years of conservative leadership previously under a Democrat President, Harry S. Truman (1945-1952). I believe he was a strong leader, regardless of being a Democrat. While serving as Vice-President, he became President upon Democrat President Franklin D. Roosevelt's death in office on April 12, 1945 (1933-1945).

I think President Truman made one of the most difficult Presidential decisions in the history of our country. Seventy three years later, few people realize its importance. He was famous for his off the cuff quotes like, *"If you can't stand the heat, get out of the kitchen"* and *"The buck stops here"*. He made the decision on bombing Japan with atom bombs. His decision was based on the projected loss of Allied troops along with the enormous cost involved in invading Japan like we did in Germany. Military leaders were predicting it would be a blood bath as the Japanese would fight to the last man to protect their homeland with no surrendering.

We justified the atomic bombings as a military necessity to avoid invading Japan which would cost the lives of an estimated 300,000 or more Allied service men along with millions of Japanese troops and civilians. On August 6, we dropped an atomic bomb on the city of Hiroshima.

When no Japanese surrender was forthcoming, a second bomb fell on Nagasaki on August 9. On August 15, 1945, Japan formally surrendered. World War II was over. Father had his 43rd birthday on August 2 and I would have my 2 year old birthday on September 16. I was a World War II baby.

In 1838, one hundred and twenty two years prior to the summer of 60, our nation witnessed another chapter of our history being closed forever through "The Trail of Tears". This action resulted in a new era being established in our state's territory for good after 1858. The territory could be rapidly settled by families without fear of Indians.

President Andrew Jackson executed the Removal Act of 1830 by ordering the U. S. Army to round up the Cherokee and Seminole Indians along with other tribes. They were loaded into boats that carried them from their territories along the Tennessee, Ohio, Arkansas and Mississippi Rivers to Indian Reservations. The relocation work included long walking distances.

It was called the *"trail where they cried"* as thousands died from hunger and disease during the relocation process. It had been almost two hundred years of consistent fighting between the Native Americans and European Settlers. Their lifestyle of living off the land for centuries was over. We had three separate periods of war.

First Seminole War   (1816-1819)
Second Seminole War (1835-1842)
Third Seminole War   (1855-1858)

As a result of the three Florida Seminole Wars finally ending in 1858, the surviving Seminoles of the Everglades would be the only federally recognized tribe which never relinquished sovereignty or signed a peace treaty with the United States. A remnant of an estimated 200 Seminoles hid in the Everglades and was never captured.

These small numbers of Seminoles, along with a band of Miccosukee Indians, survived in the wilderness; living off the land and selling handmade items to tourists. Over a period of time, they had Indian villages established in Tampa and the Everglades for tourism.

They won a court ruling that made them a nation, independent of our country. Then they won their fight to build casinos. They have seven casinos including Tampa Seminole Hard Rock Hotel & Casino with 24/7 operations. They enjoy revenues exceeding two billion dollars per year. Although I do not approve of legalized gambling, the Native Americans are a major entity in our heritage and history.

The day I started classes at USF was the end of a way of life for our family. The family farming life we grew up in along with the generations going before us became history. Strawberry farming would become big business, regardless if it were a corporation or family operated. It was no longer a nickel dime family enterprise. The required workers changed from families to other labor sources where available. We didn't discuss this lifestyle change very much around the kitchen table. I remember our father accepting the change with very little feeling on his part. We continued with our lives in the 60s as we pursued our individual aspirations.

My personality, along with my way of handling life's challenges, was forged during my first five years of life. Ironically, I experienced the summer of 48 picking cherries in Michigan before starting the first grade and picking strawberries (our last hurrah) in New York after completing the twelfth grade in the summer of 60.

We had two wonderful out of state "vacations". It was like a sandwich of personal growth for me along with a package of basic education for those twelve school years. The summer of '60 was a remarkable and unique experience that I now recognize as a strong link in my destiny during my journey on earth.

"Finally, my brethren, be strong in the Lord and in the power of His might." (Ephesians 6:10)

Charles, in the center of two un-identified co-workers, is connecting structural steel framing for a high rise building (circa 1972).

Greg (bottom) and cousin Jonathan sliding down a firemen's pole.
A roof was added later. This photo was taken circa 1985. The 2 story fort served generations of children before a falling tree demolished it in 2016.

Greg (with Karen) home on leave for Christmas 2001.

Heritage & Hope

———•———

Chapter 21

The Desert Years

In the day, it was expected of those graduating from high school to enroll in college, join a military service or enter into the work force. At the magic age of 18, boys were considered an adult and were expected to move out of their childhood home into their own living quarters. Girls were expected to live at home until marriage. Boys could continue living at home if they commuted to a local college.

I chose the latter option. As we lived through the 60s, our superficial innocence and culture was well on the way to being under heavy attacks. This path of destruction would progressively increase each year through the year 2000 and beyond to our present existence.

I believe my personal desert years were the eight years between my June 1960 high school and March 1968 college graduations. It was the substantial eight years of time I spent working and studying to obtain a college degree. For some unknown reason I would stay focused on that one goal. In September 1960, I started commuting to the University of South Florida in a car pool with two other students. The university did not have dormitories at the time.

I was very excited to have my own bedroom for the first time in my life. Michael and Donald shared a bedroom. We were the last three siblings living at home. I finished my freshman college year in an acceptable manner and worked during the summer on some construction projects.

I returned to USF for my second year. I attempted to live in a bedroom I rented from a family in Tampa. After struggling for a couple of months to make a go of it, I reluctantly moved back home. As I became dis-enchanted with my commuting college life, I enlisted in the Marine Corp Reserves after my fall semester. My enlistment was for six months active duty plus four and half years of active eserve duty. In February 1962, I was included in a group of twelve ther recruits from the Tampa Bay area bussed to Paris Island for our twelve weeks of boot camp training. We also completed two months of training in the operation and maintenance of amphibious vehicles for beach landing of troops) at Camp Lejeune near Jacksonville, North Carolina. I became an active Reserve training one weekend per month at the Gandy Boulevard Marine Corp Base. We also had two weeks of training at Camp Lejeune every summer.

On February 20, 1962, our boot camp training platoon was allowed to sit around a truck radio as we listened to the live broadcast of Astronaut John Glenn's landing after his 4 hour, 55 minutes space trip as he circled the globe three times. His re-entry procedure was modified to keep his capsule from burning up as he returned to earth. We cheered as he landed. We were allowed to listen to this historic event because he was a Marine Corp Officer. Being the first American in orbit; he became a national hero and received a ticker-tape parade in New York City, similar to one like Charles Lindbergh received in 1927.

One year we trained at Camp Pendleton in California. It was a very exciting summer training as we held maneuvers in the Pacific Ocean. We experienced a realistic beach landing in amphibious vehicles with troops from a transport ship. I had the opportunity to be a landing vehicle driver.

I could see the infantry troop's eyes enlarge as we drove off the ship ramp hitting the water like a submarine, then popping up to the surface. As I opened the driver's hatch, waves splashed into the vehicle creating concern within the ranks. The waves were pretty rough and it was really difficult to drive the vehicle back up the ship ramp. The Navy Officer barked commands at me on how to hit the ramp at the precise timing. And yes, we went to Disneyland on our liberty weekend. Disney World was yet to be.

What I thought was a curse for me being so tall and thin during my school and college years turned out to be a blessing. As an adult, I could eat whatever I wanted and not have to worry about gaining weight. I was 6'-1" and weighed 155 pounds when I enlisted in the Marine Corp Reserves at age 18. My boot camp drill instructors were extremely concerned about my thin physique. Three squares a day in the mess hall along with all of the physical training started my road to putting on more weight. I would feast at the boot camp mess hall. As I look back on my boot camp training, I always remembered it being the most physical fit time of my life. I thrived on the rigid disciple and training.

Since I was so thin and reserved, people had a hard time believing me when I told them I was a Marine. In watching World War II documentary battles, I noticed the Marines had their share of thin lanky young men fighting in their ranks. They went from a great depression right into a war. More than likely, they also had to endure a shortage of food in their childhood. Later in life, I would reach a consistent weight of approximately 190 pounds. My hair color gradually went from my youthful blood red, to auburn, to a brownish color, to salt and pepper, then grey, and finally to snow white.

In early 1963, President John F. Kennedy revived an earlier fifty mile military hiking challenge of President Teddy Roosevelt. He challenged Americans to get fit enough to hike fifty miles. His brother, Attorney General Robert F. Kennedy, was one of the first to respond by walking from Great Falls, Maryland to Harpers Ferry, West Virginia.

Our reserve unit held a volunteer fifty mile march in our fatigues and combat boots from Brooksville down Highway 41 to the reserve center on Gandy Boulevard, next to the St Pete Bridge. My buddy and I were two of the thirteen making it to the center without dropping out due to painful blisters. We started with thirty three men. I felt a great deal of accomplishment in going the distance. The Tampa Tribune published a feature article and photo of us on our feat. The challenge soon faded away.

At one of our weekend trainings in 1965, our reserve unit was notified verbally by our commander to be prepared to be called into immediate active duty. At that time the Vietnam War was escalating rapidly. After absorbing the shock of that announcement, I obediently accepted this possible dramatic change in life. Fortunately, the decision to call up the reserves was soon abandoned by the powers to be in Washington D.C. The Tampa reserve unit was activated during the Korean War and the Iraq War. Our reserves served bravely along with regular Marine units in those wars.

I was finally mustered out of the active Marine Reserves as I was serving in the Montgomery, Alabama unit in February 1967. I was a student at Auburn University and engaged to be married to Karen in June. My father died on January 13 of that bitter sweet year.

My parents allowed me to live at home in my bedroom after my six months active duty with no charge for my room and meals. I lived at home from August '62 till I enrolled at the University of Florida in

September '64. For two years I worked at a variety of odd jobs in phosphate plants around Bartow and Mulberry. I will always remember the thick fog during the night and early mornings between Springhead and Mulberry. It was so thick we could slice it with a knife. And we could only see about five feet in front of our vehicle. We had to creep along at about twenty mph.

Once I was an Oiler on a phosphate dragline. The work was 24/7 with swing shifts. I was responsible for maintaining the oil and grease levels. I also had to drag the thick heavy power cord clear of the dragline as it was "walked" to a new digging position. The dragline bucket was so big you could put a car in it. We would dig the soil down about seven feet stacking it onto a berm of excavated dirt. Then we would dig a layer of phosphate about seven feet deep and place it into a slurry pond so it could be pumped to the nearby phosphate plant to ship it via train to ships docked at the Tampa Port. It would then be shipped to countries all around the world.

I also worked for one phosphate plant operations for a period of time. For one employment, I was a "gopher" and Laborer/Custodian for a construction maintenance company. Most of my experience was working as a laborer for construction companies performing additions or renovations for various phosphate companies. I gained tremendous experience in working as a Laborer/Helper to Carpenters and Plumbers. I worked for a commercial plumbing company at one time. All of these employment opportunities helped me tremendously in preparing labor production and material cost estimates later in my construction estimating career.

For a brief time, I worked at a local supermarket as a bag boy and also in the vegetable department. A competitor grocery store announced that they would open on Sunday afternoons. I wrote a letter to the Plant City Courier Editor stating my opinion against the store's proposal. I emphasized that people needed to keep Sunday as a day of rest from business activities. Although my letter was printed, it obviously did not change anything. At that time, I do not remember any store being open on Sundays, and surely not 24/7. The 7 – 11 convenience stores were the first ones in our area to be opened beyond the regular Monday through Saturday hours. Since then, it evolved into today's 24/7 market place way of life. Overall, I wonder if any of this has enhanced our lifestyle very much.

I personally lived through an experience that would be a big *"No, No"* in today's overly protective society. One day in the early 60s, the west open shelter structure for the Plant City State Farmer's Market caught fire. With it being only a couple of blocks east of our house on Ball Street, we walked over to get a closer look at the fierce fire spreading down the wood structure from north to south. The fire department firemen were working the best they could to extinguish the flames. They appeared to be short-handed.

As one fireman in front of me was fighting to keep his high pressure hose steady, I jumped in to help him hold the hose still. My fire protection clothing was a tee shirt, jeans and sneakers. He gave me a nod of approval to continue my assistance for him. As the fire died down, he left me in charge of that hose at a reduced water pressure. When it was all over, we went home as if that was an every-day happening. My interaction would never be possible today. Remember the volunteer firemen we had in the day?

Another fire experience occurred about the same time. One night at about 11:00 PM, I drove our family car home and parked it in our carport. At about 1:30 AM, I heard a car horn blowing non-stop. Everyone at home jumped up and ran out the front door. Smoke and flames were rising out from under the car hood. One of our neighbors, a fireman, came over to help. He had already contacted the fire department. As the oldest brother present, I jumped in the car and managed to back it out to the street away from the house.

The nightmare got worse after the car started moving forward towards the house. I realized I had left the car transmission shift in a forward gear and the fire started the switch to be activated, thus moving the car towards the carport. I had to jump into the flaming car again and move the shift into the neutral position so we could push it back to the street away from our house. A fire truck arrived soon and the firemen quickly extinguished the flames. That experience was indeed nerve racking. I was bare foot, dressed in jeans and a tee shirt.

During those two years, I was paying for a car and saving as much money as I could to resume my college education. In September, 1964, I was able to do so, this time at the University of Florida. After completing a miserable fall semester there, I dropped out of college again. I worked eight months till I entered college at Auburn University in September, 1965. I decided to earn a BS degree in Building Technology. By that time, my family and friends were seriously asking me how much longer will it be till I graduated. Fortunately, my third university was the charm.

A high school classmate, Robert Spooner, was attending Auburn and told me how much he enjoyed the university. After a visit to the campus one weekend, I submitted my application to the university and was accepted. Another classmate, Larry Britt, would graduate from Auburn with a degree of Doctor of Veterinary Medicine.

"Auburn, Alabama – The Loveliest Village on the Plains" reflects the campus' beauty. The university was established in 1856 as the Methodist sponsored East Alabama Male College. After some harsh years, The Alabama Agricultural and Mechanical College at Auburn was located there in 1868. Women were first admitted in 1892. The college name was changed to Alabama Polytechnic Institute in 1899. The name was finally changed to Auburn University on January 1, 1960. Southern hospitality and "*Sweet Home Alabama*" made my time from September 65 to March 68 memorable.

Driving into Auburn, I turned down West Magnolia Ave and rented a second floor room in a house on that street owned by a widow. The house was directly across the street from the university and a couple of blocks west of Toomer's Corner (the Magnolia Ave and College Street intersection). It was a very convenient location. But the best part, it was full of Southern hospitality and charm. It looked like a typical setting for a good Southern novel. The building with my major was also across the street from my room. A freshman named Winston Robinson from Adel, Georgia, planning to major in Nuclear Physics, was my roommate. The house is no longer there.

I received a rude awakening when I met with the Dean of Building Technology for my major requirements. About half of the courses I had completed in my recent two years of college basics in Florida were not transferable to him. He adamantly insisted I had to take his basic courses before I could enter my major studies. With no other options available, I decided to accept that fate and I completed those courses in addition to my major courses. That unforeseeable plan of action required me to complete five years of college studies in order to obtain a four year Bachelors of Science Degree. My only option was to give up on obtaining a college degree. Maybe I could claim that I earned an honorary master's degree.

The university was on the quarter system in alignment with the four seasons. According to the 1967 university handbook, room rent for an air-conditioned room in Magnolia Dormitories was $80 per quarter. As available, private rooms were an additional 50% more. Off campus housing rates ranged from $50 to $130 per quarter.

Meals, seven days per week, in the Magnolia Dining Hall were $135 per quarter. Meals five days per week were $112. Meals in various off campus boarding houses ranged from $50 to $60 per quarter. We ate our meals at a private dorm dining hall. The Non-Resident Fee was $100 per quarter. Considering today's outrageous cost for a college education, the cost comparisons are mind boggling. The staggering cost increase is only over a fifty year time span.

When I returned for my second year at Auburn, I moved about one block north to a private owned boy's dorm. We had bunk beds for two students with five rooms per floor in a two story brick building. The rooms were small and uncomfortable. My roommate was from Mississippi and he would go home on the weekends. I was the neat freak and he never ever picked up after himself. We were like Oscar and Felix in the TV show "The Odd Couple".

We had students from all over Alabama such as Gadsden, Mobile, Selma, Eufaula, etc. We had two students from New York City along with me being from Florida. Often, we would have water balloon fights between the second and first floor students. That stress release activity was the most troublesome conflict a Dorm Manager had to deal with.

Many of the students living in Alabama would go home often on the weekends. They would stay on campus when Auburn played home games. We would be given student tickets to the games and it would be one big campus party time. There was always a lot of excitement on the campus during the football seasons.

It was thrilling to see our "War Eagle" soar around the stadium full of people ready to watch some college football on a sunny chilly fall afternoon. With no money available to spend on Saturday nights, I would stay back at my dorm room and study, or work at an Italian restaurant. I developed a friendship with another construction major student, Gary Hickman. I visited his home in Mobile.

Auburn students and staff were extremely conservative and patriotic. In my second year, the students gave more blood in a blood drive for the Red Cross than any other college in the country for that year. Auburn students also loved basketball. It was a treat to be a part of the small assembly of students with standing room only watching Auburn basketball in an old wood constructed 30s basketball coliseum. The crowd cheering level was deafening to the ears. Sadly, the historic building burned completely to the ground about twenty years later. It was replaced with a large high tech facility with tons of seats. Although I never was a basketball fan, I did know that Charles Berkley established us into the national spotlight for his basketball playing at Auburn. He was the Southeastern Conference Player of the Year in 1984 and considered the SEC Player of the Decade for the 80s. He excelled in professional basketball and is now an outspoken active TV sportscaster.

Due to a lack of money, joining a fraternity and living in their house was totally out of the question for me. I would go through my college years as an Independent living in private dormitories, and working part time to help cover expenses. I worked at various odd jobs during my three years at Auburn. One year I was a Dorm Manager with my room being no charge to me.

I also worked quite a while as a waiter at a downtown Italian restaurant. One night it burned down. The owner built a new restaurant on the east side of town, making it impossible for me to work as I didn't have a car at that time. I would also work for one of my major professors as a construction Painter and Laborer on projects in Auburn. I also obtained a few thousand dollars in loans during my first two years at Auburn.

In my last year, Karen worked fulltime as an elementary school teacher in a neighboring community named Smiths. We lived in a nice one bedroom duplex at 359 Genelda Avenue, a couple of blocks west of my private dorm. The rent was $75 per month. It was a peaceful shaded lot in a fantastic location. We lived quite comfortably.

On June 11, 1963, at the direction of President John Kennedy and federalized National Guard troops, Governor George Wallace finally submitted and allowed two African American students to enroll in the University of Alabama, forever ending the state's segregation policy. In September, desegregation of the high schools was also enforced at Tuskegee High School in Huntsville. The Civil Rights Act of 1964 signed by President Lyndon B. Johnson, outlawed discrimination based on race, color, religion, sex, or national origin. It ended racial segregation in schools, the workplace, and facilities that served the public. It also ended the unequal application of voter registration requirements. The law had to be strengthened by revisions years later before it was fully implemented into society. The Voting Rights Act of 1965 prohibiting racial discrimination in voting was signed into law by President Johnson during the peak of the Civil Rights Movement on August 6, 1965. The Act secured voting rights for minorities throughout the country, especially in the south

Six months after University of Alabama's integration, Harold Franklin became the first African American to enroll in Auburn on January 4, 1964. Anthony Lee and Willie Wyatt Jr. were also among the first African American students to enroll at Auburn. Lee was the first African American to complete all four undergraduate years and graduate in 1968.

I don't ever remember seeing him on campus. That was the same year I graduated. In 1969, a full back from Fairfield, Alabama named James Owens became Auburn's first African American football player. Thom Gossom was second one year later in 1970, the year Karen and I moved to Apollo Beach.

The March 7-24, 1965 marches from Selma to Montgomery accumulated at the Alabama State Capital on the 25th, as 25,000 people protested for civil and voting rights. Six months later, the students, administrative staff and faculty that I encountered in my 1965 fall semester at Auburn were accepting integration gracefully and moving on with their lives. In spite of all the headlines on segregation and integration issues, the students seemed more interested in beating their arch rivalry Alabama, coached by Paul "Bear" Bryan. They were glad his star quarterback, Joe Namath had graduated to fame with the New York Jets, Super Bowl III Champs.

Auburn's coach, Ralph "Shug" Jordan was beloved by everyone in spite of losing to Alabama too many times (which would have been more than one time). The stadium was named Jordan-Hare Stadium in his honor along with Cliff Hare. In 2005, the name was revised to Pat Dye Field at Jordan-Hare Stadium. As a side note, I saw Governor George Wallace giving a campaign speech one day at Toomers Corner. I listened to a portion of his speech before I had to move on to a class. His influence in politics and the Selma to Montgomery marches quickly became buried in history books throughout the South.

The Auburn Tigers played the Florida Gators at Ben Hill Griffin Stadium on October 29, 1966. I drove from Auburn to attend the game with Karen. With the score tied at 27-27 with only 2:12 minutes remaining in the game, Spurrier kicked a 40 yard field goal to give Florida a 30-27 victory. Spurrier and Purdue quarterback Bob Griese were battling for the Heisman Trophy. Most everyone believed it was his game winning field goal that won the trophy for Spurrier. As feathers in our cap; Auburn has three players winning the Heisman Trophy - Pat Sullivan, Bo Jackson and Cam Newton.

On December 2, 1967, Karen and I drove from Auburn to Legion Field in Birmingham with another college couple to watch Auburn play our arch rival Alabama in the "Iron Bowl". Auburn was winning 3-0 well into the third quarter. Hardly anyone left their seat during stormy downpours throughout the game. Umbrellas helped some, but not much. In a flash, Alabama's quarterback Kenny Stabler scored a touchdown on a thirty some yard run play, giving Alabama a 7-3 win in the unrelenting muddy downpour.

That game was very similar to the 1995 Outback Bowl game many years later that our family and some friends attended. Penn State trounced Auburn in the mud during a soaking rain. Greg and I got to see Auburn gain redemption by beating them in the 2002 Capital One Bowl. However, we can't forget USF beating ranked Auburn 26-23 in 2007. That game was one of the best for USF, while at the least, embarrassing and disappointing for Auburn. And it got worse as we lost to underdog UCF in our 2017 bowl game.

Auburn was a life changing experience for me. I hold many fond memories of those short two and half years. Although I existed on a "bare bones" budget, my life was enriched to the fullest. Deciding to attend Auburn and enduring to my graduation date are included in the list of top choices that I have made in life. It was indeed, "*Sweet Home Alabama*". I did not have a television to watch during my years at Auburn. Cell phones, smart devices and laptops were decades in the making. We had to use coins to make our phone calls in a pay phone located on the first floor of our dorm. We usually had to wait in line to use it. We had to use pay phones with booths in towns and at convenience stores infrequently located on the highways.

As we didn't have AAA cards, we learned to change our own flat tires and broken belts. We would tow each other. We made sure we never ran out of gas, especially on a road trip. Just about everyone changed the oil for their car, along with washing and waxing it. When the old car was busted until we could afford to repair it, we would leave it at home and stick out a thumb hoping an angel would pick us up and take us in the direction we wanted to go.

We used the nearby "wash it yourself" laundry mat. More coins were required for this weekly activity. We never read newspapers or watch television news so we never knew what was happening in the world around us. We would depend on word of mouth for important news.

We didn't have pocket calculators, but some of us did carry a slide rule hooked to our belt. We didn't have credit or debit cards and we didn't have a "money tree" handy when times were lean and mean. Although we had no talk radio, we did have Paul Harvey every day. We took it for granted that our God was always there for us.

During my time at Auburn, I basically lost touch with my family back home. I would make it home maybe once in the summer, at Thanksgiving sometimes, and for the Christmas holidays. Our first nephews and nieces were toddlers and always ready to play. Karen and I married on June 9, 1967, and we lived in a comfortable duplex on Genelda Avenue.

As a graduation requirement, I had to prepare a thesis on construction management. A construction organization had to be developed including an estimate, budget, purchasing, scheduling and management required to construct a local commercial building. Karen helped tremendously with all of the required typing.

Weeks before we graduated, we had interviews with recruiters representing companies looking to increase their staff. I also obtained home office trips to New York City to interview a housing developer and a railroad company. Additionally, I had interviews with Rust Engineering in Birmingham and J. E. Sirrine in Greenville, South Carolina. Of the offers given me, I chose J. E. Sirrine at a salary of $150 per week. Yes, that would be $3.75 per hour. Sirrine was a design firm for industrial projects throughout the South. I was assigned to the Field Engineering Department. During my two years with the company, I worked on project sites in Tennessee for a new tire cord plant and North Carolina for a hosiery plant addition.

In March, 1968, I finished my eight years in the desert to obtain my college degree. Mildred and Lloyd drove my mother to Auburn so she could see me receive my diploma. Karen and I loaded our possessions into a small U-Haul trailer and headed to South Carolina in her 1966 Mustang pulling the trailer. We should have kept that mustang! The generation since 1945 had "paid ahead" so my generation may be gainfully employed within a healthy economy. Thank God for their wisdom and foresight.

"Wisdom is the principal thing; Therefore get wisdom. And in all your getting, get understanding." (Proverbs 4:7)

Jerry and Karen receiving beautiful leis on arriving at Honolulu. We were visiting Greg in 2004, while he was stationed four years at Kaneohe Bay Marine Corps Air Station. He treated us to a tour of Oahu and a Luau.

Heritage & Hope

———————•———————

Chapter 22

One Journey

One of my first spiritual memories was seeing an image print of Jesus discarded in a trash burn barrel behind a neighborhood church building. The church was a few blocks from our house we rented for a year in north Plant City, near Wilson Elementary School. I was about 5 years old and the image left an impression in my mind that has always stayed with me. Even though I wanted to keep it, I felt it would be wrong to take the print with me, so I left it in the barrel.

One childhood memory included the day two men dressed in suits visited my 3rd grade classroom. They were allowed to have each class student visit with them one at a time and learn to recite John 3:16 with their coaching and help. Once each student had recited the verse to their satisfaction, they would give us a New Testament to keep for ourselves. I was their last student. To my embarrassment, I had a difficult time reciting the complete verse. I think they felt sorry for me, as they gave up and handed me a copy just to end my misery.

Another incident occurred in my 3rd grade also. The Monday morning after Easter Sunday, our teacher asked the class, "*Who attended church yesterday?*" I think everyone raised their hand except me. Then, she added, "*We should all try to attend church on Easter Sunday.*" We have changed drastically since the 50s. Either of those two incidents would ignite World War III in our present political correct culture. I now recognize that all three experiences increased the measure of faith in me that God had already given to each of us.

Mother was blessed with a supportive congregational fellowship as she was growing up with her family in the First Methodist Church of Punta Gorda from 1911 through her wedding in 1928. Soon afterwards, the newlyweds moved to Tampa. We fast forward twenty five years later. After settling into our Trapnell compound in 1953, our father (or an older brother) would drive us younger siblings to Springhead Methodist Church for weekly Sunday school classes and worship services. I was 10 years old at the time.

I do believe this new venture was instigated upon our mother's insistence. My Sunday school teacher, and later my Youth Pastor, Earnest Brunson, influenced me tremendously. He told our class one day that during combat in World War II, he prayed to God in a foxhole, *"Lord, if you get me back home safely from this war, I will serve you the rest of my days on earth."* He came back safely and he did indeed serve our Lord all the days of his life here on earth. His witness and ministry were instrumental in my journey.

In February 1961, my parents took us to a Billy Graham crusade at the old state fair grounds' Phillip's Field in Tampa. We spread a blanket on the grass to sit on and listened intently to his sermon. That weekend, my Pastor, Vernon McQueen, led me in prayer to accept Jesus as my Lord and Savior. Based on God's Word and faith, I was redeemed and restored to my Heavenly Father through His Son, Jesus. Ironically, I was blessed to serve as a counselor at the 1998 Billy Graham Crusade held in Tampa. The crusade would be the first event held at the new Raymond James Stadium. President H. W. Bush shared his faith at one of the meetings.

After enlisting in the Marine Corp Reserves in February 1962 at age 18, I discontinued congregational fellowshipping. During the next fifteen years or so, I read plenty of self-help books that only provided limited help. They were profitable, but limited. Karen and I were focused on growing in our careers and fulfilling our personal visions. Upon beginning our family with Kim and Greg; we were led to raise our children in a nearby congregation. We joined with the fellowship at St. Andrews United Methodist Church.

During the charismatic movement in the 70s and 80s, several men in the United Methodist Men's Fellowship had an impact in the restoration and assurance of my faith in Christ. A door opened for me to lead a Bible study group at the Hillsborough Correctional Institution for some twenty years, along with being active in small supportive home groups. Karen and I serve in an association distributing God's Word provided by the Body of Christ. We grew in the grace and knowledge of Jesus Christ as we were "Swimming in the River and His Ocean of Grace" at Revival Outreach Center (ROC). If we are in Christ, then we are free indeed.

Our fellowship with the Body of Christ continues at Centerpoint Church. I grow in the grace and knowledge of Jesus as I am being in

Him eternally. I am a blood redeemed Spirit filled believer of the Ecclesia (Church). I find assurance in believing this eternal truth.

I believe the following declaration written by Jim and Faith Chosa of Day Chief Ministries speaks for me also, *"I am in the supernatural what I am yet to be in the natural".* It is all based on my being in Him, not on what I do. I am holy as I am being in Him. This eternal hope is for all mankind to freely receive.

As Kim and Greg graduated from high school, we made a wall plaque for each of them with some of the "Life" ingredients we may enjoy as we live in happiness. I include an updated listing.

Happiness
Being Alive in Christ
Praising and Worshipping God
Fellowshipping with Believers
Forgiving and Forgetting
Being in a Life Support Group
Hearing and Doing His Will
Praying and Interceding
Cheerfully Giving God's Tithe
Giving Love Offerings and Alms
Always Saving Ten Percent

A Career in Construction Estimating.
With my introverted traits, my passion for construction, and a love for historic buildings such as the University of Tampa Plant Hotel and the Westminster Abbey in London; I was destined to be a Construction Estimator. I worked as a laborer on various construction projects during my college years as I obtained a degree in Building Technology in 1968.

However my work destiny wasn't confirmed until late 1977, at the age of 34. I was working for the Boston design/build company Stone & Webster since June 1970, constructing the new TECO Big Bend Unit 2 power plant and renovations to their existing Gannon Station power plant. The company offered me a transfer to a nuclear power plant project in New York. After considering our options; we decided to stay in the Tampa Bay area, and I would find employment here.

I submitted my neat one page resume to several local Contractors. During an interview with J. Allen Inc., Vice President Bob Smith told me he thought I would make a great Construction Estimator. He based this observation on my resume and behavioral traits.

The company was only a year or so old and he was looking for someone like me to handle the estimating so he could focus more on the management of their ongoing projects under contract at that time. With no small amount of anxiety, I accepted his offer and started my life work in commercial building construction estimating.

I would spend the next thirty three years with two local contractors, J. Allen Inc. and Ellis Construction Company, in this unique profession. One benefit was that I enjoyed employment security because only a handful of construction personnel would ever consider or qualify to be an Estimator. Almost everyone ran from it! Plus, most all construction companies needed a fulltime Estimator.

I was provided a corner office and given some previous estimates as a training guide. I was given my first set of plans and specifications to prepare a competitive bid within three weeks. I experienced "on the job training". I was the only employee in the estimating department, and I had to learn the work at hand quickly in order to survive. There was no other option except to succeed, which meant winning competitive bids that would provide a desirable profit for the company after the projects were completed. Our construction projects included commercial buildings such as governmental buildings, schools, churches, and office buildings.

As that period of time was years before desk top computers. Our estimates had to be prepared "long hand" written on paper with a pencil (all from scratch). Quantities of materials had to be determined from the drawings and entered onto the material work sheets. Extensions and totals were made on a calculator and recorded. Then the unit prices were listed and extended for the material, equipment and labor totals.

A summary sheet was developed for the building components such as concrete, masonry, steel, etc. During the bid preparation, subcontractors and material venders were solicited for their proposals. As we did not have email then, quotations would arrive via "snail mail" or were called in to me on the telephone. Fax machines were used by the few subcontractors that had one in their office. For the awarded projects, I was responsible for preparing the project construction budget. I had to also negotiate, prepare and execute the project subcontracts and purchase orders.

It was brutal during the first five years or so. There was so much work to be performed that I would burn the midnight oil on many nights and weekends. The percent of winning bids was horrible, with about a five percent win rate. A review of a lost bid would be performed and then I would immediately start preparing the next bid.

Over time it took nothing less than sheer fortitude to start all over again the next morning with an optimism that this bid would be the one we would win. Often, I would say *"This one has our name on it!"* Mostly all of the time, it did not! Eventually, I finally realized (and learned the school of hard knocks) it was God who provided.

As the company grew in projects, we hired a small staff of Estimators. In the 80's, desk top computer estimating software programs made the estimating process faster and easier. However, we were well aware of the old computer saying *"garbage in, garbage out"*. We used the review practice of checking and re-checking for complete and accurate estimates. Receipt of quotations and communications via email and cell phones helped tremendously.

During that time, the process for awarding many projects was drastically changing. Many Owners began to use selective invitation competition for Construction Management project awards in lieu of the old lump sum competitive bidding process. This method of Contractor selection and contract award ushered in a new era of contracting. Estimating was still crucial for these projects also.

Through the years I would also work as a Senior Estimator, Chief Estimator and Vice President of Estimating. In a search for Estimators; we looked for methodical, detailed, persistent, thorough, and competitive men and women. In spite of all the frustrations I encountered, it was very rewarding to prepare estimates that were complete and accurate, whether we won or lost them. It was a lot more enjoyable to win. I might say, *"Yes, I would do it all over again."*

I retired from my career on December 31, 2010. I now realize that I had experienced working in construction estimating and management with "horse and buggy "methods that were used throughout history, right up until the arrival of personal computers. About ten years earlier, slide rules were replaced with small calculators. Just like the loss of family farms and strawberry schools in the 50s, I witnessed the outdated methods of construction estimating and management in the 80s becoming obsolete with little fanfare. Will history prove our present high tech gadgets lacking sometime in the future?

Goals and Aspirations. Reflecting on my goals and aspirations throughout my life, I see them more as God's desires that He wants me to enjoy and fulfill. I believe He instilled my childhood desire to simply grow in the grace and knowledge of Jesus into a teenager all within the security, love and nurture of a family unit consisting of a father, mother and siblings. It is sad to see children growing up without the father being present. Regardless of our lack of material things, my childhood desires were fulfilled.

My teen years were filled with the desire of my heart to visit landmarks around the world that I had read about in school books such as the Eifel Tower, Statue of Liberty, Golden Gate Bridge, Washington D. C., Hawaii, London, Israel, India, Italy and so many more fascinating places. However, it made for good day dreams to preoccupy my thoughts as I pulled weeds from the nursery beds of strawberry plants along with working other farm chores.

At times, Karen, and I would rent a car and drive through countries like France, Switzerland and Germany, always having to ask locals how to find our way back on track after becoming lost (which usually ended up being the most rewarding time of our trips). Quite often, this divine meeting would open up a door for a getting acquainted visit, as long as they could at least speak broken English. Regardless of any place we visited, there is a life story to be told in every person. <u>Where ever they live in this world, people need Jesus.</u> Many times we had opportunities to give people a New Testament as we shared the gospel of Jesus with them.

My major goal as a young adult was to obtain a college degree. It took eight years of working and college. It became so bad that after about six years my family quit asking me when I was going to stop being a career college student and get a real job. It became just sheer determination on my part to keep on going till I made it. My college graduation after eight years was a major achievement. Life goals also included achieving excellence in my estimating career, experiencing a deeper spiritual journey, and helping others with their journey.

Fifty one years ago, I was blessed in my June 9, 1967 wedding to Karen. Presently I am being in Christ while believing for a sound mind and good health to do His wondrous works through the Body of Christ. I especially want to continue participating in distributing and sharing the gospel of Jesus to people around the world.

"Where there is no revelation, the people cast off restraint;
But happy is he who keeps the law" (Proverbs 29:18).

Kim, Carter and Greg at a Tampa Bay Rays game.

Carter picking U/ Pick strawberries at a local strawberry field in 2015.
A big difference to children being required to pick strawberries like an adult.

"We're going to Disney World, again and again." 2001

Heritage & Hope

———·———

Chapter 23

Abundant Supply

My earliest memory on the role of money in life was at age 5. Our family traveled to Michigan to pick cherries during the summer of '48. One night in our cabin tent, Father commented on my making the family egg money by working on the ground collecting the fallen cherries and picking the cherries at the bottom of the trees. That statement left a powerful inspiration in me for the rest of my life. In our finances, the insignificant becomes significant over a life time.

Another early memory of earning money was during the winter months of our strawberry school years. We were paid to pick strawberries on an "as needed basis" at neighboring farms for a nickel (maybe sometimes a dime) per quart. We would put our ticket in the bottom of each quart basket (we called them cups) so the total daily number of picked cups could be counted for each worker.

On good days, a worker could pick one hundred plus cups. The money earned would be used to help the family budget for our personal expenditures. Picking for our family farm was always on a "no payment" basis. There was no compensation for family chores.

The frequent shortage of money during my school years made a strong impression on my value of money. After my high school graduation, I spent eight years working my way through college. The role of money during that time was simply to pay the bills. I also borrowed a few thousand dollars for my college expenses.

Once I graduated from Auburn University in 1968, I began a career in the industrial and commercial construction industry. Karen was continuing her educational career as an elementary school teacher. We both were being established in the work that we each had decided upon. And we felt content in working for a salary compared to being an entrepreneur.

Over-night, the role of money in our life started to change from providing bare necessities to being able to afford some luxuries in life. We went from a "lean and mean" mode to a "free spending" one. The baby boomers generation was very blessed as our national economy was expanding very well during the 60s. During the 70s we suffered several years of slow growth, but the economy came roaring back in the 80s.

Early in our marriage, the role of money for us was to spend it on the things we wanted. Then credit cards were being flashed before our eyes as the new way of paying for personal expenditures. Like so many of us at that time, we thought the credit card was the best thing since sliced bread. In a short time; we found ourselves in credit card debt, even though we knew we shouldn't be in that situation.

At that time, I was reading self-help books and articles. So I added making money to my self-help list. We committed to paying off our credit cards and short term installment debts. We learned the hard way that the use of credit cards was ok only if we paid the monthly purchases in full each month.

We established boundaries to live within our means and invested the money being saved. It took a few years in the making; but we finally realized that as we had our savings withdrawn from our pay checks, we never really missed it because we never saw it.

We had already become adjusted to living on a budgeted amount before the excess monies were deducted from our pay checks. That method of saving was and is the easiest and most effective way to save. The saved monies were automatically credited to our investment venues.

Once we established that method of saving, it would be on auto pilot and we could forget about it, except for periodical reviews. We put that money to work making money. It was like riding a freight train, starting out slowly and gradually accelerating. I believe we need to get on the investment market roller coaster ride for life and never get off, in spite of the wild ride over thrilling mountain peaks and down through dark valleys.

Then everything gradually shifted for us. About ten years into our marriage, we confirmed our belief in Christ, giving us eternal life in Him. Our outlook on life and especially the role of money in our lives started changing. We confirmed that we really are to be good stewards of what God has blessed us with. We found His Word contained all of the knowledge and instructions for handling money.

We acknowledged that God owns everything. We are stewards of whatever He blesses us with. He allows us to use our resources as we choose. We want to see the advancement of His kingdom on earth along with providing for our needs as we fulfill our destiny on earth. We want to leave an inheritance for good works, our children, and for our children's children. We give God's tithe, and our offerings.

We can enjoy a freedom as we invest for our long term needs in life. As we follow God's plan for the role of money in our lives, we experience the freedom we have in seeing our money working continuously through us like fresh flowing water. Freely we receive, freely we give.

We have determined that the Bible contains everything we need to know about wealth, from accumulating it to how we handle it. We also have tons of self-help books available on financial planning. There are unlimited amounts of investment planning firms such as The Dave Ramsey Financial Program to choose from. We found that working with a financial planner on a simplistic approach to personal finances with a realistic and achievable lifelong financial program was best for us. We have worked with our financial investment company, Wells Fargo, to make sound investments.

In regards to saving money, one of my favorite past times in life is picking up coins I find on the ground for our piggybank, especially pennies. Kim and Greg tease me when they see me do this. I always replied with *"a penny saved is a penny earned."* It's almost impossible to find coins anymore as credit and debit cards have almost replaced the use of currency and coins.

My favorite money savers are to turn off lights in a room not in use and never leave my vehicle idling when stopped, except for traffic lights. Buying snacks and beverages at convenience stores is always a *"No, No."* Reducing eating out times can result in large savings.

Except for special occasions, we eat out modestly. We never spent a dime on lottery tickets and exotic coffee. Eating brown bag lunches is a great way to save also. I still believe the insignificant becomes the significant. Plus, God provides the increase.

As we are always being in Him, we have His peace. We may be content in whatever state we are in at the time. As recorded in Philippians 4:11, Paul the Apostle wrote "...*for I have learned in whatever state I am, to be content.*"

And as recorded in Matthew 6:21, Jesus tells us,
"*For where your treasure is, there your heart will be also.*"

Greg, Kim and I took a road trip to Auburn, Alabama to see Auburn play Alabama on November 25, 2017. Here we are standing in front of a monster truck a few hours before game time. Everyone was crying "*War Eagle! Beat Bama!*" We did beat #1 Bama 26-14. Sadly, we went on to lose out while Alabama won out to become the 2017 National Champions.

Jerry, Greg, and Kim at boot camp graduation in 2001.

Heritage & Hope

———·———

Chapter 24

We Picked / U Pick

"Puddin, quit standing around that fire all day long and git back to picking!" My precious warm up time by the inviting hot flames was now over as I could tell by the tone in Lloyd's voice. I was 11 and he was our 16 year old straw boss in 1954. He had the authority to give that unwelcomed command to me.

I reluctantly started back to work brushing the frosty leaves of each plant as my fingers quickly became icy cold again while I picked each ripe strawberry I found. I knew I had to pick down a new row and back up another one before I could heat up my freezing hands over the fire again.

Frosty weather on a late winter day could quickly turn into a near summer like day which creates distinct opposite weather extremes on the days we found ourselves still picking into the hot afternoons. We would become so hot and weary (to the point of our energy level dropping down to empty) with no escape except to finish the work before us. That would be picking the complete strawberry field.

We would remove our layered clothing as the temperature got hotter and hotter. At times we would crawl along on our knees as we picked. That slow work pace would give us some relief.

It was a way of life for children to perform the labor needed on family farms. It would indeed be child labor abuse today. We just considered it a family working together as we hoped for better days.

In eastern Hillsborough County, we had elementary, junior high and senior high "strawberry schools". Our school year ran from March through mid-December. The schedule gave the farm children time off from school to pick the strawberries during that harvesting period of mid December through March.

In 1956, the Hillsborough County School Board discontinued the "strawberry schools", which abruptly stopped the child labor. Migrants were hired for the required labor force as many family farms were discontinued.

As these memories flooded my mind in rapid succession on a perfectly sunny 2015 winter/spring day, Karen, and I watched our than 8 year old grandson, Carter, eagerly picking the biggest juiciest red strawberries he could find at a local "U Pick" strawberry field.

I absorbed the view of a beautiful eighty acre strawberry field, a modern designed house, a Migrant housing compound nearby with a wood land of pines and oaks in the distant background. Then I thought about our typical framed tenant house on a few measly acres of farmland we farmed some sixty plus years ago, and how vastly inadequate it was when compared to the present day 21st century strawberry production methods.

It also dawned on me that we left our air conditioned house, drove to the U Pick farm in an air conditioned vehicle, and picked twenty quarts of strawberries within thirty minutes or so in perfect weather.

The 50s, with its almost pioneer like living conditions, was definitely the end of a way of life that is now only found in history books. This unique lifestyle went back to the days strawberry farming was established here in the 1880s. The family strawberry farming way of life lasted some seventy five years. I now see it as a portion of our heritage and hope frozen in eternal time.

"To everything there is a season, A time for every purpose under heaven:" (Ecclesiastes 3:1)

Heritage and Hope

_____·_____

Chapter 25

The Loss of a Precious Child

As I recalled losses in life, I thought of family members, and then I thought of how our mother lived through the loss of two children during her fifth year of marriage. While living in Tampa one year after her marriage in 1928 at age 21, she gave birth to her first child, Mary, the family's only girl.

Soon afterwards, they moved back to Punta Gorda. A son, Allan Jr., was born in December 1930. As newlyweds for two years, they enjoyed being a blessed youthful family of four living in her childhood paradise. She would especially enjoy being close to her parents and high school friends again.

After a period of time, our father moved the family to his home town, Farmville, North Carolina, in search of work during the Great Depression. Raised on a farm in the state's tobacco country, he thought he would find work in his boyhood town. Unexpectedly, Allan Jr. died of pneumonia on October 21, 1932. He was almost 2 years old. Our mother was six months pregnant with her third child. In her grief, she felt her only son's death was the result of the living conditions in North Carolina. Upon her adamant insistence, the family moved back to Florida. For some unknown reason, they settled in Seffner.

On January 23, 1933, she gave birth to an unnamed baby dying after living for five days. Like a flash of lighting, within a three month period, our mother at the young age of 26 experienced the loss of two children. Twenty years later during the 50s, I remember the deep hurt she expressed in each of the very few times our parents would share that tragic family history with us. I am flooded with so many questions and empathy for my parents. How did she deal with this harsh tragedy after being a newlywed of five years along with her previously comfortable childhood in a small self-contained Florida village? All I can conclude is that she lived each day in hope.

In faith, she went back to North Carolina with the family as I would think with no small amount of concern. Our next brother, Charles, was born in August 1934, at Winterville, NC. Some three years later, they moved back to Punta Gorda where Robert was born in 1937.

During the next ten years, our mother would give birth to six more boys (of which I was the third youngest child). With a 1943 birth year, I would become our only family sibling born during WW II. The family continued to move to at least five different farming communities throughout the southwest central area of Florida.

Seventy three years following that sad year of 1933, Karen and I experienced the loss of our first grandchild, Caden Shane Goins. On January 6, 2006, Caden stopped breathing just before a scheduled C section delivery. In the weeks preceding his delivery in Atlanta, our daughter, Kim, and son in law, Tim, along with family and friends were looking forward to the birth of a healthy baby.

This expectation was not to be. We have comfort and peace in believing Caden is living a joyful eternal life in heaven. *"Before I formed you in the womb I knew you..."* (Jeremiah 1:5) Almost two years later, Carter Alexander Goins was born on December 21, 2007. He is now a loving 10 year old "All American" boy. I now know how mother endured her loss, the same way as we do. We continue on in faith.

Kim, Greg and Dad at the 2017 Auburn – Alabama "Iron Bowl."

Heritage & Hope

———·———

Chapter 26

Honoring Our Father and Mother

We honor the two who started it all as they became one together in marriage. And then along came each of us in God's timing, covering almost 20 years during the 20s, 30s and 40s. I believe our natural family here on earth is a glimpse of the eternal family of God in Jesus. He brought forth our natural family through the union of Allan Rufus Humphrey, Sr. and Frances Caroline Blazer in marriage on September 21, 1928 at Punta Gorda, Florida. He established our family unit through His eternal Word, Light and Love. We live our natural family life as we may in our eternal family of God in Christ.

I think if they were asked about all they would go through from that wedding date forward, neither one would have the slightest inclination of their forthcoming children; each one of us living our own individual journey. Looking back in time, I cannot imagine the joy along with the heartaches and hardships that they would endure through it all. I believe God was working on our behalf through His unconditional love and grace.

After WW II, our father traveled to large northern cities to work as a union construction electrician. The economy was expanding in those cities. In spite of being an 8th grade school drop-out in North Carolina tobacco country, he qualified as an electrician based on his work experience with Phoenix Utility Company in the 20s and working as a Tampa shipyard electrician building battleships during World War II.

He was a strict disciplinarian while always exhorting each of us towards excellence. He instilled in us a work ethic, a belief in work as a moral good. He was also a good fighter for us when need be. I do believe these traits were key motivations that kept me on course throughout my life. I wonder if he wasn't raised in an environment where children spoke only when they were spoken to by adults. He always expected obedience.

The disciple routine for bad behavior included a stern lecture as he fumbled around with his belt buckle. If we did something really bad, then he would give us a stern lecture, pull the belt off, double it and proceed to give us a good thrashing. Mother would try to intercede for us to little avail. We would still give respect in spite of the issue at hand. During the 50s, we had teachers (and principals) giving their bad behaving students spankings with a wood paddle. One well known teacher had holes drilled into his wood paddle to make his punishment sting more.

The worst part was the embarrassment of being paddled at the teacher's desk in front of your class mates. If your father found out about you getting a spanking at school, you would most likely get another one at home that night. Punishment was always swift with a fiery concern. Most likely, our father was using the same method of disciple as his father used on him and his siblings. I would assume it was the same method of disciple in our past generations.

Today, the teacher would be fired and the student's parents would win a law suit for a considerable amount of money. The younger family brothers did not get as many spankings as our older brothers. We learned from their punishment experiences as examples for us. That method of disciple, substantially, became one more cultural lifestyle that was eventually discontinued soon after that time in most families. In Colossians 3:20, we read, *"Children, obey your parents in all things, for this is well pleasing to the Lord."*

I think our mother had a nature and outlook on life sort of like Jody's mother in <u>The Yearling.</u> Our mother would definitely identify with the women in the <u>Strawberry Girl.</u> As a result of the ongoing economic circumstances, they had to be courageous and enduring in their share of the workload as the men provided for the family unit (whether by hunting, farming, or eventually working in the market place). The wife was a help mate and exhorter for her husband and children. I see similarities in our mother and the virtuous wife as described in Proverbs Chapter 31.

I remember one night as my parents thought we were all asleep. They talked with each other about how we would each make it on our individual strengths they saw in each of us. Those comments I overheard kept me going throughout my life. Although I didn't recognize it, I was going forward in life with a trust that everything would turn out for the best.

In my senior agriculture class, we were given an assignment to record the expenditures and the income we incurred in growing a crop. I chose to do this with our strawberry crop for that year. I determined that we actually lost money on the venture. We spent more than we made on selling the strawberries. I discussed this with my father and he didn't react too surprised as I think he already knew what my study would tell us. Today, I believe he thought he needed to provide an opportunity for us on how to experience and appreciate the Judeo-Christian work ethic. He was successful in his endeavor. We all grew into adults appreciating hard work.

During the 40s and 50s, our family was never exposed to drugs. They began to be a problem in our communities during the late 60s. Satan and his demons increased their attacks and torments worldwide in so many ways. I believe that decade was a turning point for our country. To me, one key date was the assassination of President John F. Kennedy on November 22, 1963. Then along came 1967.

One of the best memories I have of our mother is the day she took me downtown to a family owned pharmacy before they all vanished. She ordered one vanilla milkshake in one of those big decorative frosted glasses, of which we shared. That was the only time I can remember us sharing such a treat in my childhood. I was about 7 years old. It was on the same day she drove to the Plant City State Farmers Market to auction strawberries that we had picked that morning. I got to ride "shotgun!" as she drove our old floorboard shift truck. With a small load of berries, we only needed the two of us for the trip. Although we only exchanged a few words, it is one of my most treasured boyhood memories for the two of us.

I loved going to the farmers market and listening to the auctioneers singing the bids out with a microphone. I went every chance I got, which wasn't many for me. We had an old flatbed truck with a floor board shift. Mother would drive that truck only when she absolutely had to. Soon afterwards, she stopped driving, totally. For some reason she would not drive anymore. I never thought to ask why. Maybe it was too stressful or she had poor eyesight. I think it was because our older brothers always wanted to be the driver so much.

There is one particular incident with my father that is so strong in my memory it seems like only yesterday that it happened. During the Christmas morning when I was in the 5th grade, we all got a candy apple on a stick as one of our gifts. I had taken mine out into the yard and started to eat it. I ate about half of it and decided I didn't care for it anymore and I toss it on the ground. My father saw me do this and his instant method of discipline was upon me immediately. He briskly told me to wash the apple off and save it for another day. Then he lectured me on being wasteful. It was a blistering discipline that I never forgot. It helped to mold my thriftiness to develop lifelong blessings in saving money.

Our parents did the best they could for us with all that they had within themselves. We know from God's Word that love covers a multitude of sin and that He blotted out all of our sins forever as we are redeemed back to Him through faith in Christ. We are family in the natural through natural birth and we are family of God through being born again in Christ.

In July 1958, at age 14, I was at home in Youmans with our mother. When I saw her crying after she received a brief telephone call from Charles, I asked her what was wrong. She told me that his Marine Corp unit was on immediate standby on a battle ship in the Mediterranean Sea, ready to invade Lebanon in a potential combat operation. That was only five years after the Korean War and thirteen years after World War II. She had lived through three major wars in her life. No one needed to tell her about being "In Harm's Way" during a war. Thankfully, combat action was not required as a peaceful settlement was agreed upon for that incident.

I would see her cry once again as she was hospitalized with serious blood circulation complications. I was visiting her and she asked me where was Charles. Soon afterwards, he appeared without the help of cell phones. She was called home to be with our Lord a few weeks afterwards on November 26, 1969. Karen and I were living in North Carolina. She was almost 62. With the loss of her first born son, Allan Jr, in 1932, and a five day old child the following year; I believe she developed a special bond with her oldest surviving son that she carried throughout her life. I also know she had a special motherly bond with each one of us in her own way.

Our father died at age 64 on January 13, 1967. I was a senior at Auburn University in that time and had been home for the Christmas holidays. We had enjoyed a good Christmas celebration with our family gathering. I didn't have a car, so I rode a Greyhound bus back to the university. I had hitched a ride home for the holidays.

My father drove me to the bus station in Tampa as my mother rode along with us. I remember as I boarded the bus and looked at him as we said our goodbyes; I felt that was a memorable moment in our relationship. I perceived he felt like this may be the last time he would see me. Sadly, it would be the last time.

I remember the contact we had. It was like he was saying, all is well with my soul, and I am at peace with God. I felt his love for me without having to hear it, a bond that cannot be broken in spirit, soul and body. After the funeral, I rode a bus to Auburn. It was a long trip in a haunting darkness in the midst of a cold Alabama winter.

The summer brought a new beginning in life for me. On June 9, 1967, I married Karen with mother in attendance. Although Father was not at the wedding, we did tell him in person during the holidays we were engaged to be married in June. They would have that brief one and only visit. In March, 1968, Lloyd and Mildred drove Mother to Auburn so she could attend my graduation. I am sure she shed a tear or two of joy.

I am deeply appreciative that our parents stayed together regardless of how tough things got quite often. Neither one left the family unit during some forty years of marriage. They were always there for us even if our father was working out of state. We knew they would never leave us. They taught us how to live the Judeo-Christian values and how to cherish work. Regardless of how desperate we got financially, they never asked our governmental agencies for any help. Somehow, we kept on going ok. To them, it was all about family.

They lived roughly from 1900 to 1970. They came into the 20th century as the horse and buggy days were on the way out and they lived to see the 60s jet age being ushered into our culture with high tech gadgets. Henry Ford was starting a business to provide common citizens affordable automobiles and Thomas Edison started a company to provide electricity for homes, businesses, and for street lighting. Ironically, our father made his live-hood providing Edison's electricity to industrial and commercial projects. And he could use some of his wages to buy a car from Henry Ford.

With a flying machine on a North Carolina beach, the Wright brothers were laying the ground work for a soon to be airline industry. The telephone, radio, record player, typewriter, television, household appliances and more were invented and produced in mass quantities for eager consumers to purchase and enjoy. Americans had a field day shopping for so much.

They lived through WW I, WW II, Korean War and the Vietnam War. So much for the optimistic thinking that World War I was the war to end all wars. They would survive the collapse of the nation's economy that resulted in the Great Depression throughout the '30s. Tom Brokaw's, "The Greatest Generation", was being raised up as ordinary citizens struggling for their basic needs. They won WW II and paid in full all of the war debts.

They lived to see the interstate highway system get underway to vastly improve the speed of driving long distances. They experienced the Jim Crow era ending along with seeing new waves of tourism. Incredibly, we went to the moon and back safely. Air-conditioning for our automobiles and homes was in its infancy.

One other historical perspective on our parent's lives during the 20th century is to compare their lives to the progress of commercial airline travel for our Tampa Bay area. Wilbur and Orville Wright achieved the first successful airplane flight at Kitty Hawk, North Carolina on December 17, 1903. Father at age 1 was living about one hundred miles away. Tony Jannus flew the first commercial airline flight in the world from St. Petersburg to Tampa on January 1, 1914. At age 12, Father was living on a farm in North Carolina. Mother was a 7 year old living in Punta Gorda.

In 1928, Tampa completed the 160 acre Drew Field six miles west of downtown. Our parents were married in Punta Gorda. In 1940, the city leased the airport to our national government for the Army Air Corps World War II purposes. After renaming the airport Drew Army Airfield, they modernized and expanded it.

During the war, we bought a farm in Dover and father worked at the Tampa Shipyard as an electrician building battleships. I was born at home on that farm in September 1943. After the war was over, the airport was returned to the city. As international flights began in 1950, Drew Field was renamed Tampa International Airport.

A second terminal was opened in 1952 near Columbus Drive and West Shore Blvd. Father was 50 and we lived in Cork. Although our parents lived through the air travel era, they did not live to see the new airport.

Construction started in 1968 to replace the existing terminal. The new Landside/Airside design terminal was opened in 1971. The airport has been voted the world's best for several years.

I have good memories of the old Tampa International Airport as we saw our father fly out of it one day in the mid 50s. The terminal was a small building with the control room on a third level area. Only basic services were provided with very few people present.

A man started up a conversion with me. He told me he was Ward Bond. He did look and sound like the movie actor so I took him at his word. He starred in the TV series *Wagon Train* from 1957 till his heart attack in 1960. He was a character actor playing over 200 supporting roles. He became friends with John Wayne during their football days at USC in 1926. They played in 23 movies together. He was a very talkative man. He told me about his friendship with John Wayne, describing him as a friendly "down to earth" man. We had about a 10 minute conversation, and then he had to go. I didn't even think to ask him for his autograph.

The loading and unloading of airplanes was extremely simple. The family could walk with the passenger out of the terminal under a metal canopy that had two sides of 6' high chain link fence. You said your goodbyes as the passenger walks through the chain link fence gate while the ticket agent collected their ticket. The passengers would walk about thirty feet and step up a portable staircase to the plane door. People with window seats could wave at their family.

While we were going through the departure process, the pilot was cranking up his propeller engines, producing gusty winds and deafening noise. The passenger unloading process was the direct opposite of loading. And that was the way it was in the 50s airline era. It was a very exciting day at the old TIA.

The seventy years from 1830 to 1900 era included rapid expansion, slavery, the War Between the States, the end of slavery, winning of the West, the Industrial Revolution, beginning of the Jim Crow era, and the decline of the agricultural society. We can only imagine what their parents, grandparents and great grandparents experienced.

Mother actively participated in fellowship with her family at the Methodist Church of Punta Gorda. She was 4 years old in 1911 when her family settled into a home in that small town. I believe the fellowship she enjoyed with the church youth group was instrumental in her life through the very day of her wedding in 1928, a bonding of friends for seventeen years.

She had high school friends and especially her teammates on the girl's high school basketball team. She wanted each of us to enjoy a similar fellowship in our youth. Father, raised in a rural North Carolina Baptist fellowship, agreed with her desire to lead us in that direction.

She did see us participate in a small youth group at the Springhead Methodist Church from age 10 through 18. Because they led us into this experience, we were exposed to the grace and knowledge of Jesus during our youth. I am grateful to our parents for that exposure.

Church at the Crossroads
by Mildred Humphrey

"There's a church on the corner with a steeple tall,
From its bow there is anchored a cross.
A bright light from it beams and at night it seems,
It is shining to beacon the lost.

There's a church on the corner of the crossroads;
With stain glass windows set apart.
And my friends in the church, at the crossroads,
Are so very, very, dear to my heart.

In my life one day here I came to stay,
It has nursed me for many a year.
It has filled my needs, helped fulfill my dreams,
Always ready to dry away my tears.

It's homecoming day at the little church,
Many folks are returning to find,
Friends and family are here, fellowship sincere,
And they're ready for dinner on the grounds."

The *"Church at the Crossroads"* is Springhead United Methodist Church (intersection of Clemons and Sparkman Roads). Established in 1939, the sanctuary stands gracefully in the midst of farms, pastures and woodlands. Beautiful orange groves prospered in the community, especially during the 50s decade. Then little by little, they all vanished over time from freezes, developments or the greening disease.

I grew in the grace of God through my preteen and teenaged years in that fellowship. Our sister-in-law, Mildred (Lloyd) wrote the poem as a testimony for herself and so many others such as me. I see it also as being in honor of our parents for leading us to this countryside refuge in the 50s. It was here that I accepted God's gift of eternal life in Christ by faith. It was here on June 9, 1967, that Karen and I married in faith as God was giving Israel a victory against their enemies in the 6 Day War. We celebrated our fiftieth year anniversary in June 2017.

"Honor your father and your mother, as the LORD your God has commanded you, that your days may be long, and that it may be well with you in the land which the LORD your God is giving you." (Deuteronomy 5:16)

We are the present generation with more generations already here with us today and more to come as we approach the Day of the Lord. May all generations honor their parents to God's glory and honor.

Left photo: Karen as Teacher/Wife /Mom/Grandma.
Right photo: Karen stands in our back yard flower garden enjoying her time out space. As I finish writing <u>Heritage & Hope,</u> I keep remembering Marjorie Kinnan Rawlings quote, *"I do not know how anyone can live without some small place of enchantment to turn to."* The Garden is God's creation to His glory and honor for present and future generations.

"Bring it on, Rocky."   A Marine in the making.

Greg as a Marine Corp Infantry Machine Gunner 2001-2006.
Preparing to fire a M240B machine gun with belts of 200 rounds each.
Kaneohe Bay Marine Corps Air Station in Hawaii, 2001-2004.
Camp Lejeune at Jacksonville, North Carolina, 2005-2009.
Marine Barracks, Washington, D.C. Presidential Support/Security 2010-2011.
29 Palms Marine Base at San Bernardino County, California 2012-2014.
Rifle Squad Leader Sgt. 2006-2009/Platoon SSgt. 2010-2014.
Completed three tours (2005, 2006, 2007) in Iraq.
Completed one tour (2013) in Afghanistan as a Platoon Staff Sergeant.

Chapter 27

Our Continuing Heritage

Governor LeRoy Collins. Without hesitation, I give special recognition to one of the outstanding Governors in our state's history. LeRoy Collins (1909 - 1991) was the first Governor in the South to speak out on the moral necessity to end segregation. He took a moderate position during the civil rights movement and is remembered as a voice for civil rights. Collins was born and raised in Tallahassee. Collins was 1 year old and my mother was 3 when her parents moved their family to Florida.

The Grove, known as the Call/Collins House at The Grove, is an antebellum Greek revival architectural plantation house located across the street from the Governor's mansion. Governor Richard Keith Call constructed The Grove around 1840 with slave labor. Substantially, the Grove stayed in the hands of the Call family until 1985. The mansion was similar in design to Andrew Jackson's Hermitage in Nashville.

In 1932, LeRoy Collins married Mary Call Darby, great-granddaughter of Richard K. Call, who served as Territorial Governor from 1841-1844. One hundred plus years later in 1941, LeRoy Collins and his wife, Mary Call Darby Collins bought The Grove. They owned it until 1985 when the state acquired the property to establish a historic house state museum. During LeRoy Collins' time as governor, The Grove served as the unofficial executive residence while the current Governor's Mansion was construed from 1955 to 1957. Governor Collins was a Democrat.

In 1954, Collins won a special election to fill the remaining two years in the term of Governor Daniel McCarty, who had died in office in 1953. Our state did not have an office of Lt. Governor at that time. After those two years of service, he was elected to a full four-year term in 1956, serving through 1960. Collins focused on strengthening the state's school system. Democrats had dominated our state's politics for ninety years from 1877 to 1967, when flamboyant Republican Claude Kirk, Jr. was elected Governor.

In the racial unrest resulting from the civil rights movement, Collins took a moderate approach with a progressing obedience to the law in order to prevent trouble. Florida had minor violence compared to other Southern states. He was the first Southern Governor to speak in support of the moral need to end segregation. We ushered out the "Old South" as we ushered in the "New South" along with the good and bad. His stance on civil rights was not popular.

With a reputation as a moderate, he was selected to be Chairman of the 1960 Democratic National Convention. He had a good chance to secure the vice-presidential nomination until Lyndon Johnson was nominated in order to win Texas voters to support the ticket with Kennedy from Boston.

After Johnson became President upon Kennedy's death, he appointed Collins to be the first Director of the Community Relations Service established under the 1964 Civil Rights Act. He worked with Reverend Martin Luther King, Jr. and the Alabama authorities during the 1965 march from Selma to Montgomery in order to avoid acts of violence to the nonviolent demonstrators. In 1971, he wrote a book on Florida history entitled Forerunners Courageous Stories of Frontier Florida. He served as our Governor during my high school years. I remembered him as a bold leader for civil rights regardless of what many thought otherwise.

The State's Capitol campus includes the Old Capitol Building, the House and Senate chambers and a 22 story Executive Office Building (the New Capitol Building). When the New Capitol was built in the 1970s, the plan was to demolish the Old Capitol Building that was built in 1845. After "a no small" public outcry, a decision was made to restore it to its original 1902 condition. The restoration work was completed in 1982, and listed on the National Register of Historic Places. A visit to these historical buildings and the state museum is well worth the time to do so. And you may also want to include the Florida State University campus in your visit.

One hundred years prior to Collins being elected in 1956, the Seminoles were making a last minute desperate effort to not be captured and taken to Oklahoma via the "trail of tears". A remnant would travel deep into the Everglades where they were left alone and survived as a nation.

A native Floridian, **John Carney, Sr.** born in 1804, was one of the last settlers in our local area to be killed by Indians. He settled with his large family on a farm on Stearns Road near Pittwood Road. During the Third Seminole War (1855-1858) he was killed at age 52 on April 17, 1856 while he was plowing his field. On the day before, he sent his family to neighbors for safety. His stone marker included *"Cruelly Massacred"*. I think he was also scalped. The Indians were killed a few days later, as one did escape. A year later Carney's wife died at age 30. They had six children ranging from ages 3 to 18. The historical headstone placed a few feet from Stearns Road was sadly taken by someone around 1985. The site is less than two miles from our house which we built during 1973 in Valrico.

The Brooker Elementary School Connection. In the summer of 1961, I worked for a brief time on the school construction just before it opened in the fall. Seven years prior, I was a student at Trapnell Elementary. Upon being hired, I was instructed to take Highway 60 to Bryan, go south a mile and a half, turn east on DeWolf, and the school is on the left after a short distance. Once I left 60 in Brandon and started south, I was driving on twenty foot wide two lane gravel on asphalt county road with pastures, orange groves and wooded areas. I saw a scattering of wood framed farm houses and 50s masonry houses. I don't recall seeing a single subdivision. At the time it seemed like the school site was out in "the sticks". That was decades before GPS, cell phones, AAA, duct tape, air conditioning, and owning a reliable car to drive.

If you had a flat tire, ran out of gas or had a belt break, you had to take care of it yourself. Natives would also have a shovel available in their truck to dig their way out after getting stuck when driving on dirt (mostly sand) roads. Also we would carry a one gallon gas can and a container of water for the radiator just in case. And jumper cables were always needed. Pay phone booths were only available for use on 60 to make local calls for a dime. At that time, we had 6"x6" concrete post at intersections with the street names painted on the post. They became difficult to read as the paint faded.

My work assignments included finish rubbing masonry walls and pulling nails out of the lumber used during the project construction so it could be used on a future project. It never entered my mind that one day in my future, Karen would teach at Brooker for some thirty five years till her retirement in 2008. Also, Kimberly and Greg would both attend Brooker for their elementary school years. We have lived three miles east of the school since 1973.

Our house was out in the "sticks". The drive on Durant Road to Brandon was similar to my drive to Brooker during that experience in 61. Some thirty years later, our construction company submitted a bid for an addition to the school. To my disappointment, we lost the bid. Another interesting Brooker trivia includes sidelines reporter for FOX Sports National Football League and a co-host of ABC's *Dancing with the Stars* Erin Andrews being one of Karen's 5th grade students. Erin's mother taught art at Brooker also.

Ten major events I believe that shaped our state.
1) Families homesteading as the Indian Wars ended in 1858.
2) Transportation via river boats and railroads, 1870-1920s.
3) Cigar industry and phosphate mining, 1880s to present.
4) Building winter resorts in populated areas, 1890s.
5) Land development and housing boom of the 1920s.
6) Exposure of state to men serving in World War II, 1940s.
7) Ending open range cattle with the fencing law, 1949.
8) The horrible dredging of our waterways, 1900 to 1960s.
9) The Kennedy Space Center, 1960s.
10) Most of all, air conditioning and Disney World, 1970s.

I believe our national election day of November 8, 2016 was a crucial crossroads in our country's direction. I believe many of the decisions for our losses to date were made by our Judges. Issues that affect large segments of the population are usually voted in or out by the nine United States Supreme Court Judges after they have heard pleas from both sides. Their vote is the last resort.

More conservative Senators and Congress Representatives need to be elected to increase our conservative majority. On November 6, 2018, we voted on 35 Senate seats, all 435 House of Representatives seats, 39 state and territorial governorships along with numerous other state and local elections. I believe this November 2018 Mid Term Election will be one of the most important election dates in the history of our country. Did you vote in this historic election? Make it a priority to vote on November 3, 2020. The results will determine if we will move forward as a socialistic nation or a capitalistic nation.

I see our being in the supernatural. Whoever may be elected in any election should be a real concern for Believers. As Jesus told us, we are to pray to our Father, *"Your kingdom come. Your will be done on earth as it is in heaven."* (Matthew 6:10). His will is our will as we are being in Him eternally. I personally believe there is no separation of Church and State. It is His will being done on earth as it is in Heaven through His Believers.

We will either start correcting past bad decisions and directions, or we will continue in the same downward spiral of watching America turn into a socialistic country through liberalism. I believe we will become more in line with Judeo-Christian ethic values and work ethic through President Donald Trump. There is a big difference in the two choices we have to choose between in every election.

However, as the results in our November 6, 2018 election becomes history; the real questions for us are: what happens now? Where does America go from here? What should we be doing now? During, at least, almost sixty years since 1960, I believe we were battling to keep our country's Judeo-Christian ethic values and work ethic foundation established by our forefathers. Regardless of the election results, the battle will continue.

Being under the strong influence of liberals during these past fifty eight years since 1960, we have gone from a capitalistic Christian nation to becoming almost like some socialistic countries in Europe, Cuba and Venezuela. I foresee this fierce battle between conservatism and liberalism continuing for generations to come in all of our national, state, county and municipality elections.

Our country is in a deep rooted struggle to continue with a capitalistic economy with Judeo-Christian ethic values and work ethic along with American exceptionalism or with unadulterated socialism. At the rate of our recent progression, the scale will be tipped to the far left forever in the near future with almost no possibility of turning back. I believe we may be going in the wrong direction. We simply need to return to the basics. We need to turn in the natural as well as in the supernatural as we may witness the increase in God's wondrous works being manifested through us.

I believe our issues are challenges for God's solutions through the Believers as well as those yet to receive the gift of salvation. It is also my personal belief that the separation of Church and State that has progressively destroyed the fabric of our country during the 20th century was set into motion by our past Supreme Court Justices' erroneous interpretations of the Constitution.

I believe that we who are in Christ are one in God the Father, God the Son and God the Holy Spirit. We are in the Kingdom of God on earth. As we are being in Him, He does His will on earth through us. We are in Him and we are not of this world. We are the Ecclesia (Church). We are one in Him. I believe we are to stand firm for what is rightfully ours in God's Kingdom on earth. Jesus has given us the authority to do His will on earth as it is in Heaven.

I rate the large number of potential appointments of Supreme Court Justices as the number one issue for our 2020 election. It is the same as it was for our 2016 and 2018 elections. Although it shouldn't be so, the Justices that are appointed are most likely a partisan of the President. President Trump will have a powerful influence in our country for decades to come, just on the potential of appointing possibly three future Supreme Court Justices; especially if he is re-elected in 2020 for a second four year term. If he is re-elected, he has a high probability of appointing his third Justice by 2024.

Supreme Court Justices

1. Clarence Thomas, Associate Justice, age 70, appointed by President George Bush, seated in 1991.
2. Ruth Bader Ginsburg, Associate Justice, age 85, appointed by President Bill Clinton, seated in 1993.
3. Stephen G. Breyer, Associate Justice, age 80, appointed by President Bill Clinton, seated in 1994.
4. John G. Roberts, Jr., Chief Justice of the United States, age 63, appointed by President George Bush, seated in 2005.
5. Samuel Anthony Alito, Jr., Associate Justice, age 68, appointed by President George Bush, seated in 2006.
6. Sonia Sotomayor, Associate Justice, age 64, appointed by President Barack Obama, seated in 2009.
7. Elena Kagan, Associate Justice, age 58, appointed by President Barack Obama, seated in 2010.
8. Neil Gorsuch, Associate Justice, age 51, appointed by President Donald Trump, seated in 2017.
9. Brett Kavanaugh. Associate Justice, age 53, appointed by President Donald Trump, seated in 2018.

Conservative Justice Neil Gorsuch was seated by President Trump in 2017, to the seat held by conservative Justice Antonin Scalia.

Justice Anthony Kennedy retired July 31, 2018. President Trump seated conservative Judge Brett Kavanaugh in 2018, to replace Justice Kennedy. Kavanaugh was a United States Circuit Judge of the United States Court of Appeals for the District of Columbia Circuit. His nomination was confirmed by the U. S. Senate. Kennedy served for 30 years after being appointed by President Ronald Reagan (Movie/TV actor) in 1988.

Based on their past decisions, I believe Justices Ruth Ginsburg, Sonia Sotomayor, Elena Kagan and Stephen Breyer are four liberals. Let us not forget, liberal Supreme Court Justices seated in 1973 made the Roe verses Wade decision, and just recently, those seated in 2015 for the final Obamacare decision. Chief Justice John Roberts was the swing vote in favor of that decision.

I believe he will replace Associate Justice Anthony M. Kennedy as the swing vote in future court decisions. Chief Justice John Roberts even made a shocking suggestion on how to make the Obamacare decision technically legal as he added it into his decision. There is no other authority we can turn to for an appeal of their decisions. We now have five conservative Justices appointed to the Supreme Court.

Another critical example on the state level includes our newly elected Governor scheduled to choose three (3) new Supreme Court Justices this year for our State Supreme Court. The national Court of Appeals Judges and District Court Judges are also nominated by the President and confirmed by the United States Senate. They are appointed for a life term. The Department of Justice Attorney General is also appointed by the President and confirmed by the United States Senate

The Attorney General is the key person who should see to it that the laws of our country are enforced within the Constitution regardless of political partisan. This one non-political official is crucial to maintaining our trust in government. Of all agencies to consider, it is unbelievable to lose our trust in the Department of Justice along with the FBI. I have several questionable issues that I believe will require a special counsel or investigative team to be appointed to investigate the corruption being slowly but surely discovered within our "Deep State" leadership.

For a starter, the Department of Justice and FBI's refusal to release Hillary Clinton emails gives us a lack of trust. Believe it or not, they refused to release the emails based on their belief that there was no public interest in this issue.

Also, a day before the FBI investigation was concluded, why did former Attorney General Loretta Lynch meet secretly with former President Bill Clinton on an airport tarmac in Arizona? Why did she tell FBI Director James Comely to call the investigation of Hillary Clinton's emails a "matter" rather than "an investigation"?

Why did Comely prepare exoneration for her months before his investigation was completed? Why did his FBI investigative team leader, Peter Strzok change two key descriptive words in Comely's investigation report? Strzok edited the evidence to exonerate HRC. He changed "Grossly Negligent" (a crime) to read "Extremely Careless" (which allowed the exoneration). Strzok marked through Comely's statement and wrote his own wording.

We need a new in-depth investigation of the Clinton scandals. It is a national shame and disgrace that biased superficially interviews are being forced upon the public as verified and completed investigations (according to AG Lynch, they are considered "matters"). Why were four Clinton campaign aides given immunity?

The investigation of Clinton's private email server needs to be completed. We especially need to investigate certain actions performed by certain biased FBI leadership agents along with possible other Obama administration DOJ officials. We need an investigation of the controversial uranium deal with Russia. The sale depleted 20% of our uranium reserve.

We need to investigate the "Anti-Trump Dossier" plus the "lost" emails and text messages. Also, make public and investigate the FISA Memo exposing surveillance abuses by the FBI and DOJ leadership officials. Was the special counsel Robert Mueller III investigation probe established on falsified information?

On 8/5/18, a poll was taken for positive views on Socialism and Capitalism. There was a huge difference in the results.

Positive views on Socialism
Democrats 57%   Republicans 16%
Positive views on Capitalism
Democrats 47%   Republicans 71%

Conservative Dinesh D'Souza's movie "Death of a Nation" presents the shocking story of the Democratic Party's dark past and exposes the hidden truth that racism comes not from President Trump or the Conservatives, but rather from Democrats and Progressives on the Left. He says *"it draws a provocative analogy between Presidents Donald Trump and Abraham Lincoln"*. The movie exposes truth about the century long Jim Crow era following the War Between the States and the Civil Rights movement resistance in the 60s.

Interesting revelation in my life story. As I finished writing Heritage & Hope, I noticed the #WalkAway movement consisting of liberals who are upset by what has become of their side of the Democratic Party. It is an organization of people simply walking away from the party. I find it interesting that I experienced this same "walk away" some forty years ago during the late 1970s. The year 1976 was special for all Americans as we celebrated our 200th anniversary. I voted for Jimmy Carter in 1976 because primarily he was a "born again" Evangelical Christian Southerner. In 1980, I voted for a Republican, Ronald Reagan. From that year until now, I have never looked back at where I came from as I hold true to the consistent Republican Party platform during these past thirty eight years. I believe the Democratic Party of today is not my father's Democratic Party.

Our past, present and future sin was forgiven and redeemed by His blood on that cross some 2,000 years ago. Today, the world's population exceeds 7.5 billion. It is estimated that at least two-thirds of the people do not know Jesus as their personal Lord and Savior.

People need Jesus today, more than ever before. The Lord is *"...not willing that any should perish but that all should come to repentance."* (2 Peter 3:9)

The thief (Satan) came to steal, kill and destroy.
Jesus came to give life and life more abundantly.

"if My people who are called by My name will humble themselves, and pray and seek My face, and turn from their wicked ways, then I will hear from heaven, and will forgive their sin and heal their land." (2 Chronicles 7:14).

Hugh and Ethel Davis had two sons and four daughters. Left to right: Karen (Jerry Humphrey), Gerald (JoAnn Brown), Dale (Dick Brady), Dorothy (Ken Davis), Gordon (Dottie Simmons), and Joan (Alton Fletcher). (circa 1990)

Working on an estimate at my back room desk. Circa 1980.

Heritage & Hope

———•———

Chapter 28

Our Hope

<u>2018 MidTerm and 2020 Presidential Elections Continued</u>. I believe the second crucial issue for our country is to see our families and businesses prospering and increasing our net worth on a consistent basis. This has to include creating work opportunities. We need an increase of new small businesses along with corporate expansions. We don't need more taxes on wealthy individuals or companies so that we may pay for more unnecessary governmental programs.

We can achieve this through reducing taxes and entitlements along with getting rid of the stifling regulations implemented during the past administration. This would encourage corporations to invest corporate dollars into our national economy resulting in more earnings for business owners and employees. As our economy expands, the increased flow of taxes could be used to improve our nation's military, infrastructure, and entitlements.

Another immediate concern is to become energy self-dependent. We need to use the natural resources we have within our country. This includes the use of coal, drilling for oil, interstate pipelines, fracking, nuclear power, windmills and solar energy. Global warming preventive actions need to be put on hold until our economy is strong again and we are actively reducing our soon to be twenty trillion dollar national debt.

Our debt doubled during President Obama's watch. He accumulated more debt under his two terms than all of our previous Presidents in history combined. <u>The debt went from eleven to twenty trillion.</u> It also looks to me like this annual debt growth will continue regardless of who is President. Will our debt be twenty five trillion by 2020? Why are we held accountable for our household debt, but our government is never held accountable for the national debt? Our leaders act as if they are not personally responsible. We are kicking this can down the road to our future generations to deal with. Soon we will have to deal with this nightmare and I don't think it will be very pleasant for anyone.

Wages have been stagnant for decades. The economy growth rate never reached three percent in any of the eight years of President Obama's two terms. His "Great Recession" has experienced a slow recovery. We need to jump start our economy in 2018, in order to obtain real substantial growth. This approach to correcting our economy would be similar to those used in the 60s and 80s, when my generation enjoyed bustling economies in the day.

With plenty of increased wealth, we can indeed make America great again. Will the Democratic Party economic plan be a continuation of the last eight years? We spent a trillion plus dollars of taxes to build up some of our infrastructure. This program vanished overnight. The economy freight train never left the station.

The next priority issue to me is our physical and financial protection. I, as a kid, along with my parents, took consolation in the fact that our national government had "our back" as we pursued our family happiness and prosperity in the 50s. Sadly to write, as an adult, I have less and less faith that our government has "our back" as we move rapidly through the 21st century. In my childhood, I had that trust completely in my parents and country. That security was a fore shadow of the trust that I would come to have through faith as a Spirit filled blood redeemed Believer in the family of God. We will always need a society with law and order. We need assurance that Wall Street, mega banks and yes, our government will not lead our nation into any more financial and war disasters.

Another top priority is to identify the radical Islamic terrorist including ISIS and destroy them completely. There is a saying *"If you don't name your enemy, you can't defeat it."* We should not have to be concerned with terrorist attacks at any time or anywhere in the world, especially within our country's borders. We need to build up our military in order to maintain our freedom and protection. We are now living in a world where a terrorist may ask us at any time *"Are you a Christian?"* A "Yes" answer might result in death. During 2017, ISIS lost 98% of its territory control in Iraq and Syria. They have less than 1,000 soldiers there now compared to 45,000 in 2015.

This is a giant step forward. However we have a long hard battle ahead of us as terrorist are presently gaining footholds in countries scattered around the world, and I also believe within our borders. We must never forget that their objective is to conquer the world in the name of their religion. We want to fight this enemy in their backyard rather than our country. We will need plenty of "Guns" to win. It will also require sacrificing "Butter" until we have victory in this war.

"Build the Wall", update and enforce the existing immigration laws, "Drain the Swamp" (self-serving governmental career officials) and dismantle the "Deep State" (those entrenched bureaucrats in controlling positions). I believe the immigration issue is a high priority to help protect us from terrorist and criminal attacks. We also need to stop the constant flow of drugs into our country.

We need to reduce big government and give back sovereignty to the states. We need to replace Obamacare with a competitive health care plan. Big government (the Deep State) has to be reduced. We need to renegotiate the North American Free Trade Agreement and stay out of the Trans-Pacific Partnership. The Iran and North Korea nuclear deals have to be reworked to prevent them from stockpiling nuclear bombs.

I believe the 2016 election was the most important election in our history. We chose to continue on a road towards capitalism with President Trump. We are taking a road for economic revival and prosperity for all Americans. It will be easier to fix a bad economy now than later. Capitalism needs to be protected and given total freedom to expand and increase. We work in freedom as our God brings His increase.

Do millions of Christians not bother to vote at all in our elections? Is the America we enjoy about to vanish before our eyes? Is our priority in life only about our personal gain and entertainment as corruption in high places is being totally ignored? We live in a time when they will say "*evil is good and good is evil*".

A recent report stated that 96% of the biased national TV media and newspapers donated to the Democratic Party. They attack President Donald Trump incessantly while they protect Hilary Clinton. This harsh reality has been disturbing to deal with. Our local *Tampa Bay Times* promotes liberalism in their editorials and articles. About 95% of the voters in the DC area (the swamp) voted for Clinton.

All we heard during 2017 was "*Russia / Russia / Russia*". In 2018, it was "*Impeachment / Impeachment / Impeachment*". What we really need in 2019 is to get to the bottom of questionable DOJ and FBI leadership actions for the 2016 Democratic Party campaign and throughout years 2017 and 2018. If the Democrats win control of Congress in the Mid Term election, the Republican Party will be forced to protect President Trump from impeachment proceedings during the remainder of his term in 2019 and 2020.

The Democratic Party is Pro-Choice along with providing monetary support to Planned Parenthood. I personally believe life begins before conception. God's Word tells us that He knew us before we were conceived. I believe we exist in spirt before conception. Every abortion ends the life of an innocent human being. According to the Guttmacher Institute, sixty million abortions have been performed in America from 1973 - 2015.

Polls show that about one half of the voters are deeply upset to the point of a great divide being created between the citizens of our country. The Body of Christ (on both sides) has the challenge to prevent this from happening. The substance of God's love may be shared through the Believers to bring healing and peace to our nation. Holy Spirit makes intercession for the saints that the will of God to be manifested in our country and in the nations. As we read in Ephesians 6:12, our battle is not against people. *"For we do not wrestle against flesh and blood, but against principalities, against powers, against the rulers of the darkness of this age, against spiritual hosts of wickedness in the heavenly places."*

<u>We pray America will always stand unconditionally with Israel.</u> We bless the nation of Israel as we pray for the peace of Jerusalem. Karen and I were blessed as we married during the June, 1967 Six Day War. God gave Israel a providentially victory in that war. My best man was a Jewish Marine Corp Reserve buddy, Joel Weiss. In 1998, Karen and I were blessed with a trip to Israel. As we approach the Day of the Lord, we decree our destiny and purpose is being fulfilled as the Spirit of the Lord is being poured out on all peoples in these last days.

The Ecclesia (Church) is to legislate the will of God on earth as it is in heaven. Kingdom come, bring heaven to earth. Jesus told His disciples, upon this rock (Jesus), I will build my Ecclesia. We are redeemed eternally through the blood, death and resurrection of Jesus Christ. *"For God so loved the world that He gave His only begotten Son, that whoever believes in Him should not perish but have everlasting life."* (John 3:16). He gave the Believers authority to do God's will on earth as it is in heaven. We proclaim the gospel of Jesus Christ to all nations. We give people God's love through sharing the good news of Jesus with them. As He is, so am I. We "be" in Him as He may "do" through us.

I thank God He has given us authority, in faith, to remove iniquities and curses of the fathers on the children to the third and fourth generations, through the blood of Jesus. We want to hold fast in faith to the marriage of a man and a woman. We also hold fast in faith that the fathers do not desert their family. Parents are exhorted to provide for their household.

We thank God for taking us through our times of war and troubles. Future generations will need to be prepared when called on to do the same. *"And when you hear of wars and rumors of wars, do not be troubled; for such things must happen, but the end is not yet." For nation will rise against nation, and kingdom against kingdom..."* (Mark 13:7-8a).

From 1950 to 2017, Florida grew from 2 million to 20.6 million. The area between I-4 from the Tampa Bay area to Daytona Beach and Highway 60 from Clearwater to Vero Beach has been referred to as a "Forerunner" for our nation. This narrow strip of land is considered as being the nation's spiritual and political point. This corridor has had a profound influence in our nation's spiritual direction and presidential elections. May it continue to be so. Remember, for a time, Tampa Bay was called "The Bay of Holy Spirit".

Through the years since Ponce de Leon discovered Florida in 1513, we have just about destroyed this portion of God's beautiful creation. In the mid 50s, I will never forget the appearance of a huge dragline digging our beautiful Trapnell Compound Little Alafia Creek into a straight ditch. I was devastated as I watched them inch their way across our property continuing southward. All I heard about this natural disaster was my father saying *"They are providing better drainage for the land".*

The same thing happened to Turkey Creek, the Kissimmee River, and other state waterways; especially around the Everglades earlier in the 20th century. They changed the beautiful winding river into a large straight ditch. Where was the public outcry? It was a travesty to allow this environmental destruction to be performed. We gave up God's beautiful creation with standing water to drying up the state to gain more farmland and developments during a long period of some seventy years, from 1900 – 1960s.

Then through man's wisdom, we started restoration projects to reverse the damage we did to our state's ecology environment at a cost of billions of dollars. Recently the Corp of Engineers has started a restoration of the Kissimmee River back to its natural winding creation. However the Little Alafia Creek and Turkey Creek remains the same man made ditches.

They are also planning to construct a massive reservoir on the north side of the Everglades in order to help control the water flow southward through the Everglades. We can still be good stewards of our land as we correct destructive projects.

We didn't have water hyacinth in our lakes and rivers until the plant was brought in from South America and introduced into our waterways in the latter part of the 19th century. Now we also have Burmese pythons multiplying at an alarming rate after being released in the Everglades during our recent decade of history. They are killing off the small animals throughout the Everglades. Since the 60s, another invasive reptile is the Iguana. With a recent population explosion, they are also damaging wildlife and properties.

Also in this time, we are experiencing green slime and algae in our south Florida fresh water lakes, rivers and canals. At the same time we continue to have outbursts of red tide in our backyard Gulf of Mexico. We as a state need to address these environmental problems and correct them though our resources at hand.

This brings to mind Marjory Stoneman Douglas (1890 -1998) pleading strongly for conserving our state's balance of nature. She was an American journalist, author, women's suffrage advocate, and conservationist known for her staunch defense of the Everglades in the efforts to drain it for development. After moving to Miami in 1915 to work for the Miami Herold, she became a freelance writer. She was remembered best for her 1947 book The Everglades: River of Grass. It showed the importance of the Everglades as a valuable river instead of a worthless swamp.

Evidentially we did not respond too well to her dire pleading. Some seventy years later in 2018, we are still grabbling with this concern. Are these issues more of the legacy we are leaving for our future generations to deal with? As a side note, she also wrote a complete history of our state in her 1967 book, Florida: The Long Frontier.

As she was fulfilling her destiny in south Florida, Marjorie Rawlings was writing her books in Cross Creek while our family was in pursuit of the American Dream in the agricultural west central Florida. Thomas

Edison was working in his Ft. Myers winter lavatory till his death in 1931. We were all sort of long distance neighbors. As I write about our poor stewardship of the land, I think about the 70s TV commercial showing a Native American paddling his canoe through garbage in the water. The scene brought tears to his eyes. We need to be better stewards of our state environment and animals.

I believe the following statement is one of Satan's biggest lies. *"We all have the same God"* The Bible clearly reveals God is: God the Father, God the Son (Jesus Christ) and God the Holy Spirit. He is the only true and living God of Abraham, Isaac and Jacob. One of the largest religions in the world, Islam, does not acknowledge Jesus Christ as God the Son. They acknowledge Jesus Christ as a Prophet, but they do not acknowledge Him as God the Son.

Another major lie is: *"There are many paths or ways to God in Heaven."* The Bible tells us there is only one way to be in the Family of God. "As we read in John 14:6, *"Jesus said to him, "I am the way, the truth, and the life. No one comes to the Father except through Me.""*

The Beetles hit song "Imagine" included the following words, "… *Imagine…And no religion too".* I can agree with that statement as all the religions of the world are established in mankind. We thank God that Christianity is not a religion. It is being alive eternally in Christ.

Some Cherished Memories from my Boyhood Years (1943-1960)
Baby Ruth and Coca Cola/Moon Pie and RC Cola.
A Davie Crocket Raccoon Cap that I never got/Col. Parker.
Playing "G.I. Joe" with China berries, cow chips and dirt clods.
Dodge Ball/Hit the Can/Backyard Football/King of the Hill.
Street Cars/Cigar Factories/Devil Crabs/Cuban Sandwiches.
The Ringling Brothers Circus/Strawberry Festivals/Al Berry.
The original State Fairgrounds/smelling orange blossoms.
Sunsets/the night sky full of stars/Eating fresh picked oranges.
Bare Feet and Sandspurs/Mosquitoes/Gnats/Yellow Jackets.
Growing up in a drug free community. (Drugs were Taboo).

Closing "Food for Thought"
Build the Wall/Drain the Swamp/Dismantle the Deep State/**Vote**.
Keep our historic Monuments & Statues/Respect our Flag/**Vote**.
Enforce our Immigration Laws/Explore Florida/Pray/**Vote**.
Salvation/Purpose/Destiny/Abundant Life in Jesus/**Vote**.

I know with assurance and confidence, in faith based on the Word of God that, "Our Hope is in Christ". All Glory & Honor to our God!

"...*Christ in you, the hope of glory.*" Colossians 1:27b).

I am experiencing joy and peace with thanksgivings in my eternal journey with a canoe ride on the Hillsborough River in the natural and supernatural of God's Kingdom on earth as it is in Heaven.

To personally experience the reality of what I have attempted to write about in <u>Heritage & Hope</u>, we will want to visit the fascinating self-contained community called "Cracker Country" located on the Florida State Fairgrounds property in Tampa, Florida.

The Florida State Fair Authority has established an 1870-1912 pioneer village (Cracker Country). It is a "must see" visit during the annual state fair event. The rural Florida living history museum was established in 1978 by Mr. and Mrs. Doyle Carlton, Jr. so future generations may better understand and appreciate Florida's rural heritage. From the cypress log corn crib to the grand old two story Carlton house. The village has thirteen original buildings dating from 1870 to 1912, all restored. They were moved to their present location from their original place within the state; for example the train station was moved from Okahumpka, and the Carlton house from Wauchula. <u>Take time to enjoy the music, food, culture and history of our Florida.</u>

The Lanier Family in berry field (circa 1915). **(103 years ago).**
Photograph courtesy of Plant City Photo Archives & History Center.
Everyone is wearing chilly weather attire. Fence around farming area.
Note boy crawling as he picks. He is wondering, when will we ever be done?

The Farkas Family - 1926. **(92 years ago).**
Photograph courtesy of Plant City Photo Archives & History Center.
Note their basic "cracker" house and nice new barn. New looking truck and
car in the background. They have rows on low beds. They appear determined
to be successful in their farming endeavors.

Strawberry picking - Walden/Mott. A time in the late 30s? **(80 years ago).**
Photograph courtesy of Plant City Photo Archives & History Center.
Note the young boy picking one berry at a time on his knees. Woods in the
background. I know why they look exhausted. **"Been there, done that."**

Strawberry Field, 1953. **(65 years ago).**
Photograph courtesy of Plant City Photo Archives & History Center.
Note the cattle fenced in a pasture next to the strawberry field.
1953 was a peak year for our family crops. During the first five years of the
50s we made good money picking for neighbors in addition to picking our own
family field without compensation. The County School Board discontinued
"strawberry schools" in 1956, forever and ever. **"So be it."**

47929739R00141

Made in the USA
Columbia, SC
04 January 2019